Also by Anna Politkovskaya

A Dirty War:
A Russian Reporter in Chechnya

A Small Corner of Hell:
Dispatches from Chechnya

PUTIN'S RUSSIA

PUTIN'S RUSSIA

LIFE IN A
FAILING DEMOCRACY

ANNA POLITKOVSKAYA

Translated by Arch Tait

A METROPOLITAN / OWL BOOK

Henry Holt and Company · New York

Owl Books
Henry Holt and Company, LLC
Publishers since 1866
175 Fifth Avenue
New York, New York 10010
www.henryholt.com

Originally published in Great Britain in 2004 by The Harvill Press, London.

Library of Congress Cataloging-in-Publication Data

Politkovskaya, Anna
     [Putinskaia Rossiia. English]
     Putin's Russia : life in a failing democracy / Anna Politkovskaya ;
translated by Arch Tait.—1st American ed.
          p.   cm.
     Originally published: London : Harvill Press, 2004.
     Includes bibliographical references and index.
     ISBN-13: 978-0-8050-8250-0
     ISBN-10: 0-8050-8250-6
     1. Russia (Federation)—Politics and government—1991– 2. Russia
(Federation)—Social conditions—1991– 3. Putin, Vladimir Vladimirovich,
1952– 4. Russia (Federation)—Moral conditions.   I. Title.

DK510.763.P65213 2005
947.086—dc22   2005043756

Henry Holt books are available for special promotions
and premiums. For details contact: Director, Special Markets.

First Owl Books Edition 2007
A Metropolitan / Owl Book

Designed by Victoria Hartman

Printed in the United States of America
3 5 7 9 10 8 6 4

CONTENTS

FOREWORD

She wasn't charismatic, she didn't fill lecture halls, and she wasn't much good at talk shows either. Nevertheless, at the time of her murder in Moscow, Anna Politkovskaya was at the pinnacle of her influence. One of the best-known journalists in Russia and one of the best-known Russian journalists in the world, she was proof—and more is always needed—that there is still nothing quite so powerful as the written word.

The subject of Politkovskaya's writing was Russia itself, and in particular what she called Russia's "dirty war" in Chechnya. Long after the rest of the international press corps had abandoned Chechnya—it was too dangerous for most journalists, too complicated, too obscure—she kept telling heartbreaking Chechen stories: the Russian army colonel who pulled eighty-nine elderly people from the ruins of Grozny but received no medals, or the Chechen schoolboy who was ill from the aftereffects of torture but could get no compensation. A hallmark of her books and articles was the laborious descriptions of how she tried, and invariably failed, to get explanations from hostile and evasive Russian authorities. But she had no patience for the fanatical fringe of the Chechen independence movement either. Ideologues on both sides of the war repelled her: What interested her were human stories, particularly when they concerned brave, kind, and honest ordinary people.

Over the years Politkovskaya won scores of international prizes. At home she was threatened, arrested, and once nearly poisoned by the same Russian authorities who refused to respond to her questions. The only official acknowledgment of her status was backhanded: In 2002, when Chechen rebels stormed a Moscow theater, she was called upon to help negotiate the release of hostages. She failed to keep them alive—and then she was murdered too. On the afternoon of October 7, 2006, she was shot to death in the elevator of her Moscow apartment building.

Politkovskaya was not, it is true, the first Russian journalist to be murdered in murky circumstances since 2000, when President Vladimir Putin first came to power. On the contrary, she was the twelfth. Among the worst crimes—all, of course, unsolved—were the murders of two provincial journalists from the city of Togliatti, probably for investigating local mafia; of Paul Klebnikov, the American editor of *Forbes* magazine's Russian edition, probably for knowing too much about Russia's oligarchs; and of a Murmansk television reporter who was critical of local politicians.

Nevertheless, Politkovskaya's murder marked a distinct turning point. Her assassin made no attempt to disguise his crime as a theft or an accident: He not only shot her in broad daylight, he left her body in the elevator alongside the gun he used to kill her—standard practice for Moscow's arrogant hit men. Nor could her murder be easily attributed to distant provincial authorities or the criminal mafia. Local businessmen had no motivation to kill her, but officials of the army, the police, and even the Kremlin did. Whereas local thieves might have tried to cover their tracks, Politkovskaya's assassin, like so many Russian assassins, did not seem to fear the law.

At the time of the murder, no one in Russia expected that anyone would ever be arrested for murdering Politkovskaya. When asked about her death, President Putin himself dismissed her as a "person of no importance"—an indication that Russian investigators are not likely to waste time investigating her murder. But even if the assassin were someday to come to trial, he—or whoever paid him—will have already won a major victory by killing her. As Russian history well demonstrates, it isn't always necessary to kill millions of people to frighten all the others: A few choice assassinations, in the right time and place, usually suffice. After the death of Politkovskaya, it's hard to imagine many Russian journalists following in her footsteps.

Even the most ardent fans of Anna Politkovskaya's writing did complain, on occasion, that her gloom could be overbearing: She was one of those journalists who saw harbingers of catastrophe in every story. Still, it remains difficult for anyone to write about her, now that she is dead, without employing the same foreboding tone that she herself would have used. Her life, and her death, was so much like one of the stories she would have written herself.

Anne Applebaum

AUTHOR'S NOTE

This book is about Vladimir Putin—but not, as he is normally viewed in the West, as seen through rose-colored glasses.

Why is it difficult to sustain a rosy point of view when you are faced with reality in Russia? Because Putin, a product of the country's murkiest intelligence service, has failed to transcend his origins and stop acting like a KGB officer. He is still busy sorting out his freedom-loving fellow citizens; he persists in crushing liberty, just as he did earlier in his career.

This book is also about the fact that not everyone in Russia is prepared to put up with Putin's kind of government. We no longer want to be under anyone's thumb, even if that is what best suits the West. We demand our right to freedom.

But this book is not an examination of Putin's policies. I am not a political analyst. I am just one person among many, a face in the crowd, like so many in Moscow, Chechnya, Saint Petersburg, and other places. These are my immediate reactions, jotted down in the margins of life as it is lived in Russia today. It is too soon to stand back, as you must if you want dispassionate analysis. I live in the present, noting what I see and what I hear.

MY COUNTRY'S ARMY
AND ITS MOTHERS

The army in Russia is a closed system no different from a prison. Like anywhere else, people don't get into the army or into prison unless the authorities want them there. Unlike other places, once you are in, you live the life of a slave. Armies everywhere try to keep what they do quiet, and perhaps this is why we talk about generals as if they belonged to an international tribe whose personality is the same all over the world, irrespective of which president or state they serve.

There are, however, further peculiarities specific to the Russian army or, rather, to relations between the army and the civilian population. The civilian authorities have no control over what happens in the military. A private, who belongs to the lowest caste in the hierarchy, is a nobody, a nothing. Behind the concrete walls of the barracks, officers can mistreat soldiers with impunity. Similarly, a senior officer can do anything he fancies, anything at all, to a junior colleague.

You are probably thinking that things surely cannot be so bad.

Well, not always; sometimes things are better, but only because

some humane individual has called his subordinates to order. Those
are the only rays of hope.

"But what about Russia's leaders?" you may wonder. "The president is the commander in chief, personally responsible for what goes
on, isn't he?"

Unfortunately, once they make it to the Kremlin, our leaders abandon any attempt to rein in the army's lawlessness and are more likely
to give senior officers ever greater power. The army either supports or
undermines the leaders depending on whether they indulge it. The
one attempt to humanize the army was made under Boris Yeltsin as
part of an effort to promote democratic freedom. The program didn't
last long. In Russia, holding on to power is more important than saving soldiers' lives, and under a barrage of fury from the generals,
Yeltsin ran up the white flag and surrendered.

Putin hasn't even tried. He himself is a former officer. End of story.
When he first emerged as a possible head of state rather than an unpopular director of the universally detested Federal Security Bureau (FSB), he
started making pronouncements to the effect that the army, diminished
under Yeltsin and by its defeat in the first Chechen war, would be rejuve-
nated, and that all it lacked for its rebirth was a second Chechen war. This
assertion is responsible for everything that has followed. When the second Chechen war began, in 1999, the army was given free rein, and in the
presidential elections of 2000, it voted as one for Putin. For the army, the
present war has been highly profitable, a source of medals and acceler-
ated promotions, and a first-rate springboard for a political career. Generals who leave active service are catapulted directly into the political elite.

How exactly Putin helped the army we shall see in the stories that
follow. You decide whether you would like to live in a country where
your taxes maintain such an institution. How would you feel if when
your son turned eighteen, he was conscripted as "human matériel"?
How secure would you feel with an army where every week the soldiers desert in droves, sometimes whole squads at a time, even entire
companies. What would you think of an army in which, in a single

year, 2002, a complete battalion, more than five hundred men, had been killed not by enemy fire but by beatings, and in which the officers steal everything, from the ten-rouble notes privates receive from their parents to a full tank column? In which all the officers hate the soldiers' parents because every so often, when the circumstances are just too disgraceful, an outraged mother protests her son's murder and demands retribution?

No. U-729343: Forgotten on the Battlefield

It is November 18, 2002. Nina Levurda is a heavy, slow-moving woman, a retired schoolteacher, old and tired and with a string of serious ailments. Like many other times over the past year, she has been sitting for hours in the unwelcoming waiting room of the Krasnaya Presnya District Court, in Moscow.

Nina has nowhere else to turn. She is a mother without a son: even worse, without the truth about her son. Lieutenant Pavel Levurda, born in 1975, soldier No. U-729343, was killed at the start of the second Chechen war. What has compelled Nina to spend the past eleven months doing the rounds of legal institutions is not that No. U-729343 was killed but the events surrounding his death and what followed it. Her one aim: to get a precise answer from the state as to why her son was left behind on the battlefield. She would also like to know why, since his death, she has been treated so abominably by the Ministry of Defense.

As a child, Pavel Levurda dreamed of a career in the army—not too common nowadays. Boys from poor families do apply for places at the military academies, but their aim is to earn a degree and then be discharged. The self-congratulatory reports from the president's office about the increasing competition for admission to military institutes are true. But the situation has less to do with a rise in the army's prestige than with the abject poverty of those seeking an education. A desire for training but an unwillingness to serve in the army also explains the catastrophic shortage of junior officers in the field. When they graduate from military college, they simply fail to appear at the garrisons to which they have been posted. They suddenly become "seriously ill" and send in certificates testifying to all manner of unexpected disabilities. This is not difficult to arrange in a country as corrupt as Russia.

Pavel was different. He really wanted to be an officer. His parents tried to dissuade him, because they knew how hard life is in the army. Petr Levurda, his father, was himself an officer, and the family had constantly been shifted from one remote garrison to another.

In the early 1990s, moreover, the collapse of the Soviet empire had left chaos in its wake. A high school graduate would have been mad, everyone agreed, to choose to attend a military academy that couldn't feed its students. But Pavel insisted on his dream and went to study at the Far East College for Officers. In 1996 he received a commission and was sent to serve near Saint Petersburg. Then, in 1998, he was thrown into the frying pan: the Fifty-eighth Army.

In Russia, the Fifty-eighth Army is synonymous with the army's degeneration. Its bad reputation, of course, began before Putin. He does, however, bear a heavy responsibility—because the anarchy among its officers goes unchecked; they are effectively above the law. With very few exceptions, they are not prosecuted, no matter what crimes they commit.

In addition, the Fifty-eighth was in the hands of General Vladimir Shamanov. A Russian hero who fought in both Chechen wars, he was known for his brutality toward the civilian population. When Shamanov resigned, he became governor of Ulyanovsk Province, benefiting from his role in the second Chechen war, during which he was rarely off the television screen. Daily he would inform the country that "all Chechens are bandits" who deserved to be eliminated. In this enterprise he enjoyed Putin's full support.

The staff headquarters of the Fifty-eighth Army is in Vladikavkaz, the capital of the republic of North Ossetia–Alaniya, which borders Chechnya and Ingushetia. The officers of the Fifty-eighth Army, following their general's example, were renowned for their cruelty toward both the people of Chechnya and their own soldiers and junior officers. Rostov-on-Don is the location of the general headquarters of the North Caucasus Military District, to which the Fifty-eighth Army is subordinate. The greater part of the archive of the Rostov Committee of Soldiers' Mothers consists of files relating to desertion by privates as the result of beatings by their officers, who are also well known for the blatant theft of supplies and for wholesale treason: by selling stolen weapons to the Chechen resistance, the officers aid the enemy.

I know many junior officers who have gone to extraordinary lengths to avoid serving in the Fifty-eighth. Levurda, however, decided otherwise. His letters make heavy reading; when he came home on leave, his parents saw their son becoming more and more morose. Whenever they urged him to resign, however, he would say, "What must be done must be done." Clearly Pavel Levurda was someone who could justly be described as a profoundly patriotic young Russian with a special sense of duty toward the motherland. In fact, he was hoping for a genuine, rather than Putinesque, rebirth of the Russian army.

In 2000, when the second Chechen war began, Pavel Levurda had an opportunity to avoid fighting in the northern Caucasus. Few would have blamed him. Many junior officers found ways to obtain exemptions. But, as Pavel explained to his parents, he couldn't desert his soldiers: when they were sent to Chechnya, he went as well. On January 13, 2000, Pavel reported to the Fifteenth Guards Motorized Infantry Regiment of the Second (Taman) Guards Division (Army Unit 73881), in Moscow Province. On January 14, Nina heard her son's voice on the telephone for the last time. He had signed a special contract to go to Chechnya, and it was clear enough what that portended.

"I cried. I did my best to change his mind," Nina remembers. "But Pavel said there was no going back. I asked my cousin who lives in Moscow to go straight to the Taman Division, to try to talk him out of it. When she got to the unit, she found she had missed him by just a few hours."

By January 18, No. U-729343 was in Chechnya. "At present I am on the southwest outskirts of Grozny . . . ," Pavel wrote in his only letter to his parents from the war, dated January 24.

> The city is blockaded from all directions and serious fighting is going on. The gunfire doesn't stop for a minute. The city is burning, the sky is completely black. Sometimes a mortar shell falls nearby, or a fighter plane launches a missile right by your ear. The artillery never lets up. Our losses have been appalling. All the officers in my company have been put out of action. The officer in charge of this unit before me was blown up by one of our own booby traps. When I went to see my commander, he grabbed his rifle and sent a round into the ground a few centimeters from me. It was sheer luck I wasn't hit. Everyone laughed. They said, "Pasha, we've had five commanding officers already, and you almost didn't last five minutes!" The men here are all right but not really strong-willed. The officers are on contract, and the soldiers, though mostly very young, are holding out. We all sleep together in a tent, on the ground. There is an ocean of lice. We're given shit to eat. No change there. What lies ahead we don't know. Either we'll attack who knows where, or we'll just sit around until we turn into idiots or they pull us out and pack us off back to Moscow. Or God knows what. I'm not ill, but I feel very low. That's all for now. Love, kisses. Pasha

The letter would not have helped reassure a parent, but in war you lose the ability to reassure others, and you forget what might seem shocking to someone far away, because the terror you've experienced has been so intense.

Later it became clear that Pavel had intended to calm his parents. When he wrote it, he wasn't lying in a tent wondering what lay ahead. From at least January 21, he was involved in the "serious fighting," having first taken command of a mortar unit and, shortly afterward, of an entire company. The other officers had indeed "been put out of action" and there was no one else to take command.

Nor was he "on the southwest outskirts" of Grozny. On February

19, while helping the battalion's intelligence unit escape an ambush and "covering his comrades' retreat" from the village of Ushkaloy, Itum-Kalin District (according to the citation nominating him for the Order of Valor), Lieutenant Levurda was mortally wounded and died of "massive hemorrhaging following multiple bullet wounds."

So Pavel Levurda died in Ushkaloy, where the fighting was at its fiercest—a desperate partisan war in highland forests, on narrow paths. But where was Pavel's body? The family never received a coffin containing Nina Levurda's son for burial. His remains, she discovered, had been lost by the state he had tried with such desperate loyalty to serve.

Nina Levurda then took on the tasks of military prosecutor and investigating officer. She found out that on February 19, the official date of her son's death, the comrades whose retreat he was covering did indeed get away, and simply abandoned Pavel, along with six other soldiers who had saved them, by breaking through the ambush at the scene of heavy fighting. Most of the soldiers left behind had been wounded but were still alive. They shouted for help, begged not to be abandoned, as villagers later testified. They bandaged some of the wounded themselves, but could do no more. There is no hospital in Ushkaloy, no doctor, not even a nurse.

Pavel Levurda had been deserted on the battlefield and then forgotten. Nobody cared that his body was lying there, or that he had a family awaiting his return. What happened after his death is typical of the army, a disgraceful episode that stands for an ethos in which a human is nothing, in which no one watches over the troops, and there is no sense of responsibility toward the families.

The military only remembered Pavel Levurda on February 24, when, according to information provided by general headquarters in Chechnya, Ushkaloy was cleared of Chechen fighters and "came under the control" of federal forces. (This explanation was actually presented later, to prove that "there was no objective possibility" of recovering Pavel's body.)

On February 24, the army collected the bodies of six of the seven soldiers. They couldn't find Pavel Levurda, so they forgot about him again.

Back home, Pavel's mother was in a dreadful state. The only communication she had had was Pavel's letter, which she had received on February 7. The Ministry of Defense's "hotline" wasn't much help: talking to the duty officers there was like talking to a computer. "Lieutenant Pavel Petrovich Levurda is not on the list of the dead or missing," was the invariable reply she received. Nina went back to the "fully updated" hotline over the course of several months: even after she had located Pavel's remains through her own efforts, even after official notification of his death, she continued to hear the same information.

But to return to the story of Pavel's body. On May 20, three months after the fighting in Ushkaloy, the village police discovered "the body of a man showing signs of violent death." However, it was only on July 6, after another one and a half months of Nina's calls to the hotline and the local army commissariat, that the same police filed the relevant form, "Orientation/Task No. 464," in response to the ordinary missing-person's inquiry Nina had registered with her own local police. On July 19 the Ushkaloy report finally reached Bryansk, where Pavel's family lived. Thus on August 2, Detective Abramochkin, an ordinary police officer, came to see Pavel's parents.

The only person at home was another Nina, Pavel's fourteen-year-old niece. Abramochkin asked her some questions regarding the belongings Pavel might have had on him, and was surprised to find he was talking to a soldier's family. To Abramochkin, what had begun as a routine investigation became something quite different. It was Abramochkin—and not an official from the Ministry of Defense— who came to inform the mother of a hero that her son's entitlement to all provisions and allowances had been canceled. And it was Abramochkin who was sent to the parents in Bryansk to ask for "the permanent postal address of Army Unit 73881 in which Levurda, P. P. had been serving" so that the Itum-Kalin police could contact the unit's commanding officer to establish the circumstances relating to the death of a person who, from his mother's description, appeared to resemble one of their officers. (The quotation is from the official correspondence. It reveals a good deal about the realities of the army and the nature of Putin's war in the Caucasus.)

Seeing the state the family was in, Abramochkin strongly advised Nina Levurda to go to the main military mortuary in Rostov-on-Don as soon as she could. He had heard that the remains of the unknown soldier from Ushkaloy had been taken there for identification by Colonel Vladimir Shcherbakov, director of the 124th Military Forensic Medical Laboratory and a well-known and respected man. Shcherbakov, it should be noted, does this work not at the behest of the army but because his heart tells him it is the right thing to do. Abramochkin also advised Nina not to expect too much, because, as we say, "anything can happen in Russia," where mix-ups involving dead bodies are only too common. In the meantime, the Bryansk Committee of Soldiers' Mothers was helping with the Levurda saga, and it was only through its good offices and the efforts of Abramochkin that the elite Fifteenth Guards Regiment and the even more elite Taman Guards Division finally twigged that the seventh body just might be that of Pavel Levurda.

"We arrived in Rostov on August 20," Nina said. "I went straight to the laboratory. There was no security at the entrance. I walked in and went into the first autopsy room I found. I saw a severed head on a stand next to an examination table. More precisely, it was a skull. I knew immediately that it was Pavel's head, even though there were other skulls nearby."

Is there any way to assess this mother's distress or compensate the distress her for it? Of course not. Nina was given sedatives after the encounter with her son's skull, which she had correctly identified. At this moment a representative from Pavel's unit came rushing in to see her; the commanding officer had received a telegram from Abramochkin and then sent someone to Rostov to take care of the formalities. This representative soldier showed Nina a letter. She looked at it and, despite the sedatives she had just taken, she fainted. She already knew the news contained in the letter; the army's callousness, however, was a fresh blow. In the letter, the acting commanding officer of Army Unit 73881 and the unit's chief of staff requested that "Citizens Levurda" be informed that "their son, while on a military mission, true to his military oath, showing devotion and courage, has died in battle." The unit was trying to cover the tracks of its forgetfulness.

When Nina recovered, she read the notice more carefully. There was no indication of when her son had died.

"Well, what about the date?" Nina asked the soldier.

"Write it in yourself, whatever you like," he replied.

"What do you mean, write it in?" Nina shouted. "The day Pasha was born is his date of birth. Surely I have a right to know the date of his death!"

The soldier shrugged and went on to hand her a further document: an order to "remove Lieutenant Levurda from the list of members of the Regiment." This paper, too, bore no date and indicated no reason for removing Pavel's name, but it did have various stamps and signatures at the bottom. Again, with the artless gaze of a child, the unit's representative asked Nina to fill in the blanks herself and hand the paper in, when she got home, to the local army commissariat so that Pavel could be removed from the register.

Nina said nothing. What was the point of talking to a person with no heart, brain, or soul?

"But surely that's easiest, isn't it? Rather than me having to go all the way to Bryansk?" the soldier continued uncertainly.

Of course it was easier. There is no denying that soullessness makes life easier. Take the minister of defense, Sergey Ivanov, a crony of the president since Putin's FSB days in Saint Petersburg. Every week Ivanov appears on television to deliver the president's war bulletin. Nobody will make us "kneel down before terrorists," he says; he intends to pursue the war in Chechnya to its "victorious conclusion." Minister Ivanov has nothing to say about the fate of the soldiers and officers who allow him and the president to avoid seeming to kneel down before terrorists. Their line is wholly neo-Soviet: humans have no independent existence; they are cogs in a machine whose function is to implement unquestioningly whatever political escapade those in power have dreamed up. Cogs have no rights, not even to dignity in death.

Not being heartless is much harder work. But that would mean seeing beyond the general policies of the party and government to the details of how these policies are implemented. In the present instance, the details are that, on August 31, 2000, No. U-729343 was finally buried in the city of Ivanovo, to which Pavel's parents had moved to escape the dark associations of Bryansk. The forensic analysis in Rostov passed Pavel's head on to Nina. Unfortunately, that seemed to be all the remains they had to return.

MANY RUSSIANS HAVE heard of Nina Levurda because, on the ninth day after the funeral, having committed what was left of her son to the earth, she set off to the headquarters of the Fifteenth Guards Regiment, in Moscow Province. Her initial intention was only to look Pavel's commanding officers in the eye and to find in them, when confronted by his mother, at least some remorse for all the things they had forgotten to do.

"Of course, I didn't expect them to apologize," Nina said, "but I did think I might at least see some sympathy in their faces."

When she arrived at the Taman Guards Division, however, nobody wanted to see this mother. The commanding officer was simply unavailable. Nina sat for three days waiting to meet him, without food, tea, sleep, or any attention paid to her. Senior officers scurried to and fro like cockroaches, pretending not to notice her. It was then that Nina Levurda vowed to sue the state, to bring an action against the Ministry of Defense and Ivanov for the suffering they had caused. Not in connection with her son's death—he had, after all, perished in the line of duty—but because of what had happened subsequently. Translated from convoluted legal jargon into plain speech, she wanted to know who was responsible.

What happened next? First, the Order of Valor awarded post-humously to Nina's son was presented to the family in the army commissariat in Ivanovo. Second, the army took its revenge. The Ministry of Defense and the Taman Guards Division went on the warpath against this mother who had dared to express her outrage at their behavior.

This is how they went about it. In just under a year, there were eight court hearings, the first on December 26, 2001, the last on November 18, 2002, none of which came to any conclusion. The court never even got around to considering the substance of Nina's writ, because the Ministry of Defense ignored the hearings completely. And in the view of at least one court, they were right to do so. The case of "Nina Levurda against the state" first came before a judge in the Krasnaya Presnya Intermunicipal Court, Moscow. He decreed that a mother "has no right to information" about her son's body, and the Ministry of Defense was, accordingly, under no obligation to supply her with such information. Nina went to the Moscow City Court, where, in view of the manifest absurdity of the previous verdict, the case was referred back to the Krasnaya Presnya Court for a new hearing. The state machine's assault on the bereaved mother continued to take the form of a boycott of the court sessions by Ivanov's representatives and by the Land Forces Command, of which the Taman Guards Division and the Fifteenth Guards Regiment are a part. They simply failed to appear, brazenly and systematically. So Nina Levurda kept going from Ivanovo to Moscow, only to find herself confronted by an empty dock, her journey wasted. An ordinary woman dependent on her state pension, whose purpose is only to keep you from starving, Nina also found that her husband had taken to the bottle after Pavel's funeral as a way to escape from their suffering.

In the end, Judge Bolonina of the Krasnaya Presnya District Court, to whom the case had been referred from the Moscow City Court, became exasperated. At the fifth hearing, she fined the Min-

istry of Defense 8,000 rubles—at taxpayer expense, of course—for
failing to appear. Then, on November 18, 2002, after the imposition
of the fine, Ministry of Defense representatives finally turned up in
the courtroom, but they knew nothing about the case and declined to
identify themselves, complaining that chaos at the ministry was the
cause of the problems. The upshot was that the court was again ad-
journed, this time to December 2.

Nina was in tears as she stood in the grim corridor of the court
building.

"Why are they doing this?" she asked. "You'd think they had done
nothing wrong."

How enviable to be Sergey Ivanov, head of the pitiless Ministry of
Defense. How straightforward his life must be, not having to bother
with mothers whose sons have died in the "war on terror" about which
he waxes so lyrical, not having to hear their voices or feel their pain.
He knows nothing of the lives he has destroyed, nothing of the thousands of parents deserted by the system after their children have given
their lives for it.

"Putin can't do everything!" the president's admirers protest.

Indeed he can't. But as president, he is the person who shapes policies. In Russia, people imitate the man at the top. We know how he
views the army. He is entirely to blame for the brutality and extremism
endemic in both the army and the state. Cruelty is an infection that
can easily become pandemic. First inflicted on people in Chechnya, it
is now used against "our people," as the patriotically inclined like to
describe Russian citizens—including the soldiers, those Russians who
fought patriotically against the Chechens, who experienced the state's
atrocities first.

"Well, he made his choice and followed his destiny," says Nina,
wiping the tears from her face as Judge Bolonina stalks past in her
robes, inscrutable. "But for heaven's sake, aren't these people human
beings?"

FIFTY-FOUR SOLDIERS,
OR RUNNING HOME TO MOM

People leave Russia when staying either becomes life-threatening or involves massive injury to their integrity and dignity. On September 8, 2002, such was the situation in the army. Fifty-four soldiers gave up and tried to leave.

The Twentieth Guards Motorized Infantry Division training grounds are situated on the outskirts of the village of Prudboy, in Volgograd Province. The men of the Second Section of Army Unit 20004 had been taken from their permanent base in the town of Kamyshin, also in Volgograd Province, to the grounds in Prudboy.

The move seemed unexceptional: the troops were to receive training. Their instructors would be their commanding officers. On September 8, however, these role models, Lieutenant Colonel Kolesnikov, Major Shiryaev, Major Artemiev, Lieutenant Kadiev, Lieutenant Korostylev, Lieutenant Kobets, and Sublieutenant Pekov, decided to conduct an inquiry outside their authority. The soldiers assembled on the parade grounds were told there was to be an investigation to find out who had stolen a fighting reconnaissance and landing vehicle (FRLV) during the night.

The soldiers later insisted that nobody had stolen the FRLV. It was right there in its usual place in the divisional parking lot. The officers were just bored. They had been drinking for days, were probably feeling ill as a result and decided to divert themselves with a bit of bullying. It was not by any means the first time this sort of thing had occurred at the Kamyshin training ground, which has a bad reputation.

After the announcement, a first batch of soldiers was led into the officers' tent: Sergeants Kutuzov and Krutov, Privates Generalov, Gursky, and Gritsenko. The others, who were ordered to wait outside, soon heard the cries and groans of their fellow soldiers. The officers were beating them. The first batch was thrown out of the tent. They told their comrades that the officers had beaten them on their buttocks and backs with the hafts of entrenching tools, and kicked them in the belly and the ribs. The description was unnecessary. The signs of the beatings were clearly visible on the soldiers' bodies.

The officers announced that they would now take a break. The lieutenant colonel, two majors, three lieutenants, and one sublieutenant would be having dinner, and they informed the remaining soldiers that failure to confess voluntarily to having stolen the FRLV would result in being beaten in the same way as those now sprawled on the grass outside their tent.

Their announcement made, the officers departed to take soup.

And the soldiers? They walked out. They mutinied, choosing not to wait like sheep for the slaughter. They left the soldiers on sentry duty behind, since deserting your post is a criminal offense involving a court-martial and sentencing to a disciplinary battalion, and they also left Kutuzov, Krutov, Generalov, and Gritsenko, who were incapable of walking.

Forming a column, the soldiers marched out of the training ground toward Volgograd to get help.

It is a fair distance from Prudboy to Volgograd but the fifty-four soldiers marched the entire journey in an orderly manner, making no attempt to hide, on the edge of a busy highway along which officers of the Twentieth Division were traveling to and fro. Not one vehicle stopped. No one thought to ask where the soldiers were going without an officer, which is against army regulations.

The soldiers marched until dark. They lay down to sleep in the strip of woodland beside the highway. No one came looking for them, despite the fact that when the lieutenant colonel, two majors, three lieutenants, and one sublieutenant emerged from the dining room after finishing their meal, they discovered a marked thinning of the numbers of the Second Section. They had almost no one left to command.

The officers went to bed, having no idea of the whereabouts of the soldiers for whom, by law, they were personally responsible, but knowing full well that in Russia no officer is ever punished for something that has happened to a private.

Early on the morning of September 9, the fifty-four soldiers set off again along the highway. And again army officers drove insouciantly by.

This detachment of soldiers blessed with self-respect was on the march for one and a half days, and nobody from the Twentieth Division missed them. On the evening of September 9, they marched quite openly into Volgograd. They were observed by the police, but still nobody took any interest.

The soldiers marched to the city center.

"It was about six in the evening, and we were preparing to go home when the telephone rang suddenly. 'Are you still open? May we come to see you?'" Tatyana Zozulenko, director of the Volgograd Province Mothers' Rights organization, tells me. "I said, 'Come right in.' Of course, there was no way I was expecting what happened next. Four young privates came into our small room and said there were fifty-four of them. I asked where the others were, and the boys led me down to the little basement of our own building. The rest were all standing there. I have worked in this organization for eleven years but had never seen anything quite like that before. The first thing I worried about was where we were going to put them all. It was already evening. We asked them whether they had eaten. 'No,' they replied, 'not since yesterday.' Our members ran off to buy as much bread and milk as they could. The boys fell on the food like hungry dogs, but that was something we are used to. Soldiers are very badly fed in their units. They are chronically undernourished.

"When they had eaten, I asked, 'What do you want the result of your action to be?' They replied, 'We want officers who beat up soldiers to be punished.' We decided to put them up for the night in Mothers' Rights, all of them in together on the floor, to give us time to sleep on it. First thing in the morning we would go to the garrison prosecutor's office. I locked the door and went home. I live nearby and thought I could come around quickly if I was needed. At eleven that evening I phoned them, but nobody answered. I thought they must just be tired, probably asleep or afraid of answering the phone. I was awakened at two in the morning by our lawyer Sergey Semushin. He said someone who hadn't identified himself had called to ask him to 'secure his premises.' I was around there within minutes. There were small military vehicles outside with officers in them. They did not introduce themselves. The soldiers had disappeared. I asked the officers where they were and got no reply."

The Mothers' Rights workers also discovered that their computer system, with information about crimes committed in the Twentieth Division, had been broken into and stripped. They found a note under the carpet from a soldier saying they didn't know where they were being taken; they were being beaten and needed help.

There is a little more to add. The officers at the training ground "missed" their soldiers only after being telephoned by their superiors. This was late in the evening of September 9, after Tatyana Zozulenko had contacted journalists in Volgograd and information about the AWOL soldiers had first gone out on the airwaves. The regional staff headquarters naturally demanded an explanation from the officers. Then, during the night, vehicles drove up to Mothers' Rights, and all fifty-four soldiers were removed to the guardhouse in the military commandant's office. They were then returned to their unit under the supervision of the very officers whose bullying had made the soldiers leave the training ground in the first place. Zozulenko asked Volgograd garrison prosecutor Chernov, whose duty it is to ensure that the law is upheld in the garrison's units, why he had returned the soldiers to the Twentieth Division, and he replied, without flinching, "Because these are *our soldiers.*"

That's the key phrase in the saga of the fifty-four. "Our soldiers" effectively means "our slaves." Everything remains just as it always has been in the Russian army, where a perverse understanding of an officer's honor means the negligible value of the life and dignity of any private.

The march from the training ground was the result of the abhorrent tradition that a soldier is an officer's slave. An officer can treat a soldier exactly as he pleases. It also stemmed from the sad fact that civilian control of army procedures, about which much was said in the Yeltsin years, and a draft law was even written, is non-existent. President Putin shares the army's view of its officers' rights and considers civilian monitoring of the armed forces inappropriate.

Underlying this story is the fact that the Twentieth Division—also called the Rokhlin Division after its commander, Lev Rokhlin, a hero of the first Chechen war and today a deputy of the state duma—and particularly Unit 20004, have long been notorious in Volgograd, and indeed throughout Russia.

"For an entire year we sent information to the military prosecutor's office, primarily to Mr. Chernov, the garrison prosecutor, but also to everyone higher up the hierarchy, right up to the chief military prosecutor's office in Moscow, about the crimes committed by the officers of Unit 20004," Tatyana Zozulenko says. "In terms of the number of complaints we receive from soldiers, Unit 20004 is top of the list. The officers beat their soldiers and extort their active service payments from those who have returned from Chechnya. We have yelled about this from the rooftops, but nothing has happened. The prosecutor's office has decided to keep everything quiet. The episode at the training ground is a wholly predictable result of army officers' lack of accountability."[1]

A Few Shorter Stories

Misha Nikolaev lived in Moscow Province. His family saw him off to the army in July 2001. He was sent to the Border Guards, to a frontier post ten hours' flying time from Moscow, at the village of Goryachy Plyazh, on Anuchina Island in the Lesser Kurils—the Pacific islands that have vexed Russian and Japanese politicians since the end of the Second World War.

While the two nations argue, someone has to police the border. Misha was one of those doing the job. He lasted just six months at this outpost of the Russian Far East and died on December 22, 2001. By the autumn he had already been writing alarming letters home, having discovered festering sores on his body. He asked his family to send medicine: Vishnevsky's Balm, sulfanilamide, "in fact, any medicines for treating suppuration, metapyrin, antiseptic, bandages and as much sticking plaster as possible. There is nothing here." His parents sent off the parcels without complaining; aware that the army is under-funded, they assumed that things could not be all that bad, since Misha was still working as a cook in the army's kitchens. If he was seriously ill, his parents supposed, he wouldn't be allowed anywhere near food preparation.

Even when his skin was covered with oozing sores, though, Misha continued to cook meals for the troops. The pathologist who conducted the autopsy reported that the unfortunate soldier's tissues literally split apart under the scalpel. At the beginning of the twenty-first century, a Russian soldier rotted alive under the eyes of his officers, receiving no medical attention at all. What killed Misha was the complete lack of responsibility of his superiors.

DMITRY KISELEV WAS posted to serve in the Moscow Province village of Istra. In Russia such an assignment is regarded as a stroke of luck. He was close to Moscow; his parents, being Muscovites, could visit their son and battle their way through to his commanding officer if he needed help. It was not the Kuril Islands. The location did not, however, save Dmitry from his officers' depravity.

Lieutenant Colonel Alexander Boronenkov, Private Kiselev's

commanding officer, had a lucrative sideline. Nothing too unusual about that in today's army. People are up to all sorts of tricks, because their wages don't amount to much. This particular lieutenant colonel's enterprise was trading in soldiers. Istra is a dacha settlement of second homes, and Boronenkov sold his soldiers to the owners of nearby plots of land as cheap labor. The soldiers worked only for food; their pay went straight to their commanding officer. This moneymaking scheme is by no means unique. Indeed, it is widespread: soldiers become the unpaid laborers—that is, slaves—of wealthy people for the duration of their military service. In some cases, the officers use the troops as a means of bartering with people they think of as useful. If an officer needs his car repaired and has no money, he herds a few soldiers along to the local body shop. They work there, unpaid, for as long as the shop requires; in return, the officer gets his car fixed.

In late June 2002, it was the turn of the newly conscripted Dmitry Kiselev to be sold into slavery. Private Kiselev was sent to build a house for a certain member of the Mir Horticultural Association in Istra District. Initially he was constructing a house, but then he and seven other conscripts were required to dig a deep trench the length of the plot. On July 2 at seven in the evening, the sides of the trench collapsed, burying three of the troops, including Dmitry, who suffocated under the earth. His parents tried to have Lieutenant Colonel Boronenkov brought to trial, but he wriggled out of it. He knew a lot of useful people. Dmitry was the Kiselevs' only son.[2]

ON AUGUST 28, 2002, Army Unit 42839 was deployed in Chechnya, not far from the village of Kalinovskaya, a place where there had been no fighting for a long time. The Granddads were drinking themselves silly. Granddads—ordinary soldiers about to be demobilized into the reserves—are the most terrifying, murderous force in the army. In the evening it seemed to the Granddads that they were running short of vodka, so they told the first soldier who came along, Yury Diachenko, to go into the village and "get some more from wherever you like." The soldier refused. In the first place, he was on duty guarding a section of the perimeter and had no right to leave his post. In the second place, as he explained, he had no money. The Granddads told him to steal something in the village and get them the vodka that way.

Yury, however, said firmly, "No. I won't go." They beat him brutally until five in the morning, and between beatings subjected him to cruel and disgusting humiliations. They dipped a floor cloth into the latrine and rubbed the filth in Yury's face. They forced him to clean the floor, and when he bent over, took turns ramming the handle of the mop into his anus. To conclude their training session, as they called it, the Granddads dragged Yury into the canteen and forced him to eat a three-liter can of kasha, beating him if he tried to stop.

Where were the officers? That night they, too, were drinking themselves senseless and were physically incapable of being in charge of anything. At around six in the morning, Yury Diachenko was found in the provisions depot. He had hanged himself.

ALTHOUGH SIBERIA IS not Chechnya—it is far removed from the war—the distance makes no difference. Valerii Putintsev, a young man born in Tyumen Province, was posted to the Krasnoyarsk Region to serve in the district town of Uzhur, in the elite units of the strategic missile forces. His mother, Svetlana Putintseva, was delighted. Because they were dealing with the most up-to-date and dangerous weaponry on the planet, officers in the missile units were considered to be the best educated in the army, not likely to get drunk or to beat up conscripts, and likely to maintain discipline. Soon, however, she, too, began to receive distressing letters from her son, in which he wrote that the officers were no better than "jackals":

Hello, Mom! I don't want this letter to be seen by anyone other than you. In particular, please keep what I am writing from Gran. We both know the score there, and I'm sure you won't undermine what health she has left. I worry about her a lot. I can't accept that I have to work as a slave to benefit people I despise. More than anything in the world, I want to work for the good of my own people, to better my family. It's only since being here that I have understood how important you all are. . . .

Valerii was never to return to work for the good of his people. The officers in the Uzhur barracks robbed the soldiers of everything they had, degrading any who, like Valerii, tried to defend their dignity. In the half year he spent in his unit, four soldiers were carried out in coffins, all of them privates, all of them beaten to death.

The officers' first game was to confiscate Valerii's uniform (the soldiers have no clothing apart from their uniforms). They told him that now he had to ransom it. They assumed he would write home and ask for money to be sent as a matter of urgency. Valerii resisted. He knew that his mother lived very modestly with his grandmother, an old-age pensioner, his sister, and her little daughter, and could ill afford to send him money. As a result of his concern for his family, he was brutally and repeatedly beaten. In the end, he had had enough. He turned on the officers and was sent to the guardhouse for insubordination. Pretending he was attempting to escape, they wounded him badly. Svetlana Putintseva became anxious and called the unit's commanding officer, Lieutenant Colonel Butov, who she says informed her that he knew how to beat people so as not to leave any trace. Svetlana dropped everything and flew straight to Uzhur, where she found her son at death's door. He had gunshot wounds to the pelvis, the bladder, the ureter, and the femoral artery. In the hospital his mother was told to find blood for a transfusion: "Urgently! We have no blood here." Alone in a strange town, she was expected to find donors. She rushed back to the army unit to ask for help. The commanding officer refused. She scrambled through the city, trying to save her son. She failed. Valerii, lacking a transfusion, died, on February 27, 2002. In one of his last letters, he had written to Svetlana, "I wasn't expecting much help from the officers. All they are capable of is humiliating people."

BACK TO MOSCOW Province. It is the morning of May 4, 2002. Army Unit 13815, in the village of Balashikha. Two boilerwomen working in the plant that provides heating for the unit hear cries for help from nearby. They rush out and see that a trench has been dug in the middle of the courtyard, in which a soldier has been buried up to his neck. The women dig down, cut the rope binding him hand and foot, and help him out of the pit.

At this moment an army major appears in a towering rage. He shouts at the women to leave the soldier alone. He is teaching Private Chesnokov a lesson, and if they do not go back to the boilerhouse immediately, he will have them sacked.

Private Chesnokov, having escaped from the pit, deserted from the unit.

THE RUSSIAN ARMY has always been a fundamental pillar of the state. To this day, it is mostly a prison camp behind barbed wire where the country's young are locked up without trial. It has prisonlike rules imposed by the officers. It is a place where beating the hell out of someone is the basic method of training. This, incidentally, is how Putin, when he first took the Kremlin throne, described the way he would deal with enemies within Russia.

It may be that the president finds this state of affairs agreeable, with his lieutenant colonel's epaulettes and his two daughters who will never have to serve in such an army. The rest of us—apart from the officer caste, who revel in their status as petty gangsters above the law—are deeply unhappy about the situation. This is especially true of those who have sons, and all the more so if the young men are of conscription age. These families have no time to wait for the military reforms they have been promised for so long. They fear that their sons will leave home only to be sent straight to a training ground or to Chechnya or to some other place from which there is no return.

OUR NEW MIDDLE AGES, OR
WAR CRIMINALS OF ALL THE RUSSIAS

We currently have two kinds of war criminals in Russia. The crimes of both relate to the second Chechen war, which began in August 1999 just as Vladimir Putin was appointed prime minister. The war—a feature of his first presidential term—continues to this day.

All the war-crimes prosecutions that have occurred have had one common attribute: their outcome has been determined on ideological rather than on legal grounds. *Inter arma silent leges:* In time of war, the laws are silent. Those found guilty have been sentenced, not after due process but in accordance with the ideological winds blowing from the Kremlin.

The first kind of war criminal is someone who was, in fact, involved in military conflict—for example, an army soldier engaged in the "antiterrorist operation" in Chechnya, or a Chechen fighter who opposed the army. The former is always cleared of his crime; the latter, treated with scant regard for the law, is charged with a crime. The former is acquitted by the judicial system even where there is manifest proof of guilt (which is rare, since the prosecutor's office usually makes no attempt to collect evidence). The latter is given the severest sentence possible.

The best-known federal case is that of Colonel Yury Budanov, commanding officer of the 160th Tank Regiment. On March 26, 2000, the day Putin was elected president, Budanov abducted, raped, and murdered an eighteen-year-old Chechen girl, Elza Kungaeva, who lived with her parents in the village of Tangi-Chu, on the outskirts of which Budanov's regiment was temporarily deployed. We'll examine Budanov's experiences later in this chapter.

The best-known Chechen case is that of Salman Raduev. Raduev was a renowned Chechen field commander, a brigadier who had been carrying out terrorist raids since the first Chechen war, when he had commanded what was known as the army of General Dudaev. Raduev was caught in 2001, sentenced to life imprisonment, and died in mysterious circumstances in Solikamsk high-security prison. Solikamsk is an infamous prison city, nestled among salt mines in Perm Province, in the Urals, a place of exile since czarist times. Raduev was a symbol of those fighting for Chechen freedom from Russia. There are many cases like his; as a rule, they are heard behind closed doors, to conceal information from the public. The need for such hush-hush activity is often obscure. Occasionally it is possible, with great difficulty and in great secrecy, to obtain the court records of cases brought against Chechen fighters. The accused are usually found guilty; no time is wasted on the collection and consideration of evidence.

Thus, no one in the first category of accused war criminals, whether federal or Chechen, gets a fair trial. After sentencing, Chechen fighters are sent off to remote labor camps and prisons and do not survive for long. Opinion polls show that even those who support the government's war in Chechnya believe these prisoners are "gotten rid of" at the behest of the authorities. Almost nobody in Russia believes that the judicial system is fair, while almost everybody believes that the judiciary is subordinate to the executive branch.

Then there is the second kind of war criminal: the individual who

is in the wrong place at the wrong time, someone run over by the jug-
gernaut of history—not a soldier on either side but a Chechen who
becomes a convenient scapegoat. A typical case is that of Islam Hasuhanov. Everything about his story is redolent of Stalin's purges.
Witness statements are beaten out of people; torture and pyschotropic
drugs are used to break the will of the accused. This is the hellish path
traveled by the majority of Chechens who have found themselves in
the torture chambers not only of the FSB but of all the other security
agencies rampaging in Chechnya. Individuals were tortured by the
henchmen of the late Ahmat-Hadji Kadyrov, who, until his assassina-
tion, was head of the pro-Moscow Chechen puppet government; they
are tortured in the military commandant's posts, in pits on the territory of army units, in solitary-confinement cells at police stations.

All these practices are coordinated and managed by the FSB. These
are Putin's people, they enjoy Putin's support, and they carry out
Putin's policies.

STALIN WILL ALWAYS BE WITH US

The File

Islam Sheikh-Ahmedovich Hasuhanov was born in 1954 in Kirghizia.
Beginning in 1973, he served in the Soviet army. He graduated from
the Kiev Higher Naval Political College, and in the 1980s served in
the Baltic Fleet, and from 1989 in the Pacific Fleet. In 1991 he graduated from the Lenin Political Military Academy, in Moscow. As a
submarine officer who had graduated from a military academy, Hasuhanov would have been regarded as the elite of the Russian navy. He
retired to the reserves in 1998, with the rank of captain first class,
from the position of deputy commander of a B-251 nuclear submarine. From 1998 he lived in Grozny, where he was head of the Military
Inspectorate in the government of Aslan Maskhadov and head of
Maskhadov's operational staff. He is married to Maskhadov's niece, his

second wife, and has two sons. Hasuhanov took no active part in the first or the second Chechen war and was never in hiding from the federal authorities. Arrested on April 20, 2002, in the district center of Shali by special units of the FSB as an "international terrorist" and "one of the organizers of illegal armed formations [IAFs]," he was sentenced by the Supreme Court of the republic of North Ossetia–Alaniya to twelve years' detention in a strict-regime labor camp.

The Prehistory of the Trial

What happens to a man after he is picked up by the FSB? Not the Cheka of 1937, not the Cheka of Aleksandr Solzhenitsyn and the Gulag, but the one funded by today's taxpayers? Nobody has any hard facts, but everybody is frightened, just as people used to be.

And just as under the Soviet regime, only rarely does any information get out. One of those rare instances is the case of Islam Hasuhanov.

According to the file of Criminal Case No. 56/17, Islam Hasuhanov was arrested on April 27, 2002, on Mayakovsky Street in Shali, and charged under Article 222 of the Criminal Code of the Russian Federation with "being in possession of and bearing firearms." The wording would lead one to expect some evidence of the alleged weapons.

In fact, armed individuals wearing masks, as is usual in Chechnya, burst at dawn into the house of Hasuhanov's relatives, where he was living with his family. They dragged him off to an unknown destination without bothering to plant any firearms on him; he had none of his own. The federal special units operating in Chechnya in the search for "international terrorists" have long been confident that they can behave, no matter how despicably, with impunity. This time they were acting on a tip-off from an informer, and had no doubt they were picking up one of the leaders of an IAF whose fate was already sealed. As he would not be surviving, no pistol, no assault rifle was registered as material evidence.

The charge under Article 222 was allowed to stand anyway. The false date of April 27 was also left intact. Missing weeks are characteristic of the antiterrorist operation in Chechnya. A man is arrested and goes missing. The first seven days of his detention are the most brutal. No organization is responsible for him; none of the security agencies admits to knowing anything about him. His relatives search desperately, but it is as if he does not exist. It is during this time that the intelligence services beat everything they need out of him.

Hasuhanov has barely any recollection of the period between April 20 and 27. Beatings, injections, more beatings, more injections. Nothing beyond that. The record of the court hearing ten months after that terrible week states: "For the first seven days I was held in the FSB building in Shali, where I was beaten. Dating from that time I have 14 broken ribs, one rib in my kidney."

What did the authorities want to get out of Hasuhanov before he died from his injuries? They demanded that he lead them to Maskhadov.[3] After that he could die. The trouble was, Hasuhanov didn't take them to Maskhadov, and with the robust good health of a submarine officer, he didn't die, either.

On April 30 it was decided to formalize the case against him. He was dragged off (the public prosecutor of Chechnya at the time was Alexander Nikitin) to a temporary interrogation unit in another Chechen district center, Znamenskaya. This village was blasted from the face of the earth by a female suicide bomber on May 12, 2003. Afterward there was general satisfaction in Chechnya, where most people felt that justice had been done at last. How many people had been tortured there and were secretly buried in the area?

When Hasuhanov arrived in Znamenskaya, he looked like death. His body resembled a sack, but he was breathing. The torture continued under the supervision of Lieutenant Colonel Anatoly Cherepnev, deputy head of the investigative section of the directorate of the FSB for Chechnya. Cherepnev was to be the main investigator in the

Hasuhanov case, deciding on the level of torture and directing the process to obtain the required evidence.

From the court record:

> "Why were violent means being used against you?"
> "In all the interviews, all they were interested in was where Maskhadov was and where the submarine was that I supposedly was intending to hijack. Those were the two questions in connection with which violent means were used against me."

Hasuhanov could not lead his questioners to Maskhadov because he had last seen him in 2000 and subsequently had contact with him only on audiocassettes. When necessary, Maskhadov would record one and send it to Hasuhanov by courier. Occasionally Hasuhanov would reply. One of the couriers had become an FSB informer. The last time before his arrest that Hasuhanov had received a cassette was in January 2002, and he had replied two days earlier. On the tapes, Maskhadov usually asked Hasuhanov, apparently for the record, to confirm how much money he, Maskhadov, had transferred to which field commanders. We shall see why Maskhadov was interested in this subject.

Let us turn to the submarine. Its story deserves to be told in some detail. As noted earlier, Hasuhanov had been a high-ranking submarine officer before retiring. He was the only Chechen who ever became an officer in the nuclear submarine fleet, in either Soviet or post-Soviet times. Accordingly, Lieutenant Colonel Cherepnev set about trying to incriminate him in the "planning of an IAF to hijack a nuclear submarine, gain possession of a nuclear warhead, seize Deputies of the State Duma as hostages, demand changes to the constitutional system of the Russian Federation by threatening to use a nuclear warhead and to kill hostages." This is a quotation from a form returned by Cherepnev to the public prosecutor's office in Chechnya with a request for permission to continue the detention of Hasuhanov. The request was not refused.

Cherepnev did his utmost to incriminate Hasuhanov, but the results were unspectacular. Hasuhanov would not, and indeed could not, give in. In 1992 he himself had "built," as they say in the navy, the very submarine Cherepnev was accusing him of planning to hijack. Hasuhanov had monitored the submarine's construction, knowing that he would be serving on it. Thus he had supervised the project on behalf of its future crew.

Cherepnev worked hard on the story of the submarine hijacking. The FSB forged documents supposedly written by Chechen fighters on the basis of intelligence supplied by Hasuhanov. There was a "Working Plan of Chechen IAFs for carrying out an act of sabotage on the territory of the Russian Federation and hand-drawn maps of the bases of 4 Nuclear Submarine Flotilla of the Pacific Fleet" and a "Plan for conducting a terrorist act on the territory of Russia." There was a helpful note added to the effect that "detailed planning of the operation was carried out on the basis of visual and reconnaissance intelligence of the region of interest to us during December 1995." It was under these words that Hasuhanov was meant to place his signature.

The trouble was, the authorities could not get him to sign. The FSB set about beating him more ingeniously, although there was little they hadn't already tried. Now, however, they were punishing him for disrupting their plans.

The only things Cherepnev ever got Hasuhanov to sign ("endorse" was the term used in the verdict), out of his mind from a combination of pain and psychotropic drugs, were blank sheets of "orders and operational instructions of Maskhadov." Cherepnev wrote in whatever it seemed would go down well. Here is an example of one such fabrication:

> On September 2, 2000, Hasuhanov issued a combat instruction ordering all field commanders to scatter small nails, nuts, bolts, and ball bearings on highways and routes of deployment of federal forces in order to disguise mines and explosive devices. Thus, availing himself of his leading role in the IAF, by his deliberate actions

Hasuhanov incited other participants of the IAF to commit terrorist acts directed at opposing the establishment of constitutional order on the territory of the Chechen Republic.

Cherepnev also demanded that Hasuhanov sign the minutes of his interrogations without reading them. Here is an example of their quality:

> Question [supposedly asked by Cherepnev]: You have been shown a photocopy of an Address to Russian Officers, No. 215 of November 25, 2000. What testimony can you give? Answer [supposedly given by Hasuhanov]: The preparation and distribution of such documents was a component part of the propaganda carried out by the operational directorate of the armed forces of the Chechen Republic of Ichkeria under my immediate leadership. The Addresses referred to were intended to counteract the Russian mass media in respect of their coverage of the progress of the antiterrorist operation. I understood that distribution of such documents could lead to destabilization of the situation on the territory of the Chechen Republic, but continued my activities. . . .

This document is typical of the army's literary style. For a month Hasuhanov was tortured in Znamenskaya so that material of this caliber could be accumulated.

From the court record:

> "And when as a result of these beatings I no longer understood or reacted to anything, I was given injections and transferred to the FSB in North Ossetia. They didn't want to admit me to the interrogation unit there because their doctor said that, as a result of the earlier beatings, I would die within 48 hours. I was then taken to a timber mill, Enterprise No. YaN 68–1."
> "Were you given any medical assistance?"
> "I just lay in the timber mill recovering for three months."

What timber mill is this? Mention is occasionally made of it in stories about people who have vanished without a trace after purges in Chechnya. Some who have been there and survived call it a lumber camp, a term from Stalin's times; others call it a timber mill. Its official title is Enterprise No. YaN 68–1, and it comes under the administration of the Ministry of Justice of the Republic of North Ossetia.

What we do know about the timber mill is that it is the destination of people who have been beaten half to death by officers of the law-enforcement agencies (primarily FSB agents). The enterprise closes its eyes to the fact that these individuals have no identification documents. They are nonpersons who have vanished without a trace after their encounter with the feds.

We owe a debt of gratitude to those who work at the timber mill for illegally accepting the outlawed into their enterprise. They have saved many from certain death: those who were supposed to die but whom the feds simply couldn't be bothered to shoot as they were brought from Chechnya to Ossetia, and those who were sent to the mill to die without the FSB getting its hands dirty. Nobody knows how many people have died there in the course of the second Chechen war or who they were. They have left behind not so much as a grave mound. On the other hand, we do know how many survived. Hasuhanov is one of these. A guard took pity on him, no more than that, and every time the man was on duty he would bring Hasuhanov milk from his home.

Hasuhanov thus survived yet again, and yet again found himself facing Cherepnev. In the Chechen directorate of the FSB, there is a rule that anyone who survives interrogation is put on trial. Not many do, and hence trials of "international terrorists" are few and far between. Nevertheless, for the sake of expediency, at least, some trials are held: within the antiterrorist operation, it is thought desirable to sentence the occasional "terrorist." Western leaders ask Putin questions from time to time; he demands information from the FSB and the prosecutor general's office, and they do their best to oblige. Only, of course, when someone survives.

Vladikavkaz

Vladikavkaz is the capital of the republic of North Ossetia–Alaniya, which borders on Chechnya and Ingushetia. Ossetia, too, is a fully paid-up member of the antiterrorist operation. Mozdok, in North Ossetia, is the main military base where federal groups are formed before being sent to Chechnya. It was the scene of two major suicide bombings in 2003: on June 5 a woman got on a bus transporting military pilots and blew herself up and on August 1 a man crashed a truck loaded with a ton of explosives into a military hospital.

In Vladikavkaz, the traditional setting for many fabricated court cases against international terrorists, the local lawyers act less as counsels for the defense than as functionaries in close liaison with the court, the FSB, and the prosecutor's office. Vladikavkaz is also where agents of the Chechen directorate of the FSB often have extended tours of duty, preferring to bring their victims there to interrogate them, as far away from the war as possible.

Cherepnev now went to Hasuhanov in Vladikavkaz and found him a lawyer. Since June 1, 2003, Russia has had a progressive code of criminal procedure in conformity with the highest European standards. Among other things, it prohibits interrogating a suspect without a lawyer being present, but of course, "when necessary," everything continues as before. In any case, from April 20 until October 9, 2002, for almost six months, Hasuhanov had no legal representation at all. Not until his skull had healed over and his fractured ribs and broken hands had recovered at the timber mill could he be readied for a court appearance.

Here again, the details are of interest. On October 8, Cherepnev summoned Hasuhanov to an interrogation and instructed him to address an application to him. Cherepnev dictated the following: "I request you to provide me with a lawyer for the preliminary investigation. Up to the present time, I have had no need of the services of a lawyer, and in this connection I have no complaints against the investigative services. I request you to appoint an advocate chosen at the investigator's discretion. . . ." On October 9, then, Hasuhanov had his first interrogation in the presence of a Vladikavkaz legal-aid attorney. Hasuhanov suspected the attorney was an FSB agent.[4] The lawyer did nothing to cause him to change his mind. He gave Hasuhanov no advice, sat passively at the interrogations, and said nothing.

From the court record:

> "You may say whether there is a difference between the evidence you gave before a lawyer was present and after, and if so, what that difference is."
> "There is a difference. Before, I was not given the record to read at the end of an interrogation. After the appearance of a lawyer, I was."

In all, Hasuhanov had three such interrogations in the presence of a defense lawyer, on October 9, 23, and 24, 2002. More precisely, in the course of these three days, Cherepnev simply copied the testimony beaten out of the defendant in Znamenskaya onto new forms, which became "testimony in accordance with the code of criminal procedure."

Cherepnev declared that October 25 would be the final day of the investigation. He informed Hasuhanov that he would shortly receive the text of the indictment and that he was to sign it as quickly as possible. So that he should have no illusions. Hasuhanov was taken from the solitary-confinement unit for two days, October 29 and 30—naturally, without a lawyer. He did not know where he was being taken. He had a hood put over his head and was led out as if to be executed. "That's it, the end," the guards said, cocking their rifles.

His execution was a hoax, designed to frighten him into signing the indictment.

Of course he signed. But he remained unbroken, and at the trial he retracted everything on which the indictment was based. The indictment was nonetheless confirmed by the new prosecutor of Chechnya, Vladimir Kravchenko, and the text migrated, virtually intact, into the verdict of Judge Valerii Dzhioyev.

Here are quotations from both the indictment and the verdict, with my comments. It is easy to see how criminal cases are fabricated, and also that none of the counterfeiters are the least bit worried about being exposed or about the fact that these records will remain as the raw material of history (which, in accordance with Russian tradition, will surely be rewritten in the course of time).

> In April 1999, Hasuhanov . . . voluntarily entered an armed formation not permitted under federal law. Hasuhanov made contact with Hambiev Mahomed, an aide of Maskhadov, who proposed that he provide assistance to Maskhadov using his experience to organize the work of "Military Audit," an IAF then being created.

After retiring, Hasuhanov had returned home to Grozny. Unique in being a Chechen officer with an academic education, he was invited by Maskhadov to work in the Chechen government, which, in 1999, was the official republican government, financed from Moscow, and Maskhadov was the lawfully elected president of Chechnya, recognized by Moscow. The "Military Audit" that Maskhadov invited Hasuhanov to join was an urgent requirement. The Chechen bureaucracy was shamelessly corrupt, as indeed were the bureaucrats in Moscow, and the republican government needed a knowledgeable person to monitor the flow of military funds, in particular those coming from the Russian Federal Treasury. What kind of IAF is that?

From the court record:

> "Did you consider the actions of President Maskhadov to be lawful?" [the prosecution asked].
> "Yes. I had no way of knowing that Maskhadov, the government, and security ministries would later be considered illegal. I knew that Maskhadov was the president. He was recognized as such by the Russian leaders. There were meetings with his ministers, financial resources were allocated, so of course I did not know that I was joining an IAF."
> "Was it your job to inspect the finances and general adminis-

tration of the Ministry of Internal Affairs of the Chechen Republic of Ichkeria?"

"Yes, I reported the results of the audit to Maskhadov in June
1999. I listed everything money had been spent on. I received this
information from the Ministry of Internal Affairs of the Russian
Federation. All the information was received through official
channels. I had no reason to suppose anything was unlawful."

Hasuhanov's work before the war did indeed include the inspection
of finances and administration as well as the setting up of a system to
audit and monitor the financial resources allocated for maintaining the
security services of Chechnya: the Ministry of Internal Affairs, the national and presidential guards, and the army's staff headquarters. In
the summer of 1999, Hasuhanov established that considerable sums of
money were passing through staff headquarters for the purchase of
weaponry and uniforms but that, for example, the rocket launchers
the Ministry of Defense was ordering from the Grozny Red Hammer
Factory were known to be militarily useless. This was a blatant mis-
appropriation of funds, as was the purchase of uniforms. They were
being sewn in the Chechen town of Gudremes at a price of sixty rubles
per outfit, but the accompanying documentation stated that they were
"made in the Baltic States" at a higher price.

Hasuhanov reported all this to Maskhadov, and the director of the
military audit office immediately ran into trouble with the president's
security forces, who were involved in all phases of the embezzlement.
After Hasuhanov had worked in the military audit office for just a
week, Maskhadov appointed him chief of staff, simply because he
needed honest people around him.

It was the end of July 1999. Chief of Staff Hasuhanov began work
in August, a few days before the start of the second Chechen war, in
which he refused to take part.

As you read the record of the court hearings (which took place behind closed doors), you cannot help feeling that the trial was a put-up
job. Someone had decided that Hasuhanov had to be sent down for a

very serious offense, but no one would characterize that offense. Had
Hasuhanov, back in 1999, found out something that came back to haunt
him three or four years later? Was it the secret of those embezzled federal funds? There is even some suspicion that the fraud itself was, to a
large extent, the reason the second Chechen war was started, perhaps a
war to ensure that the tracks of the wrongdoers would be covered forever. And is this a reason why the upper echelons of Russia's armed
forces are still so set against peace negotiations?

Here is a further quote from the indictment:

> Hasuhanov was actively involved in the work of the IAF and in 1999
> was engaged in matters relating to the financing of the IAF. He de-
> vised and implemented an auditing system for the financial resources
> provided to maintain the National Guard, general headquarters, and
> Ministry of Internal Affairs IAFs of the self-proclaimed "Republic
> of Ichkeria." Having demonstrated organizational ability and effi-
> ciency in this position, Hasuhanov was appointed by Maskhadov to
> the post of his chief of staff in late July 1999. Actively engaged in the
> work of the above-named IAF, Hasuhanov was involved in formulat-
> ing the basic decisions relating to opposition to the forces of the fed-
> eral government, by means that included armed opposition, in its
> task of restoring constitutional order to the territory of the CRI.

The charge would be laughable if we did not know the price ex-
acted from Hasuhanov for this brazen falsification of history by the
forces of the FSB.

From the record of the court hearing:

> "Tell the court what necessity there was for you personally to be
> in Chechnya from the beginning of combat operations until the
> day of your arrest."
> "I did not consider it possible to turn my back on Maskhadov
> because I considered him the legally elected president. I could not
> stop the war and did everything in my power. . . . I sometimes ful-
> filled his requests. I was not in a fit condition to march through the
> forests, but what I could do I did. I saw people dying. I know what

is meant by 'restoring constitutional order.' I will not conceal the fact that this entire war is genocide. However, I never called for the carrying out of acts of terrorism."

"Did you call for the killing of federal troops?"

"In order to call for that, I would have had to have men under my command. I had no men under my command."

"Were any of the field commanders directly subordinate to you?"

"No."

In front of me I have documents marked OFFICIAL USE ONLY. When he was preparing the court case, Cherepnev sent out inquiries to every local FSB department in Chechnya requesting information on terrorist acts committed in its district on "combat instructions from Chief of the Operational Headquarters of the Armed Forces of the CRI Hasuhanov." Recall the "combat instructions" Hasuhanov signed during his interrogation: blank sheets of paper, on which Cherepnev then wrote in whatever he wanted. Not surprisingly, every local department head replied that Hasuhanov was not wanted for any terrorist acts. These responses came back to Cherepnev not from Chechen fighters but from his own people.

The negative feedback did not, however, halt the machinery that was to proclaim the guilt of "a leading member of the IAF," as Hasuhanov, after he had survived, now began to be called. The court paid not the slightest attention to this pile of papers for OFFICIAL USE ONLY, and neither did the prosecutor general's office.

The Trial

The Hasuhanov case was heard behind closed doors and at great speed, from January 14 to February 25, 2003, in the Supreme Court of the Republic of North Ossetia–Alaniya, Judge Valerii Dzhioyev presiding. The court found nothing untoward—not in the fact that the accused had had no access to a lawyer for six months, or that the lawyer invited to act on his behalf had been chosen by those who had been beating his client, or that there was no information on the whereabouts of the accused between April 20 and 27. The court noted that he had been tortured but had no comment to make on the subject. Here is a quote from the verdict:

> Hasuhanov made no admission of guilt during the investigation but under physical and psychological pressure from officers of the FSB was forced to sign previously prepared records of the interrogations.
>
> "You have said that violent means were used against you," the judge told Hasuhanov. "Can you give the names of those who used violent means against you?"
>
> "I cannot give their names because I do not know them."

The court passed over this detail, since the torturers had failed to identify themselves to their victim. It even refused to commission a medical report, despite the fact that the accused had a dent in his skull. The court confined itself to asking Tebloev, the director of the timber factory, whether Hasuhanov had stayed in his hospital section. He replied, "Yes. He was there from May 3 until September 2002 with a broken rib cage." The court took this information in stride. To quote again from the verdict:

> At the court hearing the accused, Hasuhanov, did not admit to being guilty of the crimes committed. He stated that he considered it his duty to carry out certain requests and missions for the legally elected President Maskhadov. He denied making preparations for the committing of terrorist acts or providing financial resources for field commanders. He acknowledged only that he authenticated certain orders and instructions of Maskhadov, annotating them "True copy" in his own hand.

Was that it?

Yes, that was it. The sentence was twelve years in a strict-regime labor camp without eligibility for amnesty. The prisoner's final comment was, "I wish to state that I have no intention of repudiating my beliefs. I consider what is going on in Chechnya to be a flagrant violation of people's rights. Nobody makes any attempt to catch the real criminals. While the present situation continues, there will be many more people like me in the dock."

THE SHROUD OF darkness from which we spent several decades during the Soviet era trying to free ourselves is enveloping us again. More and more stories are heard of the FSB using torture to fabricate cases to suit its ideological needs, implicating the courts and the prosecutor's office as its accomplices. This practice is now the rule rather than the exception. We can no longer pretend that the occurrences are random.

The implication is that our constitution is on its deathbed, in spite of the guarantees intended to safeguard it, and the FSB is in charge of the funeral arrangements.

When I learned that Hasuhanov had been brought to the notorious Krasnaya Presnya transit prison in Moscow, a kind of distribution center from which those already sentenced are sent off in convoys to other parts of the country, I rang the Moscow office of the International Red Cross. Those who work there are among the few people allowed to visit particular prisoners. I called because I knew that after the torture Hasuhanov had endured, he was in poor health indeed. I asked the agency to visit him in Krasnaya Presnya, to provide him with medicine, to ask the prison authorities to ensure that he received treatment, and to get their consent for regular visits.

A week passed, during which the Moscow office of the IRC considered my appeal. Then the charity rejected the request, mumbling something about the situation being "very complicated."[5]

THE PRECEDENT OF COLONEL BUDANOV

On July 25, 2003, in a North Caucasus district military court in Rostov-on-Don, sentence was finally passed on Yury Budanov, a combatant in the first and second Chechen wars and recipient of two Orders of Valor. He was sentenced to ten years in a strict-regime labor camp for crimes committed in Chechnya in the course of the second war. He had abducted a Chechen girl, Elza Kungaeva, and murdered her in an exceptionally brutal manner. The court further resolved to strip Budanov of his rank and state awards.

As noted earlier, the Budanov case began on March 26, 2000, the day Putin was elected president; it continued for more than three years. It became a test for all of us, from the Kremlin down to the smallest villages. We tried to make sense of the soldiers and officers who, every day, had murdered, robbed, tortured, and raped in Chechnya. Were they thugs and war criminals? Or were they unflinching champions in a global war against international terror, using all the weapons at their disposal, a noble aim justifying their despicable means? The Budanov case became highly politicized, turning into a symbol of our time. Among the Russian people, many crucial events that happened in those three years, in Russia and elsewhere, were seen in the light of this case: September 11, 2001, in the United States; the wars in Afghanistan and Iraq; the creation of an international antiterrorist coalition; terrorist acts in Russia; the seizing of hostages in Moscow in October 2002; the endless succession of Chechen women blowing themselves up; and the Palestinization of the second Chechen war.

This striking, tragic case brought our difficulties into the open. Most important, it revealed the changes that the Russian justice system has experienced under Putin and as a result of the war. The legal reform that the democrats had tried to implement and that Yeltsin had done all he could to promote collapsed under the pressure of the Budanov case; for over three years we were treated to a demonstration of the fact that we did not have an independent judiciary. Instead, the judicial system took its marching orders from the Kremlin. Moreover, we discovered that a majority of the population saw nothing out of the ordinary in this state of affairs. Today's Russian, brainwashed by propaganda, has largely reverted to Bolshevik thinking.

On July 25, Kungaeva's parents—who, more than most, understood what was going on—did not even bother to attend the court. They were certain the man who had butchered their daughter would be acquitted.

But then a miracle occurred, both a miracle and a courageous act by Judge Vladimir Bukreev. The judge dared to find Budanov guilty and, furthermore, to sentence him to a far-from-token period of detention. Bukreev thereby set himself against the military establishment, which had been actively working on Budanov's behalf. The military courts come under the jurisdiction of the armed forces, whose commander in chief is the president. Yet, despite immense pressure from the Kremlin and the Ministry of Defense, Bukreev decided that Budanov should receive the sentence he merited. In the process, however, the judge showed beyond a doubt that the judicial system is fully in thrall to the politicians.

The Case

To dispel the myths surrounding the Budanov case, I will quote from the indictment. Despite the dry language of the prosecutor's office, the following excerpts testify more eloquently to the climate of the second Chechen war than many journalists could. They convey the situation in units deployed in the "Zone of Antiterrorist Operations," where anarchy rules. Lawlessness was the ultimate cause of the crimes committed by Yury Budanov, colonel of a tank regiment and commander of an elite army unit, a graduate of the military academy who had been awarded the country's highest honors for his distinguished service.

Indictment in respect of Colonel Yury Dmitrievich Budanov, Army Unit 13206 (160th Tank Regiment), accused . . .

The preliminary investigation has established that:

Yury Dmitrievich Budanov was appointed on August 31, 1998, to the post of commander of Army Unit 13206 (160th Tank Regiment). On January 31, 2000, Budanov was awarded the military rank of colonel. Ivan Ivanovich Fedorov was awarded the rank of lieutenant colonel on August 12, 1997. On September 16, 1999, Fedorov was appointed to the post of chief of staff and deputy commander of Army Unit 13206 (160th Tank Regiment). On September 19, 1999, on the basis of Order of the General Headquarters of the Armed Forces of the Russian Federation No. 312/00264, Budanov and Fedorov left as part of Army Unit 13206 for duty in the North Caucasus Military District and were thereafter deployed to the Chechen Republic to engage in a counterterrorist operation. On March 26, 2000, Army Unit 13206 was temporarily deployed on the outskirts of the village of Tangi. . . . During dinner in the regimental officers' mess, Budanov and Fedorov imbibed spiritous liquor to celebrate the birthday of Budanov's daughter. At 19.00 hours that day, Budanov and Fedorov proceeded in a drunken state, together with a group of officers of the regiment and at Fedorov's suggestion, to the intelligence company of the regiment under the command of Lieutenant R. V. Bagreev.

Having inspected the state of orderliness in the tents . . . , Fedorov desired to show Budanov that the intelligence company, to whose command Bagreev had been appointed on Fedorov's recommendation, could be relied upon in a combat situation. He proposed that Budanov check their readiness for action. Budanov at first declined, but Fedorov insisted. After Fedorov had repeated his suggestion several times, Budanov gave permission to test the company's combat readiness and proceeded with a group of officers to the Signals Center. Permission having been given, Fedorov decided, without telling Budanov, to order the use of regimental armaments to open fire on Tangi. Fedorov's deci-

sion . . . was taken . . . without any actual necessity, since no fire
was incoming. . . . Implementing his plan in flagrant violation of
the requirement of Order of the General Headquarters of the
Armed Forces of the Russian Federation of February 21, 2000,
No. 312/2/0091, which forbids the use of intelligence subsections without thorough preparation . . . , Fedorov gave orders for
firing positions to be taken up. . . . Obeying orders, Lieutenant
Bagreev gave the command to the company's personnel. . . .
Three combat vehicles took up combat positions. After completing targeting, some members of the crews declined to carry out
Fedorov's order to open fire on a populated position. Continuing
to exceed the authority of his rank, Fedorov insisted that they
should open fire. Angered by the refusal of his subordinates, Fedorov began complaining to Bagreev. In a coarse manner he demanded that Bagreev should get his subordinates to open fire.
Not satisfied with Bagreev's actions, Fedorov began personally to
direct the activity of the company's personnel. . . . The crew
opened fire . . . and a house . . . was destroyed. Having succeeded
in getting the company's personnel to carry out his unlawful order, Fedorov grabbed Bagreev by his clothing and continued to
address him in a vulgar manner. Bagreev offered no resistance . . .
and returned to the tent of his subsection.

Budanov . . . ordered Fedorov to stop firing and report to
himself. Fedorov reported that Bagreev had deliberately failed to
carry out his order to open fire. Bagreev was summoned to Budanov. Budanov . . . insulted him and then punched Bagreev at
least twice in the face.

At the same time, Budanov and Fedorov ordered the soldiers
on guardhouse duty to tie Bagreev up and place him . . . in a
pit. . . . Budanov then seized Bagreev by his uniform and threw
him to the ground. Fedorov booted Bagreev in the face. The soldiers on duty bound Bagreev, who was lying on the ground. Budanov, together with Fedorov, then continued to kick Bagreev. . . .

After this beating, Bagreev was put in the pit, where he was left
sitting with his hands and legs tied. Thirty minutes after the beating, Fedorov went back to the pit, jumped in, and punched him in
the face at least twice. . . . This beating was stopped by officers of
the regiment. . . . Several minutes later, Budanov came to the pit.
On his orders, Bagreev was pulled out. Seeing that he had succeeded in untying himself, Budanov again ordered the soldiers on

duty to tie him up. When this order had been carried out, Budanov and Fedorov again began beating Bagreev. . . . Bagreev was again put in the pit, bound hand and foot. . . . Fedorov jumped down and bit him on the right eyebrow. Bagreev was left . . . until 08.00 hours on March 27, 2000, after which, on Budanov's orders, he was freed.

At 24.00 hours on March 26, Budanov, acting without instructions from his superiors, decided to go into Tangi personally in order to check out the possible presence, at No. 7 Zarechnaya Street, of members of an IAF. In order to drive to Tangi, Budanov ordered his subordinates to ready armored personnel carrier (APC) No. 391. Before departing, Budanov and the members of the crew armed themselves with standard-issue Kalashnikov-74 assault rifles. At this time, Budanov informed the crew of the APC, namely Sergeants Grigoriev, Yegorov, and Li-En-Shou, that their mission was to arrest a female sniper. . . .

Budanov arrived at Tangi before 01.00 hours. . . . On his orders, the APC stopped outside No. 7 Zarechnaya Street, where the Kungaeva family lived. Budanov entered the house together with Grigoriev and Li-En-Shou. In the house were Elza Visaevna Kungaeva . . . along with her four younger brothers and sisters. Their parents were not present. Budanov asked where the parents were. Not receiving an answer, Budanov continued to exceed his authority and in contravention of Federal Law No. 3, "The Struggle Against Terrorism," Article 13, ordered Li-En-Shou and Grigoriev to seize Elza Visaevna Kungaeva.

Believing themselves to be acting lawfully, Grigoriev and Li-En-Shou seized Kungaeva, wrapped her in a blanket taken from the house, carried her from the house and placed her in the assault compartment of APC No. 391. . . . Budanov took Kungaeva back to the compound of Army Unit 13206. On Budanov's orders, Grigoriev, Yegorov, and Li-En-Shou took Kungaeva, still wrapped in the blanket, to the prefabricated officers' accommodation which Budanov occupied and placed her on the floor. Budanov then ordered them to remain in the vicinity and not to let anyone through.

Remaining alone with Kungaeva, Budanov began demanding information from her as to the whereabouts of her parents and also information about the routes by which fighters passed through Tangi. When she refused to talk, Budanov, who had no right to interrogate Kungaeva, continued demanding information. Since she refused his demands, Budanov began beating Kungaeva, punching and kicking her many times on her face and different parts of her body. Kungaeva attempted to resist, pushing him away and trying to run out of the accommodation.

As Budanov was convinced that Kungaeva was a member of an IAF and that she had been involved in the deaths of his subordinates in January 2000, he decided to kill her. For this purpose, Budanov seized Kungaeva's clothing, threw her down on a camp bed, and, clasping the back of her neck, began to squeeze it . . . until he was sure she no longer showed signs of life. . . .

Budanov's deliberate actions caused . . . asphyxia. . . . Budanov called Grigoriev, Yegorov, and Li-En-Shou into his quarters and ordered them to remove the body and secretly bury it away from the unit. Budanov's order was obeyed by the crew of APC No. 391. They secretly transported Kungaeva's body and buried it on one of the forest plantations, as Grigoriev reported back to Budanov on the morning of March 27, 2000.

The accused Budanov and Fedorov, when questioned to respect of the present criminal charges, partly admitted to being guilty of the acts of which they are accused. They changed the testimony they had given at the initial stage of the investigation.

Accused: Yury Dmitrievich Budanov

Questioned as a witness on March 27, 2000, Budanov explained that he had driven to Tangi, . . . discovered mines in one of the houses, and detained two Chechens. . . . Budanov asserted that nobody had beaten Bagreev up. While carrying out a check of the combat readiness of the intelligence company . . . , the company had reacted incorrectly to the command "Attack." A conflict had arisen. Bagreev had insulted Fedorov. . . . He had then ordered the arrest of Bagreev. Budanov denied that Fedorov had given orders to fire on Tangi, or that the village had been fired on. At the end of the interrogation, Budanov requested permission to write an admission of guilt regarding his having terminated the life of a female relative of citizens who were members of illegal formations in Chechnya.

Further, in an autograph admission of guilt . . . , Budanov gave the following information. On March 26, 2000, he had departed for the eastern outskirts of Tangi in order to take out or capture a woman sniper. . . . When they returned to the unit, the girl was carried to his quarters. . . . A conflict ensued, as a result of which he tore the girl's blouse and brassiere. The girl continued trying to escape. . . . He strangled her. . . . He did not remove the clothing from the lower part of her body. . . . Budanov called the crew, ordered them to wrap the body in a blanket, drive with it to a forest plantation in the vicinity of the tank battalion and bury her.

Questioned on March 28, 2000, Budanov testified that on March 3, 2000, he had learned from operational sources that a female sniper was living in Tangi. . . . He had been shown a photograph of her. This information had been made known to him by an inhabitant of Tangi who had personal scores to settle with the fighters. . . . Detaining the girl, they returned to the regiment. . . . He dragged her to a far corner of his quarters, threw her down on the camp bed, and began to strangle her. . . . The commanding officer of the APC came in with the signaler. The girl was lying in the far corner of his quarters, wearing only her pants. . . . Budanov had been infuriated that she would not say where her mother was. According to information in his possession, on January 15–20, 2000, her mother had used a sniper's rifle in the Argun Ravine to kill twelve soldiers and officers.

When questioned on March 30, 2000, Budanov partly admitted his guilt. . . . Budanov partially changed his testimony about Kungaeva's conduct, saying that she had told him they would get around to him in the end, and that he and those under his command would never get out of Chechnya alive. She had mouthed obscene remarks about his mother and run to the door. Her last remarks had completely infuriated Budanov. . . . His pistol lay on a table next to the bed. She had tried to seize the pistol. Throwing her back on the bed, he held Kungaeva by the throat with his right hand and with his left hand held her arm to prevent her from reaching the pistol. . . .

[These gradual changes to Budanov's testimony occurred because the Kremlin and the military establishment, having recovered from their shock at the unexpected audacity of the prosecutor's office in allowing itself to arrest a decorated, serving colonel, began to pressure the officials conducting the investigation. As a result, they started coaching Budanov as to what he should say, to minimize the legal consequences and possibly even escape criminal responsibility completely.]

In the course of a further interview . . . , Budanov gave additional detailed testimony as to how he knew that the Kungaevs were members of an IAF. Information to this effect had been received from one of the Chechens he had encountered in January–February 2000 after the fighting in the Argun Ravine. This Chechen had passed him a photograph which showed Kungaeva holding a Dragunov sniper's rifle.

Interviewed on January 4, 2001, Budanov testified that he would plead not guilty to abducting Kungaeva. He considered that he had acted properly, given the operational information in his possession. . . . He had arrested her in order to pass her on to the law-enforcement agencies. He had not done so because he hoped himself to discover from the detainee where fighters were located. . . .

He was also aware that if the fighters learned that Kungaeva had been detained, they would do their utmost to free her. It was for this reason that he decided to return to the regiment immediately. . . . He did not accept that he was guilty of premeditated murder. . . . He was in a highly emotional state, and he was at a loss to explain how it came about that he had strangled her.

Accused: Ivan Ivanovich Fedorov

Interviewed on April 3, 2000, as a witness, Fedorov testified that on March 26, 2000, he, Arzumanyan [a comrade in arms], and Budanov went to inspect the intelligence company. Having completed the inspection, he gave Bagreev an interim order: "Command post under attack: Take up firing positions" and indicated the location of the target. He then summoned Bagreev and asked why the combat vehicles had not taken up their firing positions. He could not remember what Bagreev replied. . . . He then seized Bagreev by his clothing.

[Fedorov] did not remember who gave the order to tie Bagreev's arms and legs. . . . He then went up to Bagreev and struck him several times. . . . On his, Fedorov's, orders, Bagreev was then put in the pit. He jumped down into the pit in order to tell Bagreev exactly what he thought of him.

He, Fedorov, was pulled out of the pit by Arzumanyan. He learned only the following morning that Budanov had driven to Tangi that night. . . .

On or around March 20, 2000, he saw a photograph Budanov had of a woman who, Budanov told him, was a sniper. According to Budanov, this woman lived in Tangi. . . . The woman appeared to be not more than 30 years old. On or around March 25, 2000, Budanov drove to Tangi, and a Chechen showed him houses where fighters lived. . . .

Aggrieved Party: Visa Umarovich Kungaev . . .
agronomist of the Urus-Martan Soviet Farm,
father of Elza Visaevna Kungaeva

Elza was the eldest child in the family . . . modest, calm, hard-working, decent, and honest. She had to undertake all the house-work, since his wife was ill and not allowed to work. For the same reason, Elza had the responsibility of looking after the younger children. She spent all her free time at home and did not go out. She had no boyfriends. She was awkward with members of the male sex. She had no intimate relations with them. His daughter simply was not a sniper. She was not a member of any armed for-mation. The suggestion was absurd.

On March 26, 2000, he went, together with his wife and chil-dren, to vote in the elections.

They busied themselves about the house. His wife got ready to go and see her brother Alexey in Urus-Martan. . . . He remained with the children.

They went to bed at about 21.00 hours, since there was no elec-tricity. . . . At about 00.30 on March 27, he was awakened by the roar of a military vehicle. . . . He looked out of the window and saw strangers coming toward their house. He called his eldest daughter, Elza, and asked her quickly to rouse all the children, get them dressed, and take them out of the house, telling her that it was being surrounded by soldiers. He, Kungaev, ran outside to find his brother, who lived some 20 meters away.

His brother was already running to see him. . . . On entering the house, his brother saw Colonel Budanov, whom he recognized because his photograph had been published in the *Red Star* news-paper.

Budanov asked him, "Who are you?" Adlan replied that he was the brother of the owner of the house. Budanov replied rudely, "Get out of here." Adlan ran out of the house and began shouting.

From what his children told him, Kungaev knew that Budanov then ordered the soldiers to take Elza. She was screaming. Wrapping her in a blanket, they took her outside. His relatives immediately came running and woke everybody to look for his daughter.

He went to the head of the village administration, the military commandant of the village, and the military commandant of Urus-Martan District. At 6 A.M. they drove to Urus-Martan to find his daughter. On the evening of March 27, 2000, they learned that Elza had been murdered. In Kungaev's opinion, Budanov abducted Elza and then raped her because she was a pretty girl.

Witness A. S. Magamaev testified that he was a neighbor of the Kungaevs. They were a poor family. They worked mainly in the fields. He had known Elza since she was born. She was a shy girl and did not associate with boys her own age. He could say with certainty that Elza had never been a member of any armed formations.

The investigation has been unable to discover any evidence that E. V. Kungaeva was associated with or a member of any IAF.

Witness: Ivan Alexandrovich Makarshanov,
former private in Army Unit 13206

On the evening of March 26, 2000, the guardhouse duty squad was called out to an emergency. On the orders of the commanding officer of the regiment, the personnel of the guardhouse duty squad bound the commanding officer of the intelligence company. Bagreev, the commanding officer of the intelligence company, was lying on the ground. Budanov and Fedorov each kicked Bagreev at least three times. Everything happened very quickly. After this, Bagreev was put in a pit, the so-called *Zindan*.

After a time, when it was already dark, Makarshanov heard shouts and groans and came out of his tent. He saw that Budanov and Fedorov were in the pit where they had put Bagreev. (The tent was about 15–20 meters from the *Zindan*.) Fedorov was punching Bagreev in the face. . . . Somebody shone a torch into the pit, so he saw everything clearly. Someone then pulled Fedorov out of the pit.

Until 02.00 hours on March 27, Makarshanov was in Fedorov's tent, keeping the stove lit. At about 01.00 hours he heard an APC drive up to Budanov's quarters. . . . He saw four persons enter Budanov's accommodation, one of whom was Budanov. One was carrying something on his shoulder, like a roll, its dimensions approximately those of a human body. He, Makarshanov, saw long hair hanging down from one end of the roll. . . .

The person carrying the roll opened the doors, carried the roll inside, and put it on the floor. A light was burning in the accommodation. Accordingly, Makarshanov was able to see Budanov enter. The distance from the place where he was (in the tent) to Budanov's quarters was some 8–10 meters. . . . The whole time after Budanov came to his quarters, he had three members of the crew of his APC standing by. . . .

Other Witnesses

Witness Alexander Mikhailovich Saifullin testified that he had served with Army Unit 13206 from August 1999. From late January 2000 his duties were to act as stoker in Budanov's quarters. At approximately 05.00–05.15 hours on March 27, he entered the commander's quarters. . . . Budanov was lying on the camp bed on the right and not, as usual, on the far one. The rug on the floor had been moved and was rumpled . . . and he saw that Budanov's bed was not made up. Budanov was asleep. At about 7 A.M. he entered the quarters and poured the commander a bucket of water to wash himself. . . . The commander told him to tidy up in the quarters and, indicating the bed with his head, ordered him to change the blanket and all the bed linen. Saifullin set about tidying up and noticed that the blanket was damp. . . . Budanov gave him an hour to clean the premises from top to bottom. When he took the bed linen from the far camp bed out of Budanov's quarters, the left corner of the sheet was wet.

Witness Valerii Vasilievich Gerasimov testified that from March 5 until April 20, 2000, he was acting commanding officer of the West Group of Troops. On the morning of March 27, he learned from the commandant of Urus-Martan that a girl had been abducted from Tangi during the night and that it was suspected that soldiers were responsible. He communicated with the commanding officers of three regiments, including Budanov of the 160th Tank Regiment, and ordered that the girl should be returned within 30 minutes. With General Alexander Ivanovich Verbitsky, he himself drove first to the 245th Regiment, then to the 160th Regiment.

In the 160th Regiment he was met personally by Budanov, who reported that everything was in order and that he had been unable to learn anything about the girl. Together with Verbitsky, [Gerasimov] drove to Tangi, where at that moment some villagers were gathered. From the explanation of the father of the girl, it appeared that a colonel had driven into the village during the night with soldiers in an APC, had wrapped the girl in a blanket, and carried her off. They knew this colonel: he was the commanding officer of the tank regiment. At first [Gerasimov] and Verbitsky did not believe this. They returned to the regiment. Budanov was not to be found. Gerasimov ordered that Budanov should be detained.

There is a rule in the Russian armed forces that serving personnel can be arrested only with the permission of their superior officers. For Budanov, only General Gerasimov had this status. Accordingly, we are obliged to Gerasimov for the fact that there ever was a Budanov case. The majority of commanding officers in Chechnya do not give the prosecutor's office permission to arrest those under their command who have committed war crimes and go to great lengths to protect them. Given the situation in the Zone of Antiterrorist Operations, Gerasimov's act must be regarded as very courageous. It could well have cost him his career. Perhaps because the affair became a major focus of public attention, the general was not punished. Indeed, Gerasimov was appointed commander of the Fifty-eighth Army, a significant promotion. The indictment continues:

After his arrest, Budanov was taken to Hankala [the main military base in Chechnya]. On that same evening, the driver of the APC who had driven Budanov to the village admitted that on the night of March 27, they had brought a girl back and dragged her into Budanov's quarters. Some two hours later, Budanov had summoned them. The girl was dead. Budanov had ordered them to take the body and bury it.

On the morning of March 28, the body was exhumed, taken to the Medical and Sanitary Battalion, medically examined, washed, and returned to the parents.

When interviewed as a witness, Igor Vladimirovich Grigoriev

testified that on March 27, 2000, when they returned to the unit,
Budanov ordered them to carry the girl, wrapped in a blanket,
into his quarters and themselves to stand guard. . . . Budanov remained in his quarters with the girl. Some ten minutes after they
had left the quarters, a woman's cries were heard coming from
within, and Budanov's voice was also heard. Then music was heard
coming from the accommodation. A woman's screams were heard
for some time more, coming from the same place.

Budanov was together with the girl in his quarters for between one and a half and two hours. Some two hours later, Budanov called all three of them into his quarters, where the
woman they had brought was lying naked on the bed. Her face
was a bluish color. The blanket they had wrapped the girl in was
spread on the floor. Her clothing was lying on it in a heap. Budanov ordered them to take the woman away and bury her in secret. . . . Wrapping the body in the blanket, they drove the girl
away in APC No. 391 and buried the body. Grigoriev reported
this back to Budanov on the morning of March 27.

Interviewed on October 17, 2000, Grigoriev elaborated that ten
to twenty minutes after their leaving Budanov's quarters, Budanov
began shouting. What, exactly, he did not hear. There were also several screams from the girl, screams indicative of fear. When, at Budanov's summons, they entered his quarters, they saw the girl lying
naked on the camp bed without signs of life. . . . The girl had
bruises to her neck, as if she had been strangled. Pointing to her, Budanov said with a strange expression on his face, "That's for you, you
bitch, for Razmakhnin and the boys who died up that mountain."

The examination of Kungaeva's body revealed . . . injuries . . . on
the . . . neck . . . , the face . . . , bruising in the right suborbital area,
on the inner surface of the right thigh, hemorrhaging into the . . .
mouth and . . . of the left upper jaw. The corpse was unclothed. . . .

The medical examination of the corpse . . . established that the
injuries discovered on the neck had been caused ante-mortem. . . .
The cause of death was pressure on the neck from a blunt object.
The bruising on Kungaeva's face and left thigh, the hemorrhaging
into the . . . mouth, the injury to the right eye resulted from the
action of a blunt object(s). . . . The act causing injury was a blow.
The injuries referred to occurred ante-mortem. . . .

Interviewed as a witness, Captain Alexey Viktorovich Simukhin, investigator, military prosecutor's office, testified that on

March 27, 2000, he received orders to bring Budanov to the landing strip of Army Unit 13206 in order for the latter to be transported to Hankala.

During the flight Budanov was very agitated, inquiring how he should behave, what he should say, and what he should do. On the morning of March 28, 2000, Simukhin traveled out as a member of the investigating team to . . . locate the body of Kungaeva. . . . Simukhin wished to note that the burial site had been very carefully camouflaged, covered with turf. . . . The body was in a half-sitting "fetal" position and was completely naked.

Aggrieved Party: Lieutenant Roman Vitalievich Bagreev . . . deputy chief of staff of Tank Battalion, Army Unit 13206

From October 1, 1999, as a member of the 160th Regiment, Bagreev took part in the counterterrorist operation. He had no scores to settle with Budanov and Fedorov.

On March 20, 2000, the intelligence company moved from . . . Komsomolskoe to . . . Tangi. It had been decided to hold a competition between the regiment's subsections to decide which company was the most orderly. The antiaircraft section came in first. Fedorov disagreed with this result and assured everybody that the intelligence company was better. . . . In order to persuade Budanov of this . . . , Fedorov insisted an inspection should be carried out of the company's site.

After 18.00 hours Budanov, Fedorov, Silivanets, and Arzumanyan arrived at the site. Budanov was intoxicated but entirely able to control himself. Fedorov was very drunk, his speech was slurred, and he was unsteady on his feet. Fedorov tried to persuade Budanov to check the combat readiness of the company. Budanov refused three or more times but Fedorov continued to insist. Budanov yielded to Fedorov's demands, ordering, "Firing positions. Prepare for combat."

Bagreev immediately ran toward the company's trenches. Fedorov ran behind him. The vehicles took up their firing positions. Budanov was at the Signals Center. He knew that each vehicle always had a high-explosive fragmentation shell in its rammer tray ready for firing. There were no grounds to open fire on the village at the time, other than Fedorov's order.

After the vehicles' gun crews had taken up their positions, he gave orders to the crews to unload the fragmentation shell, load a hollow-charge shell, and fire it over the houses. Such a shell, shot upward, if encountering no obstacle, self-destructs. A fragmentation charge has no such self-destruction mechanism. . . .

Vehicle No. 380 fired once over the roofs of the houses in the village. Fedorov saw this, leapt on to the second APC, and ordered the gun layer to fire at Tangi. Dissatisfied with Bagreev's actions, Fedorov seized him by his clothing and abused him with obscene language. Bagreev was summoned by Budanov. When he arrived at the Signals Center, Budanov and Fedorov were both there. They beat him up.

Inspection has established that to the southwest of the staff headquarters of Army Unit 13206, at a distance of 25 meters from the regimental command post on March 27, 2000, there was a pit above which three square-edged planks had been placed. The pit was a hollow in the ground 2.4 meters long, 1.6 meters wide, and 1.3 meters deep. The walls were faced with brick, and the bottom was earthen.

[Thus the first description in a Russian legal document of a *Zindan*. These special torture pits were introduced on an extensive scale during the second Chechen war. They are to be found in almost every military unit in Chechnya and are generally used for detaining arrested Chechens, as well as privates who are in disgrace. It is rare for them to be used against junior officers.]

Witness Private Dmitry Igorevich Pakhomov testified that on March 26, 2000, at about 20.00 hours, Fedorov shouted at Bagreev, "I'll teach you to carry out my orders, you puppy." Bagreev was deluged with insults. . . . Fedorov gave the order to tie Bagreev up and put him in the pit. There had been earlier occasions when the squad had tied up drunken contract soldiers before putting them in the pit, but for such a thing to be done to the commanding officer of the intelligence company was unbelievable.

Approximately one hour later, the squad was again alerted to an emergency by Budanov. When they arrived, Bagreev was lying on the ground. Budanov and Fedorov once more started kicking him. After this, on Budanov's orders, Bagreev was again tied up and put in the pit. Fedorov then jumped down and began beating Bagreev up in the pit. Bagreev was shouting and groaning. . . . Silivanets jumped down into the pit and pulled Fedorov out. At about 02.00 hours Pakhomov was in his tent when he heard rifle fire. As he later learned, this was Suslov shooting in order to bring Fedorov to his senses. He was again trying to reach Bagreev.

Budanov and Fedorov were charged. The criminal case against Grigoriev, Li-En-Shou, and Yegorov was closed as the result of an amnesty.

The expert conclusion of the Standing Interdepartmental Forensic Psychological and Psychiatric Board was that Budanov was not, at the time of the act with which he was charged in respect to Bagreev, in a transitory pathological state of dysfunction or in a state of pathological or physiological incapacity. At the time of the murder of Kungaeva, Budanov was in a transitory, situationally induced, cumulative psychoemotional state and was not fully aware of the nature and significance of his acts or able to use his free will to control them.

The Trial

In the summer of 2001, Budanov's case moved to trial. The first judge was Colonel Victor Kostin of the district military court of the North Caucasus, in Rostov-on-Don, in the same location as the North Caucasus Military District staff headquarters, which, as Russians say, is "fighting the war in Chechnya." The influence of the military on every aspect of life in Rostov-on-Don is enormous. The main military hospital, through which thousands of soldiers crippled and wounded in Chechnya have passed, is located there, and the city is home to the families of many officers posted to Chechnya. In a sense this is a frontline city, and this circumstance had a significant impact on the development of the Budanov trial. Pickets and demonstrations outside the courtroom, in support of Budanov, provided the trial with a running commentary, with slogans like "Russia in the Dock!" and "Free Russia's Hero!"

The first phase of the hearings lasted for more than a year, from the summer of 2001 until October 2002. The purpose of the proceedings seemed not to be to decide whether Budanov was guilty or not but to absolve him of all sins and crimes. Throughout the hearings, Judge Kostin displayed manifest support for Budanov, turning down all representations on behalf of the Kungaevs and finding reasons to refuse to admit any witness who might speak against Budanov. He even refused to question Generals Gerasimov and Verbitsky, on the grounds that they had given permission to arrest the murderous colonel.

During this time, the prosecutor, too, appeared openly on the side of the accused, effectively acting as his defense lawyer, although his duty was to act on behalf of the victims.

The situation inside the courtroom was mirrored by the situation outside it. Public opinion was generally on Budanov's side. There were meetings outside the court with red Communist flags, and flowers for Budanov as he was being led into the building. The top brass at the Ministry of Defense joined in, with public pronouncements by Minister Sergey Ivanov to the effect that Budanov was "quite clearly not guilty."

The ideological basis for absolving Budanov was that, although he had committed a crime, it was a crime he had a right to commit. His treatment of Elza Kungaeva was justified on the basis that he was taking revenge on an enemy in war, because he believed the girl to be a sniper responsible for the death of officers.

The Kungaev family had major problems with lawyers from the beginning. The family was very poor, had many children, and no work, and was obliged to move to a tent in a refugee camp in the neighboring Republic of Ingushetia after their daughter's tragic death. Family members were afraid of reprisals from the army for having gone to court (they were threatened on more than one occasion). As a result, they found themselves without a lawyer. At this point, the Memorial Civil Rights Center, based in Moscow, with a branch in

Rostov-on-Don, found them attorneys and, for a long time, covered their fees.

The first lawyer who thus became involved in the case was Abdullah Hamzaev, an elderly Chechen who had been living in Moscow for many years and who was, moreover, a distant relative of the Kungaevs.[6] It must be said that his efforts were not effective; rather, the reverse was true—not because of any fault of Hamzaev's but because Russian society is becoming increasingly racist. It does not trust people from the Caucasus, let alone from Chechnya. The press conferences Hamzaev called in Moscow, to describe how difficult it was to move matters forward in the military court in Rostov-on-Don, went nowhere. Journalists did not believe what he said, and, accordingly, no public campaign in defense of the Kungaevs was mounted. And a public outcry was, of course, the family's only hope of making any headway.

The Memorial Civil Rights Center invited a young Moscow lawyer, Stanislav Markelov, to assist Hamzaev. Markelov was a member of the same Interrepublican College of Lawyers to which Budanov's attorneys belonged. The major cases Markelov had defended before and that had attracted Memorial's attention were the first in Russia to involve accusations of terrorism and political extremism: the blowing up of memorials to Emperor Nicholas II in the vicinity of Moscow, an attempt to blow up the monument to Peter the Great, and the murder of Russian citizens of Afghan descent by skinheads.

Markelov was Russian, and, at the time, his background was crucial. Memorial had made a good selection, because subsequently it was his energy, choice of tactics, and ability to communicate with the press that focused attention on the trial. Here is a summary of what Markelov himself has to say about what he saw in the court just after taking on the case. At this point, the trial was effectively occurring in camera, and journalists were banned:

"The court was in a great rush. It did not want to go into the details of any of our requests and rejected anything that could be interpreted to be against Budanov. . . . All our petitions, for example, to call witnesses, to call in experts, to have independent examinations, were rejected. I had the impression that Judge Kostin was not even reading them. We discovered that one of the informers who supposedly pointed out the Kungaevs' house was a deaf mute, physically incapable of hearing Budanov's question about the female sniper . . . and physically incapable of replying. The second informer was in fact photographed talking to Budanov one day earlier than alleged. Thus Budanov's spontaneous reactions, feelings that overwhelmed the colonel and justified his behavior, are no longer valid. Witnesses also testified that on both March 25 and until midday on March 26, when the officers in the regiment began the binge drinking Budanov had organized in honor of his daughter's birthday, the colonel was calm and showed no intention of taking revenge on some female sniper."

The second informer turned out to be Ramzan Sembiev, a convict serving in a maximum security labor camp for kidnapping. What matters here is that there should have been no difficulty at all in bringing him to the court for cross-examination.

"The court's approach to the case was ideological. The Kremlin was applying pressure for Budanov to be absolved of his sins. Nothing was important or relevant if it could be to Budanov's disadvantage. The prosecutor's office decided not to behave in . . . accordance with its role as defined by the Constitution. . . .

"During Nazarov's speech to the court, a number of other inexplicable things came out. For example, a prosecutor in Dagestan was said to have approached Sembiev in the labor camp after our application and to have asked whether he knew Budanov. Sembiev reputedly denied it and said the first time he had seen him was on television."

"Was this conversation forwarded to the court as an official document?"

"No, of course not . . ."

Following in Budanov's footsteps, the court decided to apply customary law instead. Budanov had acted entirely in accordance with Chechen customary law: he considered the murder he committed to be retribution. The court, and Russian society, supported him in this. What the case shows is that the authorities in Russia, and the state as a whole, accept that Russian law is in abeyance in Chechnya.

Playing Games with Psychiatric Reports

One of the main features of the Budanov case was the games played with the forensic psychological and psychiatric reports.

During the three years the case ran, the colonel had the benefit of four psychiatric reports and, when the initial verdict was set aside, of a further two. The conclusions of nearly all these documents were politically slanted and supported whatever the current Kremlin line happened to be.

The first two reports were compiled in the aftermath of the crimes, in May and August 2000, during the preliminary investigation. The first examination was carried out by the psychiatrists of the military hospital of the North Caucasus Military District and the Central North Caucasus Forensic Laboratory of the Ministry of Justice of Russia. The second investigation was produced by doctors of the civilian Novocherkassk Provincial Psychoneurological Hospital. According to these reports, Budanov was responsible for his actions—that is, he was answerable for his crimes. The documents were released during a period when Putin was talking a great deal about the "dictatorship of law," which needed to be established in Russia. Under this doctrine, soldiers who committed crimes in Chechnya would be punished in exactly the same way as Chechen fighters who were members of IAFs.

Moreover, it was a time of courting the Chechens after the fierce

assaults of 1999–2000 and the appointment of a new head of administration of the republic, Ahmad-Hadji Kadyrov. He had been one of
the fighters and the mufti, or interpreter of Muslim law, for Djohar
Dudaev, the first president of Chechnya, who had been assassinated in
1996 by a smart missile targeted by federal officers. Having earlier declared jihad on Russia, Kadyrov had subsequently become a friend of
the Kremlin after "fully appreciating the situation."

These two reports noted, however, that when Elza Kungaeva was
strangled, Budanov was probably mentally unbalanced, and that he appeared to be exhibiting symptoms of brain damage resulting in a "personality and behavioral disorder."

The Ministry of Defense took exception to these conclusions because they had two serious implications. One was that since Budanov
was in his right mind at all other times, he could be prosecuted to the
full extent of the law. The other was that the army was employing
people with brain damage that nobody bothered to assess, that such
people were fighting in battles, and that people with personality dis-
orders had command of hundreds of individuals and had cutting-edge
weapons at their disposal.

It soon became clear, when the trial began, that the psychiatrists'
conclusions did not suit Judge Kostin either. As a military judge, employed by the Ministry of Defense, Kostin was beholden to the military establishment for his living accommodations, salary, and any
prospects of promotion. So Judge Kostin's apartment and pay would
have to come from the same headquarters to which the accused, Colonel Budanov, was subordinate. Also, by the time Budanov came to
trial, political circumstances in Russia had begun to change. The
Kremlin had gradually stopped playing at democracy and worrying
about the "dictatorship of law." In consequence, all those who had
fought in Chechnya were declared heroes, irrespective of what they
had done there. The president began dishing out medals and orders
right, left, and center, assuring those involved in the war that the state
would never betray them. These highly charged words meant that the

government intended to be lenient toward those guilty of war crimes in Chechnya, to the point of forgiving the most sordid offenses, and that any prosecutor trying to bring criminal proceedings against federal military personnel should pipe down.

Stories from the state-controlled television channels explained how scrupulously Budanov had fulfilled his duty, and General Shamanov was continually in evidence making patriotic speeches in praise of his comrade in arms. The claim that the eighteen-year-old Chechen girl whom the colonel had murdered was a sniper was no longer subject to doubt. Nobody now recalled that neither the investigation nor Budanov's counsel had been able to find a shred of evidence to suggest that Elza Kungaeva had had anything to do with IAFs.

The politically inspired brainwashing of the Russian population was going full tilt, paving the way for Budanov's acquittal.

At this very moment, the court in Rostov-on-Don, stricken by doubt as to the competence of the experts who had carried out the first two psychiatric reports, commissioned a new one. This time it was a joint military and civilian enterprise, in Moscow, moreover, uniting the efforts of the Central Forensic Medical Laboratory of the Ministry of Defense and the Serbsky State Research Center for Social and Forensic Psychiatry, popularly known as the Serbsky Institute.

The Serbsky's reputation in Russia dates from Soviet times, when dissidents would be certified insane. The doctors of the Serbsky Institute were invariably conscientious in carrying out the tasks they were allotted by the KGB. It was to the Serbsky Institute that Budanov was sent. When the decision became common knowledge, there were few doubts as to why the state research center had been chosen. Everything possible was being done to free Budanov of criminal responsibility, his supporters—and his opponents—said.

The official reasons for commissioning a third report were given by the court as "imprecision, contradictoriness and factual incompleteness"; in addition, "new and more accurate data" had appeared that were important for "determining Budanov's true mental state."

No matter that a series of episodes described to the new commission had never happened. Because the information favored the colonel, it was put before the experts, who then treated it as incontrovertible.

Not to mince words, this was blatant falsification and the Serbsky experts' response was tailored to produce the requisite image of a hero.

> According to Budanov, his was a difficult birth. . . . According to the testimony of his mother and sister, he was vulnerable and liable to flare up in response to a slight. He would respond coarsely or start a fight. He was particularly sensitive toward unfair remarks and in such cases always tried to defend the weak, those smaller than himself, and the poor. . . .
>
> Budanov's service references show him in an exceptionally favorable light. He was disciplined, effective and tenacious. In January 1995, during the first military campaign in Chechnya, while taking part in combat operations, Budanov suffered a concussion, losing consciousness for a short time. He did not seek medical attention. According to his mother and sister, after he returned from the first Chechen war, Budanov's personality and behavior changed. He became more nervous and irritable. . . . In his subsections Budanov created a spirit of intolerance of shortcomings and passivity. He had a highly developed sense of responsibility. . . .
>
> None of his comrades has noticed mental aberrations in Budanov. He has never been under the observation of a psychiatrist or neuropathologist.
>
> Budanov testifies that when his regiment arrived in Chechnya . . . , it was involved almost constantly in combat operations. In October and again in November 1999, Budanov suffered a concussion with loss of consciousness. After this he began to suffer incessantly from headaches and dizziness with loss of vision. He became unable to tolerate sudden loud noises, became liable to flare up, lacking in restraint and irritable. He suffered mood swings, with outbursts of rage. He committed acts which he later regretted.
>
> Budanov testifies that the most severe fighting was in the Argun Ravine from December 24, 1999, to February 14, 2000. From January 12 to 21, the regiment lost nine officers and three

other ranks. Many of these were killed, Budanov testifies, by a shot to the head from a sniper. On January 17, 2000, Budanov's comrade Captain Razmakhnin died at the hands of a sniper. . . .

Budanov was extremely upset by the fact that the majority of officers in his regiment had died not in open battle but at the hands of a sniper. He said he would return home only after they had "wiped out the last fighter."

On February 15, without completing his leave, Budanov returned to Chechnya. His mother and sister testify that Budanov looked in on them . . . and had changed beyond recognition. He smoked constantly, hardly spoke and "flew into a rage over nothing at all." He could not sit still. Showing photographs of those who had died and of their graves, he wept. They had not seen him in such a state before.

Budanov led attacks himself, his rifle in his hands, and took part in man-to-man combat. After the battles in the Argun Ravine, he tried personally to retrieve the bodies of those who had died. After the death of officers and soldiers of the regiment on Hill 950, Budanov blamed himself and was in a state of constant depression. He might strike subordinates or hurl ashtrays at them. In mid-March 2000, having demanded that his tent should be tidied, he threw a grenade into the stove. . . .

From mid-February 2000, the regiment was deployed in the vicinity of Tangi. Budanov was ordered to carry out intelligence and search measures, lay ambushes, carry out supplementary passport checks of the inhabitants of the village, and detain suspects.

Budanov and those under his command commented that at that time the situation was very confused, and it was impossible to tell friend from foe or where the front line was. . . .

The report continued with a highly variant account of events on the night of March 26 and concluded by noting, "When questioned, . . . Budanov explained the contradictions in his statements by saying that he had been in a very bad state.

"On the basis of the above, the commission has come to the conclusion that Budanov was not responsible for his actions, on the grounds of diminished responsibility. . . . The acts of the victim, Kungaeva, were one of the factors causing Budanov's temporary mental breakdown. . . . There is no conclusive evidence regarding Budanov's being in a state of intoxication. . . .

"Budanov . . . should be kept under observation and treated by a psychiatrist on an outpatient basis. Category C: Partially fit for military service."

The commission's conclusions gave the judge all the ammunition he needed under Russian law to do the bidding of his political masters and acquit the colonel. Just as in Soviet times, what the experts report to the courts depends not on the facts but on who is presenting them. Among the cast of characters who provided the psychological and psychiatric grounds for exculpating Budanov was Professor Tamara Pechernikova, doctor of medical science (commission chairman), director of the Consultancy Section of the Serbsky Institute, a doctor with an international reputation, a psychiatric consultant of the highest standing, with fifty years of consultancy experience. This choice was far from random, I believe, because in Russia such appointments do not just happen. This is the way things were done in Soviet times. The worst of Communism is with us again; in Putin's era the appalling practice of political-psychiatry-to-order has returned.

On August 25, 1968, a famous demonstration took place in Red Square, Moscow. Seven people entered the square and unfurled banners reading FOR OUR AND YOUR FREEDOM! and SHAME ON THE OCCUPIERS! One of the seven was Natalia Gorbanevskaya, a poet, journalist, and dissident who, on this occasion, was pushing a pram with her baby in it. In a country where nobody had protested for a long time, people were stepping forward who had it in them to protest the Soviet invasion of Czechoslovakia.

The demonstration of the Seven lasted only a few minutes before they were seized by the plainclothes KGB agents who constantly patrolled Red Square. A court subsequently sentenced two of them to terms in labor camps, sent one to a psychiatric hospital, and three into exile. Gorbanevskaya was at first released, since she was breast-feeding her baby.

Some time later, she was rearrested for continuing civil-rights activism. It was then that Tamara Pechernikova made her mark. It was she who, at the behest of the KGB, interrogated Gorbanevskaya in the same Serbsky Institute where, three decades later, Budanov was examined.

Pechernikova produced the medical verdict on Gorbanevskaya the KGB required: "schizophrenia"—which is to say that anyone displaying a banner in Red Square, protesting Russian tanks in the streets of Prague, must have been insane. Pechernikova also supplied the KGB its diagnosis that Gorbanevskaya was a danger to society and should be subjected indefinitely to compulsory treatment in a specialized psychiatric hospital.

Natalia Gorbanevskaya, the founder and first editor of the underground *Chronicle of Current Events*, a samizdat bulletin of Soviet civil-rights activists, was to spend grim years of incarceration in the Kazan Specialized Mental Hospital. Imprisoned there from 1969 until 1972, she emigrated with an Israeli visa in 1975. She now lives in France.

The Gorbanevskaya case was among the first of the psychiatric repressions against dissidents in the Soviet Union. The 1970s, an era when the Communist regime fought a war of attrition against dissidents, was a heyday for Colonel Budanov's would-be savior. To understand what is happening in Russia now, we need to be aware not only of the revival of political psychiatry, with diagnoses to order, but also of the way it functions.

In the files of almost all of Pechernikova's cases, from Gorbanevskaya and well-known Soviet dissident Alexander Ginzburg to Budanov, we find the leitmotif of the search for social justice. Today these words are used in an entirely different context, however. In the Soviet era, Pechernikova regarded evidence of a search for social justice as a symptom of mental illness dangerous to society. Today she considers a brutal murder to be justified by the murderer's search for social justice. The colonel was overwhelmed by feelings of guilt over the death of his comrades at the hands of a sniper. As a result—understandably, according to Pechernikova—he killed a woman.

Can it be mere chance that Pechernikova figured in the cases of Ginzburg, Gorbanevskaya, and Budanov?

For the past three decades, the KGB/FSB has known that Pechernikova could be relied upon. She bided her time in the shadows during the "late democratic" period of Mikhail Gorbachev and under Boris Yeltsin, but then a KGB officer with a twenty-year service record became president. In the wake of Putin's rise to power, every nook and cranny in the power structure was filled by people who had been employed by the KGB.

Information from independent sources (not surprisingly, there is none from official ones) suggests that more than six thousand ex-KGB/FSB people followed Putin to power and now occupy the highest offices. These include the key ministries, in which they hold the most important positions: the president's office (two deputy directors, the heads of the staffing and information departments); the Security Council (deputy secretary); the government administrative apparatus; the ministries of defense, foreign affairs, justice, the nuclear industry, taxes and revenues, internal affairs, press affairs, television, radio and mass media; the State Customs and Excise Committee; the Russian Agency for National Reserves; the Committee for Financial Recovery—and so on.

Like cancer, bad history tends to recur, and there is only one radical treatment: invasive therapy to destroy the deadly cells. We have not done this. We dragged ourselves out of the Soviet Union and into the New Russia still infected with our Soviet disease. To return to our central question: Is the resurrection of Professor Pechernikova in the Budanov case a coincidence? Well, is the return to power of the secret police a coincidence?

It is not. Back in 2000, people were saying, "What if Putin did start out in the KGB in the Soviet period? He'll shape up once he is in office."

By then it was already too late. Now we find ourselves surrounded by people trusted by Putin and Putin's friends. Unfortunately, they trust only their own kind. The result is that the power structures of the New Russia are overrun with citizens from a particular tradition, brought up with a repressive mentality and with an understanding of how to resolve governmental problems that reflects this mentality.

Pechernikova both embodies that tradition and is a mechanism for perpetuating it. In the two decades she spent patriotically, as she would see it, defending the Soviet social and state system, she put in place a mechanism for controlling medical science, molding psychiatry to fit the needs of the state security apparatus. Now, more than a decade after the fall of the visible structures of the Soviet system, she has found herself and her special skills in as much demand as ever.

These are not abstractions of political theory. Pechernikova's contribution to the Budanov case had life-and-death consequences for real people, just as it did in the 1970s and 1980s. Whether Budanov did or did not go free was a matter of fundamental importance, not least for the army, which, in Chechnya, has become an instrument of repression. The army was waiting for a precedent from the court in Rostov-on-Don. Could the military continue to behave like Budanov?

Pechernikova, who effectively said, "Go right ahead," provided crucial ammunition to enable Judge Kostin also to say, in law, "Go right ahead."

Their signals were certainly interpreted that way in Chechnya, where officers picked up exactly where Budanov had left off. We could cite enough examples to fill another book.

MORE THAN A year passed. The Budanov case files were augmented by three additional expert reports. Pechernikova's conclusions were rejected as untenable. The Supreme Court sent the case back for a retrial, and a newly appointed military court in Rostov-on-Don commissioned new reports. The prosecutor, who had effectively defended the accused, was removed from the scene, and social justice began to emerge from behind the clouds.

And Pechernikova? Was she reprimanded? No chance—she was left in place.

LET US TURN now to the evidence Pechernikova did not address: the subterranean foundation of the Budanov case.

On the last night of her young life, Elza Kungaeva was not only strangled but also raped. From the forensic report:

> The burial site is a plot in the forest plantation 950 meters from the command post of the tank regiment. The body of a naked woman is discovered wrapped in a tartan blanket.
>
> The body is lying on its left side, the legs pressed to the stomach, the arms bent at the elbows and pressed to the trunk. The perineum in the region of the external genital organs is smeared with blood, and the blanket in this place is also bloodstained.
>
> A forensic investigation of Kungaeva's body was carried out on March 28, 2000, . . . by Captain V. Lyanenko, director of the Medical Section, 124th Laboratory Medical Corps. On the external genital organs, on the surface skin of the perineum and on the rear surface of the upper third of the thigh, are moist smears of a dark-red color resembling blood and mucus. . . . On the hymen there are bruised radial linear tears. In the buttock crease there are dried traces of a red-dark-brown color. Two cm from the anal aperture there is a tear of the mucous membrane. . . . The tear is filled with coagulated blood, which indicates it occurred antemortem. On the side of the blanket turned toward the corpse, there is a damp patch of dark-brown color resembling that of blood. . . .
>
> Together with the body there were recovered: 1. Blouse, woolen. Back torn (cut) vertically the full length . . . 5. Underpants, worn. Removal of specimens for forensic examination not undertaken in view of the lack of suitable conditions for preserving and conserving them. . . .

> The tears in the hymen and mucous membrane of the rectum . . .
> resulted from the insertion of a blunt, hard object (objects). . . . It is
> possible that such object might have been an engorged (erect) penis.
> It could, however, have been the haft of a small entrenching tool. . . .

From the very beginning of the investigation Budanov had cate-gorically denied rape. But someone had clearly violated Elza Kun-gaeva before she was murdered. Since during the last hours of Elza's life Budanov was alone with her, and since he allowed his sol-diers to enter his quarters only after she was dead, one conclusion seems inescapable.

Two forensic analyses were performed during the preliminary inves-tigation. When the court set about its whitewash of Budanov, it commis-sioned a third report for the same purpose as the new psychiatric report commissioned from the Serbsky Institute: to deliver the conclusions the military establishment and the Kremlin wanted to hear, and to avoid having an officer awarded two Orders of Valor shown to be a rapist.

According to the third report, which contradicts everything the original medical corps examiner had seen with his own eyes, "The tears of the hymen and mucosa of the rectum occurred postmortem when the retractive capacity characteristic of living tissue had been completely lost." In other words, while someone had abused this girl, it most certainly had not been Budanov. He had an alibi. After mur-dering her, he had gone peacefully to sleep.

To make this explanation seem more plausible, the profuse bleed-ing Lyanenko had seen was interpreted as follows: ". . . the presence of bloodstains in the region of the external genital organs does not con-tradict the conclusion regarding the postmortem origination of these injuries. . . ." These experts augmented their conclusions with a side-swipe at the earlier report: "The unexplained decision by the consul-tant not to collect material for forensic histological analysis does not allow us to conclude more definitely at the present time. . . ."

In a war zone, with nowhere to conserve histological specimens, the absence of definitive proof strengthened the colonel's alibi. Without a tissue analysis, as the latest pathologists asserted, any attempt to prove that a rape had occurred, and that the perpetrator had been Budanov, was doomed to failure.

The desired conclusion could now be delivered: "There are no data supporting the hypothesis that the posthumous injuries were caused by an erect male sexual organ. The results of the forensic examination of the body and the material evidence give no grounds for concluding that a forcible sexual act was committed against Kungaeva."

In other words, the report acquitted Budanov.

The experts who signed the report evidently imagined their efforts had removed a stain from the Russian army's uniform. From the jacket perhaps, but not from the trousers.

Russian Public Opinion

As the Budanov case dragged on, the reaction of Russia's women became more and more disturbing. Women comprise more than half the population; thus one might expect a majority of Russians to despise a rapist. Apparently not. Tens of millions of Russians have young daughters, and, if only for that reason, one might expect them to understand and identify with the Kungaev family's grief. Again, apparently not. Budanov's wife was interviewed on television. She talked about her poor husband having to endure all those examinations and a trial, and about their little daughter who was tired of waiting for her daddy to come home. The country sympathized with the colonel's wife—not, it seemed, with the Kungaevs, who, wait as they might, would never see their daughter again.

In 2002, when the experts accepted that Budanov had been temporarily insane at the moment of committing the murder, he was cleared of rape. No storm of indignation swept the country. There was not a single protest demonstration, not even from women's organizations. No civil-rights defenders took to the streets. Russia thought what had happened was fair enough. The report acquitting the colonel triggered a wave of war crimes in Chechnya, committed by soldiers who used the disastrous situation and the cruelty perpetrated by both sides as a cover. Throughout 2002, "purging" of territory continued in Chechnya on a massive scale and with extreme brutality. Villages were surrounded, men taken away, women raped. Many were killed, and even more disappeared without a trace. Retaliation was elevated to justification for murder. Lynch law was encouraged by the Kremlin itself—an eye for an eye, a tooth for a tooth. We discovered that we were moving backward, from stagnation under Leonid Brezhnev to the out-and-out arbitrariness of Joseph Stalin. Terrifying as the thought was, we probably had the government we deserved.

Budanov's final address to the court was scheduled for July 1, 2002, indicating that the judicial mummery of the case was about to conclude. Elza Kungaeva's parents and their lawyers left the courtroom, unable to stomach the perverse traducing of morality and the desecration of the law. Supporters of the colonel and his colleagues were braying outside the walls of the courtroom, in the expectation that another couple of days would see them and Budanov toasting their victory with vodka.

Suddenly, something happened. Budanov's final address was abruptly canceled. The verdict, which had been expected on July 3, was not delivered. To everyone's surprise, a break in the hearings was announced until the beginning of October, and Budanov was taken off to Moscow again, back to the Serbsky Institute for a further, by now fourth, medical report. What was going on?

Perhaps the strong pressure exerted by the German Bundestag, with letters and appeals addressed to Putin personally, had some effect. Chancellor Gerhard Schröder himself had been inquiring at summit meetings as to why those trying Budanov the war criminal seemed interested only in getting him acquitted. Sources within the president's office say Putin had no answer. None of this should be too surprising. In Russia, with its byzantine traditions of servility, such trivia are often sufficient to change the course of history.[7]

The hearings started up again on October 3. Attention was focused on the new psychological and psychiatric report. Many were anticipating a sensation, but, in fact, there was only a rerun. Budanov was again found to have suffered a "temporary pathological dysfunction of his mental activity." The verdict was delivered on December 31, 2002—a day when few Russians have anything very serious on their minds—and thus entirely predictable: he would not bear criminal responsibility, and the court would insist on psychiatric treatment, the length of which would be decided by the doctor treating him.

The Kungaevs' lawyers, naturally, lodged an appeal, but were not very optimistic. Abdullah Hamzaev pinned most of his hopes on the European Court of Human Rights, not on the Russian judicial system, and the appeal to the Supreme Court was made primarily because that step was procedurally necessary before an appeal could be lodged in Strasbourg.

But then, a sensation: early in March 2003 the Military College of the Supreme Court unexpectedly annulled the verdict, acknowledged irregularities, and decreed that a retrial should take place. The case was to go back to the start of the investigation and convene in Rostov-on-Don in the same district military court, but with a different judge presiding.

On the Russian political map, the Supreme Court has long been regarded as no more than a department of the president's office rather than as the highest level of an independent national judicial authority. Thus this turn of events could mean only one thing: the winds in the Kremlin had changed direction and the president had turned his back on the notion that a Russian officer in Chechnya was always in the right. Again, as in spring 2000, Putin was trying to position himself publicly as the champion of the dictatorship of law, and the 2004 pre-election presidential campaign was about to begin. Putin's United Russia Party also faced parliamentary elections in December 2003.

The front-running slogan for both campaigns was "The law rules supreme."

On April 9, 2003, the court in Rostov-on-Don reconvened. The colonel was a changed man. There was little sign of the brazen lout who almost spat at the judge and insulted the parents of the murdered girl. He complained he had been betrayed. He was plainly nervous. He demanded a trial by jury but was refused. He then ceased to reply to questions, stuck cotton in his ears, and sat in the dock reading. Colonel Vladimir Bukreev, deputy chairman of the district military court, now presided over the bench. For the first time, witnesses were called for cross-examination. This was a revolution.

First to be questioned was General Gerasimov. He reported that Budanov, as the commanding officer of a tank regiment and hence a representative of the Ministry of Defense rather than of the Ministry of Internal Affairs, had had no right to search the village of Tangi-Chu looking for a female sniper. Arresting suspected members of IAFs was a matter for the prosecutor's office, the FSB, and the police. Moreover, General Gerasimov testified that the regiment had received no orders to conduct search operations in February and March 2000. Budanov himself had "no right to be checking passports and accommodations in populated areas, and no right to be gathering intelligence there."

Then Yakhyaev, the head of the municipal administration of Duba-Yurt, was called to give evidence. According to Budanov, Yakhyaev was the one who had given him the photograph of men and women carrying snipers' rifles, which had been the main reason why Budanov had gone looking for a sniper in Tangi-Chu. Yakhyaev now told the court he had given no such photograph to Budanov. His statement was corroborated by a certain Pankov, who had been in Chechnya as a senior FSB agent in late December 1999 and early January 2000. Pankov testified that Budanov had indeed met Yakhyaev several times in his presence but that Yakhyaev had not given Budanov any photograph or said anything to him about a female sniper.

Neither had Budanov himself made any mention to Pankov of a photograph or a sniper.

As a result, all Budanov's testimony in his own defense was discredited. On July 25, 2003, sentence was passed: ten years' detention in strict-regime labor camps. Budanov is due for release on March 27, 2010.

Budanov undoubtedly got what he deserved, and even if his comeuppance was as the result of preelection maneuvering and opportunistic political intrigue, one can only welcome the court's just verdict, of which there are so few in Russia. The trial certainly cut against the grain. The majority of the army top brass, and virtually all of the officers' corps, especially in the Caucasus, categorically rejected the verdict. Greatly incensed, they were convinced that Budanov had suffered only because he had honorably defended the motherland. They took the ten-year sentence and the stripping of Budanov's awards and rank as a personal insult. Since the military courts are, to all intents and purposes, part of the military, not the judiciary, Judge Bukreev's position was a brave act, because he was simultaneously passing sentence on himself.

What About the Others?

No matter how dramatic the controversies surrounding the Budanov case, the story of his conviction is an exception to the rule. Political circumstances placed his crime in the limelight and brought the case to the public's attention, with important political consequences. The authorities were forced to give permission to the court to find Budanov guilty. In other war-crimes trials in which the accused were members of the Russian federal forces, the charges were frozen, and the security services exerted themselves only to enable the criminals to escape punishment, even when monstrous acts had been committed.

For example, on January 12, 2002, six military groups landed in the vicinity of the Chechen highland village of Dai. They were searching for fighters, among them Field Commander Hattab, who, according to operational intelligence, had recently been wounded and was in the region.

What happened then came to be called Budanov Case II. Ten men from a special operations unit tied to the Central Intelligence Directorate (GRU) of General Headquarters, landed from helicopters. Seeing a minibus on the road, they stopped it and ordered everybody to get out. They first tortured the passengers, trying to get them to reveal the whereabouts of fighters, then killed all six, and finished by burning the bodies.

The official agencies promptly dubbed this brutal, lawless execution "a military clash with IAFs." There were witnesses, however, who quickly made that story untenable. All six passengers proved to be ordinary civilians returning on a scheduled trip from the district of Shatoy to their homes. Among them was forty-year-old Zainap Djavathanova, the mother of seven children, ages two to seventeen years, and expecting her eighth. All that remained of her was one foot in a shoe, from which her husband and older children identified her. That day she had been to Grozny to be examined by a gynecologist.

Then there was the headmaster of the Nokhchi-Keloy village school, Said Mahomed Alskhanov, sixty-nine years old, and Abdul-Wahab Satabaev, the history teacher at the school. They were returning from a teachers' meeting in Shatoy. The fourth body belonged to Shahban Bahaev, a forester. The fifth was that of a nephew of the pregnant Zainap, Djamalaili Musaev, accompanying her on the journey as was customary in that region. The sixth body was the bus driver, Hamzat Tuburov, a father of five. The entire district knew him well, because every day he drove whoever required transport from Shatoy to the various highland villages and back.

On the evening of January 12, all the killers were arrested. The Shatoy District prosecutor's office, acting on the evidence of a chance witness, Major Vitaly Nevmerzhitsky of military intelligence, managed to obtain permission to make the arrests, which were virtually unprecedented in Chechnya. The special operations troops were handed over shortly afterward to the investigators of the military prosecutor's office, and Criminal Case No. 76002 was brought against them.

All, it would seem, was proceeding according to the rules. I met Colonel Andrey Vershinin, the military prosecutor in Shatoy District, who was conducting this much-publicized case at that time, and in the spring of 2002 he was still full of optimism. He said there was more than enough proof of guilt, and that the case would most certainly come to court. It would be almost impossible to demolish it, as happens nearly every time with similar cases. Hundreds of criminal cases waiting to be brought to court are blocked at all levels for one simple reason: army personnel accused of crimes are moved out of Chechnya by their commanding officers as quickly as possible. Investigations stall, obstacles are put in the way of the prosecutor's office, its staff members are intimidated, and so the investigation is silenced.

Prosecutor Vershinin had managed to achieve what was almost impossible: he had personnel of the GRU under arrest, while the investigation proceeded, in the guardhouse of the 291th Regiment, because the military prosecutor's office had its premises within the regiment's compound. So the suspects were under the colonel's direct, around-the-clock supervision.

Prosecutor Vershinin is not to blame for what happened next. The accused were removed from Shatoy and transferred to a prison outside Chechnya and beyond his reach. Two of the accused, Lieutenant Alexander Kalagandsky and Corporal Vladimir Voevodin, spent nine months in prison in Pyatigorsk and were then released because the central military prosecutor's office in Russia failed to apply to the court to extend their period of detention. The court was therefore automatically obliged to release them "on receipt of their signed undertaking not to travel outside the Shchelkovsky District of Moscow Province."

Why were these two killers to be found in Moscow Province? Before being sent to Chechnya, both had been serving at the end of the world in Buryatia. That they had been transferred to Moscow Province meant only one thing: the Central Intelligence Directorate in general headquarters had decided to support them, evidently considering that, like Budanov, they had loyally served a motherland that had failed to appreciate their efforts. The military has tried again to pursue the charges against them but has made no headway on getting a conviction.

Only Captain Eduard Ulman, Special Operations, remained for a while in detention. It was he who, on January 12, 2002, gave the order to carry out the massacre, although he claimed he was following orders from a superior and was later released. The suspected instigator, Major Alexey Perelevsky, remains at large.

What do you call this sort of situation? If a Chechen fighter had shot six Russians and burned their bodies, he surely would not have been freed in return for an undertaking not to change his place of residence.

Russia now faces the question, comparable to the one the United States confronted during and after the Vietnam War: how to view its soldiers and officers in Chechnya who routinely murder, loot, torture, and rape. Are they war criminals? Or are they unyielding combatants in the struggle against international terror, using every means at their disposal, with the noble end of saving humankind? Are the ideological stakes in this struggle so high that everything else should be disregarded?

A Westerner would, I hope, have a simple answers to these questions: It is for the courts to decide. As of now, Russia has no answer. Now, five years into the second Chechen war, more than a million soldiers and officers have experienced that lawlessness. Poisoned by war, they threaten civilian life; they cannot be left out of the social equation.

The Budanov case and the Dai massacre are both tragic and dramatic; they exposed Russia's problems and challenged the country to consider the impact of the second Chechen war on Russian lives. These events highlighted illogical thinking about the war and about Putin, and put Russia's notions of right and wrong in the northern Caucasus on trial. Most important, they showed the profound changes that have occurred in the judicial system under Putin and under the influence of the war.

The spirit of democratic reform lived on in the work of Judge Bukreev and Prosecutor Vershinin, but Russia has seen clearly that it does not have an independent judiciary or a prosecutor's office. Instead it has verdicts decided by political fiat and based on the imperatives of political expediency.

TANYA, MISHA, LENA, AND RINAT:
WHERE ARE THEY NOW?

So, where are we now?—we who lived in the Soviet Union, where most of us had a stable job and a salary we could rely on, who had unbounded, unshakable confidence in what tomorrow would bring. We who knew there were doctors who could treat our ailments and teachers who would help us learn. And who also knew that we would not pay a kopeck for all these benefits. What kind of existence are we eking out now? What new roles have we been allocated?

The changes since the end of the Soviet era have been threefold. First, we underwent a personal revolution (in parallel, of course, with the social revolution) at the time of the demise of the Soviet Union and during the regime of Boris Yeltsin. Everything vanished in an instant: Soviet ideology, cheap sausage, money, and the certainty that there was a Big Daddy in the Kremlin; even if he was a despot, at least he was responsible for us.

The second change came with the 1998 debt default. Many of us had managed to earn a bit in the years after 1991, when the market economy was introduced, and there were signs that a middle class was being formed. A Russian middle class, admittedly, not like what you might find in the West, but a middle class nonetheless, one that would support democracy and the free market. Overnight, it all disappeared. By then, many people were so tired of the daily struggle for survival that they could not rise to the new challenge; they simply sank without a trace.

The third change came under Putin, as we embarked upon a new stage of Russian capitalism with obvious neo-Soviet features. The economy in the era of our third president is a curious hybrid of the free market, ideological dogma, and various other features. It is a model that puts Soviet ideology at the service of big-time private capital. There are an awful lot of poor, indeed destitute, people. In addition, an old phenomenon is flourishing again: the *nomenklatura*, a ruling elite, the great bureaucratic class that existed under the Soviet system. The economic system may have changed, but members of the elite have adapted to it. The *nomenklatura* would like to live the high life, like the New Russian business elite, only their official salaries are tiny. They have no desire to return to the old Soviet system, but neither does the new system entirely suit them. The problem is that it requires law and order, something Russian society is demanding ever more insistently; accordingly, the *nomenklatura* spends most of its time trying to get around the law in order to promote its status.

As a result, Putin's new-old *nomenklatura* has taken corruption to heights undreamed of under the Communists or Yeltsin. It is now devouring small and middle-size businesses, and with them the middle class. It is giving big and super-big business, the monopolies and quasi-state enterprises, the opportunity to develop. (In other words, they are the *nomenklatura*'s preferred source of bribes.) Indeed, they represent the kinds of businesses that produce the highest, most stable returns not only for their owners and managers but also for their patrons in the state administration. In Russia, big business without patrons, or "curators," in the state administration does not exist. This misconduct has nothing to do with market forces. Putin is trying to gain the support of the so-called *byvshie*, the *ci-devants*, who occupied leadership positions under the Soviet regime. Their hankering after old times is so strong that the ideology underpinning Putin-style capitalism is increasingly reminiscent of the thinking in the Soviet Union during the height of the period of stagnation in the late Brezhnev years—the late 1970s and early 1980s.

Tanya, Misha, Lena, and Rinat are real people (although I have changed some of their names), not fictional characters, ordinary Russians who, together with the rest of the country, have been struggling to survive. They were all my friends. This is what has happened to them since 1991.

Tanya

It is early winter, 2002. The *Nord-Ost* saga has just ended. Russian society, particularly in Moscow, is in a state of shock. I appeared on television, playing a small part in these events, and, as a result, old friends reappeared in my life.

The late-night call was from Tanya. Actually she had always rung in the small hours, so late that most people were already asleep.

I hadn't seen Tanya, my sometime neighbor, for ten years or so. In those days she had been downtrodden, but now she was a queen. She looked triumphant and chic, not because she was expensively dressed, which she was, but because she was self-possessed and poised. This was something new.

In the Soviet period, Tanya's life had been one long torment. Almost every evening she would come down to see me (I lived on the ground floor of an old block of flats, and she lived at the top). She would weep over the fact that her life was ruined.

In those years Tanya was an engineer in a research institute and thus was regarded as belonging to the Soviet scientific and technical intelligentsia, a substantial social category that no longer exists.

How did one come to belong to that stratum? At the time, a young woman from a good family—Tanya was the only daughter of well-established parents—was expected to pursue higher education; if, after secondary school, she showed no particular inclinations or aptitudes, she studied at a technical institute, of which there were any number, and became an engineer. After graduating, she was required to work for three years at the speciality the state had trained her in at its expense. Accordingly, there was a whole army of people who were deeply dissatisfied with life, young specialists who had never wanted to be engineers and who now spent their working days in research institutes producing nothing useful whatsoever.

Tanya was a fully paid-up member of this army, with the profession of engineer of communal facilities in nuclear power stations. For days at a time and without the least enthusiasm, she would design projects for drainage and water-supply systems that nobody ever built, receiving a minuscule salary in return. She was always unhappy because of a chronic shortage of money. She tried to feed and clothe her family decently, frantically ministering to her two small, perpetually sick children and her husband, a rather odd young man named Andrey, a lecturer at a prestigious technical university in Moscow.

As a result, Tanya was a typical neurasthenic, endlessly tormenting herself, Andrey, and the children with her bad moods, her hysteria, her depressions, and her constant dissatisfaction.

To make matters worse, Tanya was from Rostov-on-Don. She had managed to move to Moscow by marrying Andrey, whom she had met on a Black Sea beach. She was regarded as little better than one of the *limitchiki*, menial "quota workers" who, in the mid-1970s, were granted temporary residence permits in Moscow in return for working in unpopular or undersupplied occupations. At that time there were no end of female "engineers" in the capital, women from the provinces who had married Muscovites. No one wanted to remain outside Moscow, and young women from good families did their best to move there.

Tanya did not know what she wanted, but she knew clearly what she did not want: to be an engineer and to be living in penury with the impoverished Andrey. We talked about it a lot. Tanya was angry because she saw no way out.

There were often noisy disputes at home. In accordance with Soviet tradition, Tanya, not having a place of her own in Moscow, should have lived with Andrey in his flat, but he did not have an apartment either. So they ended up sharing one large flat with Andrey's parents and his two elder brothers, each of whom had a family and a couple of children.

All in all, it was a typical Soviet beehive, but with no option to swarm and achieve independence. To make things worse, Andrey came from a genteel old Moscow family consisting of exceptional people. One, for example, was a famous professor who had taught the violin at the state conservatory. He was the second husband of Andrey's grandmother, who had also been a professor of violin there. His grandmother had died long ago, but her husband was still in the beehive. Like Tanya, he had nowhere else to go.

Andrey's parents were professors of physics and mathematics. The elder brother was a professor of chemistry at Moscow University who made one discovery after another, although his achievements had little material impact on his life.

The situation made Tanya more and more exasperated. She considered Andrey's family to be a bunch of incompetent failures despite the dozens of academic qualifications they possessed, and Andrey's family reciprocated wholeheartedly, constantly finding fault with her. Tanya, it's important to remember, was from Rostov-on-Don, where, even in Soviet times, people traded in any available product. Illegal underground workshops flourished there. Many rich men divided their time between prison and the outside world, and no one considered it a disgrace. The newspapers called them speculators and con artists, but the young women of Rostov were happy enough to marry them.

When we first met in the early 1980s, Tanya already thought she had made a mistake in marrying Andrey. Love hadn't come into it. She admitted she had simply swallowed the bait of residence in Moscow. She came out of herself only when she could produce pretty things she had picked up who knows where and was inviting you to buy them. She undoubtedly had a special gift for commercial persuasiveness. She could sell you a blouse of appalling quality at three times its value while assuring you, "It's what people are wearing in Europe." When the fraud came to light, she would not be embarrassed in the least. This talent for speculative trade was something that Andrey's traditionalist, highly educated family despised.

Now, in 2002, Tanya invited me to her home, which turned out to be that same spacious flat in the heart of Moscow.

The flat had been magnificently refurbished. The place was crammed with the latest technology, excellent copies of famous paintings, high-quality reproduction antique furniture. Tanya was almost fifty, but her skin was youthful and healthy, her clothes bright. She talked in a loud, confident voice, very openly, and although she laughed a lot her face remained unwrinkled. Obviously she had had plastic surgery, a telltale sign that she had made the big time.

Has Andrey struck it rich? I wondered. Tanya strode through the rooms. Ten years ago she had preferred to whisper in this flat, to sit in the corner of one of the rooms, avoiding her in-laws.

"Well, where is the family?"

"I'll tell you, only don't faint. All this belongs to me now."

"It's yours? Congratulations! But where do they live?"

"In a minute, in a minute. Everything in good time."

A handsome young man about the age Tanya's sons must be now, I supposed, slipped quietly into the room. The last time I'd seen her boys, they'd been children, so I blurted out, "Can this really be . . . Igor?"

Igor was Tanya and Andrey's elder son and must by then have been twenty-four or twenty-five.

Tanya burst out laughing. Peals of merriment, mischievous, echoing, youthful. Not at all like Tanya.

"My name is David," the handsome, ox-eyed young man with dark curly hair murmured. He kissed Tanya's manicured hand. I remembered a time when her hands hadn't looked like that: they had been worn by many hours of washing clothes for a large family. David drifted off into the depths of the flat. "Well, don't let me spoil things for you, girls."

Oh, dear. We really were not girls.

"All right, tell me. Reveal the secrets of your youthfulness and prosperity," I begged my old friend. "Where is your family?"

"They aren't my family anymore."

"What about Andrey?"

"We split up. My sentence of hard labor came to an end."

"Have you remarried? This boy? David?"

"David is my boyfriend, short-term, just for the sake of my health, really. He's my toy boy. I'll keep him for as long as I feel like it."

"Good heavens! Who are you working for?"

"I don't work for anyone. I work for myself," Tanya answered firmly and with a metallic edge to her voice that didn't seem to go with the image of the slightly indolent, manicured lady with a young lover who was sitting opposite me.

Tanya is a happy product of the new life. In the summer of 1992, when there was nothing to eat in the majority of homes in Moscow (the outcome of "economic shock treatment," part of the market reforms of then–prime minister Yegor Gaidar), Tanya, together with her children and the rest of the professor's family, was living in the country at the in-laws' old dacha.

In that terrible, hungry summer, Muscovites, if they had a dacha, were sitting it out in their wooden shacks in the country and growing vegetables for the winter so as to have at least something to eat. The research institute where Tanya worked had closed for the summer. The facility had no work at all and hadn't, in any case, paid anybody's salaries for ages. The employees, town dwellers all, had gone off to hoe their vegetable patches or to trade in the markets that had sprung up in large numbers on the streets of starving Moscow. Tanya was busy growing vegetables of her own and looking after the children. Andrey often stayed in the city and didn't come back to sleep at the dacha because, unlike the majority of research institutes, his technological university had not closed.

One morning, for some reason, Tanya turned up in Moscow unexpectedly, unlocked the door of their flat, and found Andrey and a young woman student in her matrimonial bed. A loud-mouthed woman from the south of Russia, Tanya bawled at Andrey so the whole apartment block could hear her.

Andrey made no excuses. He said he loved the student. She herself said nothing, got dressed, and went through to the kitchen, where she began boiling the kettle for tea as if nothing had happened.

For Tanya her rival's silence and her manifest familiarity with the layout of the flat was the last straw. She decided, then and there, that she hadn't been putting up with Andrey's pathetic family all her married life only to let a rival invade their space. She told Andrey not to imagine he could get away with it. He collected his things and left with the student.

That, in effect, was the day Tanya's new, completely independent life began. Andrey behaved abominably, giving her not a kopeck to support herself or the children. Three years later, when Tanya had made a little money, she would, in fact, occasionally feed him and even buy him clothes, but not from any feeling of sympathy. Tanya fed Andrey because revenge is sweet. She gave him red caviar, a symbol of luxury in Soviet times, which she could now afford. Andrey gobbled it up until it was coming out of his ears, not even blushing at the humiliation, because he was so hungry. At times he ate at the soup kitchens set up at churches, pretending, for good measure, to be a believer. He even learned how to cross himself.

In 1992, the summer of the free-market breakthrough, these events were still in the future. After a week, when there was nothing left to feed the children, and with her mother-in-law insisting that she must forgive Andrey and take him back, Tanya went off to trade at a nearby market.

Her mother-in-law shrieked, "The disgrace of it! The disgrace!" and took to her bed. She soon came around, however, when Tanya began buying her medicine with the disgraceful money she was making at the market. Not one of the old lady's sons, her husband, or her other daughters-in-law had been able to do anything like this for her. Matters had taken on a tragicomic aspect when it was resolved, at a family council, that they would never, come what may, sell off the family heirlooms, the antique furniture inherited from their forebears, the rare antiquarian music albums, the pictures by famous nineteenth-century Russian painters. Lying obstinately in her bed and readying herself for death rather than disgrace, Tanya's mother-in-law was the first to vote against the idea. In the early 1990s, other long-established families who had held on to their heirlooms through the Stalin years were selling them off on the cheap or, as people said at the time, "for a meal."

Meanwhile, Tanya was out at the market from six in the morning until eleven at night. It was not work but hard labor. It was pure purgatory, but it had one redeeming feature: this was slavery with a price tag. Tanya stood in the market and earned real rubles that rustled in her pocket. What was more, you got your cash on the day. You stood there and you got the money, not later but right then, and that was what mattered. Tanya always came home with money. She also came home with swollen legs, barely able to put one foot in front of the other, and with enormous swollen crab-claw hands, incapable even of washing herself or making herself look half human. But—she was almost happy!

"You may not believe it, but I was happy not to be dependent on anyone else anymore. Not on the director of the institute, who didn't pay me; not on Andrey, who was giving me nothing, not on my mother-in-law, with her family heirlooms and traditions. I depended solely on myself." Tanya, now rich and beautiful, told me the story of how it had all changed ten years ago. "My mother-in-law? Well, one fine day I just told her where to get off. 'Go **** yourself!' And what do you think? For the first time she didn't preach back at me. It was a revelation. A revolution took place before my eyes. The seemingly incorruptible old Moscow intelligentsia was being broken. It was being broken by the money I was giving my mother-in-law. She stopped lecturing me because I started feeding her. Me, the one who was always in the wrong. Gradually all of them, that whole family, which had looked down on me for so many years because I didn't come from the same sort of background and because, as they always said, I had inveigled Andrey into marrying me because I wanted to move to Moscow, the whole bunch learned to smile at me and even to listen attentively to what I had to tell them.

"And it was just because I was feeding them all by trading at that market. I gloried in it. I was prepared to continue doing it for just one reason: to get more and more money, more and more, and to humiliate them by rubbing their noses in it."

When Tanya returned home toward midnight, she would collapse on the bed. She no longer had any time for her sons. She did not check their homework. She would collapse and then she was out like a light. Early the next morning everything started again.

Her mother-in-law began looking after Tanya's children—for the first time, it has to be said, since they had been living under the same roof. Tanya was amazed yet again.

In the market, Tanya found herself working for an adroit young man who was a "shuttle," as people said then. Nikita's "shuttling" consisted of importing cheap clothes from Turkey, cheap watermelons from Uzbekistan, cheap mandarins from Georgia—in fact, anything cheap from anywhere at all. Tanya and the other women working for him sold his goods. There were no taxes, no state levies. In the market, the rules were the same as inside a prison. Disagreements were resolved at knifepoint, extortion was rife, people got beaten up. The women traders were mostly in the same situation as Tanya, single women with children abandoned at home, former members of the scientific and technical intelligentsia whose institutes, publishing houses, or editorial offices had closed. They were little better than whores for their bosses.

Soon Tanya was sleeping with Nikita. He picked her out from the others, despite the difference in their ages, and took her with him to Turkey on a buying trip. He took her once, then a second and a third time, and within two months Tanya, a woman with a commercial streak, had become a shuttle herself, having seen that the enterprise really wasn't rocket science.

Then Nikita was murdered, shot by no one knew whom. One morning they found him at the market with a bullet hole in his head, and that was that. Nikita's saleswomen migrated across the way to Tanya and were glad to do so. Tanya proved much more efficient than Nikita, and business began to boom. As a bonus, Tanya was less of a shit than the deceased.

After another six months, Tanya stopped traveling to Turkey. Not because she was tired, although life as a shuttle was hard. At that time you had to carry the goods yourself, in enormous bundles that you dragged around airports and railway stations, skimping at every turn, even on luggage carts, which had to be paid for. She stopped traveling herself because she had discovered her niche: she was exceptionally good at business.

Tanya flourished, and her business soon grew to the extent that she hired five and then another five shuttles and became the proprietor of what, in the context of a local market, was a large business. The shuttles traveled, her women traded, and Tanya managed them all. She was already going around, as people put it, "not dressed like a Turk"—in other words, like a European. She was a habituée of all the restaurants, where she ate, got drunk, threw her money about, and relaxed after work. She had plenty of money left over for herself, her family, and her workers. Takings in those years were astronomical. She had lovers befitting her income and years: virtuosos. Tanya got rid of them when she felt like it. Andrey, to be frank, had not been worth much in that department.

Another year passed and Tanya decided to refurbish the flat, having first taken over ownership of it. She bought some rather poky apartments for Andrey, his brothers, and her father-in-law, which made all of them happy. Tanya kept her elderly mother-in-law with her. Pity aside, she needed someone to look after her sons. The elder, Igor, had reached puberty and was causing problems, while the younger boy was sickly.

Tanya did, however, carry through the refurbishment as a kind of retaliation. "I just really wanted to show them who owned the place!"

She threw everything out, absolutely everything. She sold off all the heirlooms and expunged all traces of her in-laws' dusty gentry past. Nobody protested. Her mother-in-law went off to the dacha and kept out of the way. The result was a modern European flat equipped with cutting-edge technology.

After the renovation Tanya decided to move on: she abandoned the shuttle business and went into mainstream commerce, buying a number of shops in Moscow.

"What? Those shops belong to you?" I couldn't believe my ears. Tanya was the owner of two excellent supermarkets I would drive to after work. "Congratulations! But your prices . . . !"

"I know, but Russia is a rich country!" Tanya parried, laughing.

"Not that rich. You've become an imperialist. A bit hard-nosed."

"Of course. Yeltsin's gone, and with him the easy money and the romance. The people in power now are insatiable pragmatists, and I am one of them. You are against Putin, but I am for him. He almost seems like a brother to me, downtrodden in the past and getting his own back now."

"What do you mean by 'insatiable'?"

"The bribes. The endless bribes you have to give everyone. Just to keep hold of my shops, I pay up. Who don't I give bribes to? The pencil pushers at the police station, the firemen, the hygiene inspectors, the municipal government. And the gangsters whose land my shops are on. Actually, I bought them from gangsters."

"Aren't you afraid to do business with them?"

"No. I have a dream: I want to be rich. In today's Russia that means I have to pay them all off. Without that 'tax' I would be shot tomorrow and replaced by someone else."

"You aren't exaggerating?"

"If anything, I am understating things."

"What about the bureaucrats?"

"Some of the bureaucrats I pay myself, and the rest are paid by the gangsters. I give the gangsters money and they keep those other gangsters, our bureaucrats, sweet. Actually, it's quite convenient."

"Where is Andrey now?"

"He died. In the end he couldn't take the fact that I had moved up in the world and he was eating my caviar. He asked me to take him back, but I wanted none of it. I told him to find himself another student. Anyway, I don't want to live with an ugly man. I've decided I like handsome men. I go to male strip shows and choose my partners there."

"You're kidding! Don't you miss family life? Domestic bliss?"

"No. I don't. I've just started living. There is a downside. Of course there is. You may think it is all sordid, but what was so pure about the way I used to live?"

"What about the children?"

"Igor, unfortunately, has turned out a weakling, like Andrey. He's on drugs. I've sent him to a clinic. This is the fifth time already. . . . I am having Stasik educated in London. I'm very pleased with him. Very. He's first in everything there. My mother-in-law looks after him. I rent a small flat for her. Stasik lives in a student hostel during the week, and at the weekends in this flat with my mother-in-law. I paid for her to have a hip replacement. They did it in Switzerland. She's come back to life, running around like a young woman, and she absolutely worships me. I think she really does. It's a great thing, money is."

David swirled into the room bearing a tray. "Time for tea, girls," he crooned. "Just the three of us. All right, Tanechka?"

Tanya nodded and said she'd be right back. She wanted to change for tea. David exuded degeneracy and languor. It was all rather unpleasant. A couple of minutes later, Tanya returned. She was covered in diamonds, her ears ablaze, her décolletage ashimmer. Even her hair was glittering.

The show was for my benefit. I politely registered appreciation. Tanya was really pleased, as radiant as her diamonds from the pleasure of presenting herself, the new Tanya, to an old friend.

We quickly drank our tea and said our good-byes.

"Only not for ten years this time!" Tanya proposed as we parted.

"Let's make an effort," I replied, and thought as I went down the stairs that in the Putin era people really did meet up more often. Old friends, I mean. There was a time in Russia, the late Yeltsin period, when everybody was terribly busy just surviving, when people didn't phone each other for years, some embarrassed because they were poor, some because they were rich. It was a time when many emigrated forever; when many put a bullet in their brains because nobody seemed to need them anymore; when people snorted cocaine out of disgust with themselves. Now, however, it was as if everybody who had survived was meeting up again. Society had become noticeably more orderly, and people even had free time.

When the new times had arrived, women were the driving force, going into business, divorcing their husbands. The husbands became gangsters, and in the first years of the Yeltsin period, many died in shoot-outs. These things happened because, on the eve of perestroika, many Russian women had felt, like Tanya, that they would never be able to change their lives. Suddenly here was their big chance.

A week later I had to be at a press conference in connection with a special election to the municipal duma, I think. And there, quite unexpectedly, I met Tanya again. In our already rather structured and, as under the Soviets, cliquish society, owners of supermarkets just don't go to political press conferences.

Tanya manifested herself to the world of journalists with never a hair out of place, in a classic black business suit and without a single diamond to be seen. David was there as well, and he, too, gave a top-notch performance, flawlessly playing the role of Tanya's business secretary, modest but not ingratiating. No "girls" on this occasion.

I sat with the journalists. Tanya was on the other side of the barricades. Handed a microphone, she was the last to speak. She was one of the candidates running for a seat in the municipal duma. She told the journalists, including me, how she saw the problems of the homeless in Moscow, and promised to fight for their rights if the voters did her the honor of electing her to be a member of the legislative assembly.

"What on earth do you need this for? You're rich already," I asked Tanya when the press conference was over.

"I told you, I want to be even richer. It's very simple: I don't want to pay bribes to our councilor."

"Is that all?"

"You have no idea of the level of corruption nowadays. Gangsters in Yeltsin's time didn't even dream of this. If I become a councilor, that will be one 'tax' less."

"But why have you taken to defending the homeless in particular?" We wandered into a French café nearby. Tanya had chosen it; the place was too expensive for me.

"I think that backdrop will make me look good. Anyway, I really can help them pull themselves up by their bootstraps. I've done it myself."

"And why at the press conference, at the end of your speech, did you talk about Putin? About how much you love and respect and trust him? Did your image makers tell you to say that? It's in terrible taste."

"No, it isn't. It's what you have to do nowadays. I know that, without any help from 'image makers.'" Tanya stumbled over these difficult English words, which have immigrated into Russia along with the new life. "If I didn't mention Putin, our local FSB man would be around to see me in the shop tomorrow to complain I wasn't saying what everybody says. That's the kind of life we businesspeople lead now."

"So what if he came around and said that?"

"So nothing. He would just demand a bribe."

"What for?"

"To 'forget' what I hadn't said."

"Listen, aren't you tired of all this?"

"No. If I need to kiss Putin's backside to get another couple of shops, I'll do it."

"But what do you mean by 'get'? You just buy them, don't you? Pay for them, and that's it?"

"No, things are different now. To 'get' something, you have to earn the right from the bureaucrats to buy the shop with your own money. Russian capitalism, it's called. Personally, I like it. When I tire of it, I'll buy myself citizenship somewhere and move on."

We parted. Of course Tanya got elected. She's said to be not bad. She puts her heart into battling for the poor of Moscow. She's organized another canteen for the homeless and refugees, she's bought another three supermarkets, and she often speaks on television in praise of our modern times. She rang recently and asked me to write an article about her. I did. The one you are reading right now. She asked to read it before it was published, was horrified, and said, "It's all true." She made me promise not to publish it in Russia before her death.

"How about abroad?"

"Go ahead. Let them know what our money smells of."

So now you do.

Misha and Lena

Misha was married to Lena, my school friend from early childhood. She had married him when they were at college in the late 1970s. At that time, Misha was a very clever, talented young man who translated from German, who dubbed films while still a student at the Institute of Foreign Languages, and whose future seemed very bright. When he graduated, he was inundated with attractive offers of employment, not something that happened often.

Misha landed a job in the Ministry of Foreign Affairs, which was very prestigious, especially toward the end of the Soviet period. It was unusual for a man without family connections to get into such a closed corporation as our MFA. Misha had none. He had been brought up by his grandmother, a humble cleaning woman. His mother had died suddenly, from a brain tumor, when Misha was only fourteen. His father had promptly abandoned his orphaned family and run off with another woman.

So there was Misha in the MFA. We were great friends. We would go on picnics together, grill kebabs in the forest over a campfire and enjoy ourselves thoroughly. Lena and I were very close, and Misha was keen to be friends, too.

Underpinning our relationship were my two small children. When Misha came visiting, he simply couldn't take his eyes off them. He would watch them with delight no matter what nonsense they got up to, talk to them and play with them for hours at a time.

All our friends knew that Misha very much wanted to have children. He was obsessed with the idea, but Lena was a talented linguist. She was writing her dissertation and kept postponing having a baby until after she had graduated in philological sciences.

Misha was very jumpy as a result. He gradually developed a complex about the fact that they did not have any children. He began to suffer and to torment those around him, most of all Lena. However, Lena was made of stern stuff, and once she had made up her mind, nothing was going to change it. She would defend her dissertation and get her degree, and after that she would get pregnant. That was all there was to it.

Misha reacted by taking to the bottle. He put up with his disappointment for as long as he could but then just went off the rails. At first he didn't drink a lot, and people laughed at his behavior and teased him, but then his bouts began to last for several days at a time. He would disappear, and goodness knows where he was spending his nights. Later still he would drink for weeks at a time. Lena thought that perhaps she should give in and not finish her dissertation, but how do you make a baby with a man who is permanently inebriated?

Then the new times came—Gorbachev, Yeltsin—and the only reason Misha wasn't fired for his chronic drinking (he would have been sacked instantly under the Communists) was that there was no one to replace him. MFA staff who knew languages and had experience on the other side of the Iron Curtain were suddenly worth their weight in gold. They abandoned the cash-strapped MFA to work for the commercial firms and branches of foreign companies that were springing up. Misha got no offers, even though the Germans were the first to dash into the Russian market and translators fluent in German were the most sought after of all.

Even at the MFA, Misha's days were numbered, and he was eventually fired. Late one night at the end of 1996, in December when there was around thirty degrees of frost, someone rang my doorbell. It was Lena, wearing only her nightdress under a coat. You just don't walk around Moscow dressed like that in winter, and certainly not if you are Lena, who was always immaculately turned out. She was an equable, well brought up, and intelligent young woman. Now, however, one foot was bare, as if she were a destitute person without a home to go to, while on the other foot the top of a half-laced boot was flapping like a flag. My friend was shivering as if she had fallen through ice and just been pulled out of the freezing water. Something had frightened her half to death, and the shock had made her incoherent.

"Misha, Misha," she repeated over and over again, sobbing loudly, quite unlike her usual self and seemingly unaware of where she was or of the people around her.

The children had woken up by now and came quietly out of their room. They stood by Lena, spellbound by an anguish they could not understand. Lena finally noticed them, pulled herself together, took a tranquilizer with a glass of water, and began to explain what had happened.

Misha had been away from home for three nights in a row. Lena wasn't really expecting him back. She had gotten used to his drinking bouts and his absences, and so she went to bed. She had to go to the institute early in the morning. Shortly after midnight, however, Misha suddenly turned up. This was unusual.

This time he came straight in through the door and, just as he was, in his winter coat and dirty shoes, unwashed and stinking, walked into the bedroom and stood over Lena in menacing silence, staring at her in the semidarkness. He seemed out of his mind. His black eyes were shining unnaturally, and there was a silvery gleam on his cheeks. His once handsome face was contorted in a grimace. Lena pulled the covers up and said nothing. She knew from bitter experience of living with an incipient alcoholic that it was pointless to say anything. Despite appearances, you were talking to someone who could not hear. You just had to wait for him to fall asleep.

Misha moved closer to the bed and said, "That's it. . . . It's all your fault . . . that I drink . . . and now I am going to kill you."

Lena heard a note of quiet determination in Misha's voice that left no room for doubt. She jumped up and rushed around the room. At first, Misha cornered her on the balcony, and she thought she'd had it, but drunks are clumsy and she was able to slip past him, grab some things by the front door, and run out across the snow to the nearest refuge, my block of flats.

After that they got divorced, and although neither was at all maudlin by nature, they would both come to sob in my kitchen and tell me how much they loved each other but how they could never live together again.

I continued to see Misha, although increasingly less often. He would drop by once in a while, mainly to ask for money, because he was continuing to drink and very hard up. He had only the occasional translation to make ends meet.

On his rare sober visits, he told me he was trying to stop drinking and start a new life. He had developed an interest in Orthodox Christianity, was reading religious books, had been baptized, had found a confessor whom he trusted, and was going to confession and communion and finding solace in doing so. He was convinced that redemption was possible. Misha's outward appearance was not, however, that of someone on the road to salvation. He was in a bad way, his hair greasy and unkempt. He wore a threadbare, obviously secondhand black coat that was much too short for him, and when I asked where he was living, blurted out some nonsense to the effect that nobody understood him and it was difficult to live anywhere when nobody understands you.

Under Yeltsin this was not a particularly unusual or surprising sight. A lot of penniless people were wandering the streets, people who had been well educated, respectable citizens who had lost their jobs and taken to drink when they could find no place for themselves in the new reality. It was precisely on this fertile ground of general dissatisfaction, unemployment, and the laying off of many who had been members of the professions in the Soviet period that Orthodoxy became fashionable, and the failures who had lost their work, their spouses, or their reasons for being ran to the church, although not all of them, certainly, were genuine believers.

Accordingly, Misha was one of many people on that path. He came to see me one time, sober and yet joyful, and invited me to congratulate him. He had become a father the day before; he had a son. We hastened to say how pleased we were: at last his dream had come true. For some reason, however, Misha was not in the seventh heaven we expected.

The boy was named Nikita. A long time before, when Misha was still married to Lena, he had often mused that if he had a son, he would name him Nikita.

"Who is Nikita's mother?" I asked cautiously.

"A young girl."

"Do you live with her? Are you married . . . or going to get married?"

"No. Her parents don't like me."

"Then rent a flat and live with your son. That is so important."

"I haven't got any money."

"Start earning some."

"I don't want to and I can't. I just can't—it's simply not possible."

He cut off any further attempts at conversation.

More than a year passed. Yeltsin abdicated power, nominating Putin as his successor. The second Chechen war started. Putin was constantly on television. One moment he was flying a military aircraft, the next issuing instructions in Chechnya. The election, a foregone conclusion, was approaching.

Late one night Lena called. "Do you know what?" she said in a barely recognizable voice, hoarse, like the voice of a singer after a concert. "I have just had a phone call. Misha has killed the woman he was living with. She has left a fourteen-year-old son from her first marriage. The boy was in the flat when it happened. Misha got drunk. Apparently the woman was older than he, felt sorry for him and drank with him so he wouldn't feel so lonely. Anyway, they were drinking together yesterday when Misha took a knife and said what he said to me: 'I am going to kill you.'"

Lena burst into tears. "It could have been me," she said. "Do you remember? You were all trying to persuade me not to get divorced. You said he would sort himself out, that he needed treatment. But he would just have killed me."

The court was lenient on Misha, especially after the story of his life was related. He was sentenced to four and a half years. Not much for a murder. The court held that he was not mentally ill or suffering from diminished responsibility, despite his alcoholism.

Misha was sent to a labor camp in Mordovia, in the depths of the forests. Six months later, the commandant of the camp came to see Lena in her Moscow flat, where by now she was living with a new husband and the son she had finally had. The commandant was not the brightest of men but evidently had a kind heart. The decision to visit

Lena was his own. He considered it his duty, as he was in the capital on business, to find her, despite the fact that she was divorced from Misha, and tell her that "her Michael" (as the commandant described him, to the horror of her new husband) was the best prisoner he had ever met, the most literate and hardest-working person in the camp. The commandant, who evidently had a pedagogical bent, had appointed him to look after the prisoners' library, and Misha had reorganized it. He was reading a lot himself and working with the other criminals in the role of psychologist. Misha had single-handedly constructed a wooden church inside the camp's barbed wire and was preparing to become a monk. He was corresponding with a monastery to find guidance on his chosen path. The commandant also informed Lena that he supported Misha's monastic inclinations, since he could see only good coming from them for his contingent of murderers, rapists, and old convicts. At Misha's request, he was going to buy a church plate in the Moscow Patriarchate shop and take it back to the camp.

The jailer ended by promising he that would intercede to have Misha's sentence reduced on the grounds of exemplary conduct.

"Lena, are you not glad?" he asked the divorced wife, noticing that she was practically in tears.

"I am frightened," she replied.

"There's no need for that," Misha's commandant replied. "He has changed a lot. He isn't dangerous. He doesn't drink anymore, and he won't kill anyone else. At least, I don't think so."

The commandant smoothed his hair, drank his tea, rubbed his hands together as if intending to produce fire from his palms, and added, "To tell the truth, I am a bit sorry he will be leaving."

We started readying ourselves for whatever might transpire. Misha might resurface in Moscow at any moment. In any event, it was 2001 before he reappeared. For a few weeks he bobbed around, again with nowhere to stay, his German forgotten, by now completely incapable of adapting to the new life.

I had known for a long time that he was in Moscow, but we met by chance on Tverskoy Boulevard. When our paths crossed, I barely recognized the features that had once been so familiar. We sat down on a bench and spoke for three hours or so without a break. He didn't ask about my children, and I didn't ask about his son. Misha simply needed someone to talk to, someone to hear him out.

He talked the whole time about choosing the right monastery. I looked closely at the man in front of me. Of the earlier Misha, or what he had been in his youth, almost nothing remained. He looked gray, old, and flabby. Of the talent you once could have seen in him, nothing remained. There was only a grudge against fate, and a lot of prison slang. In addition, Misha treated me to a lot of banal nonsense about the meaning of life, in the way it is written about in crude brochures for the barely literate. I realized the kind of library they must have had in the camp in Mordovia.

"Have you found a job?"

"Where? The pay is low everywhere, and they expect a lot."

"Well, we're all in that situation now. We just have to put up with it—" I began.

Misha interrupted me. "Well, I don't want to be like everybody else."

He certainly had that in spades.

"How are you getting on with the monastery?"

"They can't take me for the time being. There's a waiting list and you have to pull strings even for that. You have to know people. Having been in prison doesn't help."

"I suppose it's understandable. You really haven't been out of prison for long."

"Well, I don't understand it." Misha became aggressive.

"What are you planning to do?"

"I shall go into that little church." Misha gestured behind him, and there indeed stood one of the oldest churches in Moscow, solidly rooted in the years. "I'll ask them to take me on as a watchman. They told me you need the right number of points in your résumé to get into a monastery."

We both laughed. Only someone born in the Soviet Union and who had spent a fair part of his conscious life there knew how typically Soviet that approach was to getting a good job when you couldn't do it through string-pulling. And here we were, talking about a monastery, faith, religion, the rules of the church, which couldn't be further removed from the everyday reality of the Soviet way of life. We fell to laughing at the idea.

"It's weird," Misha said, "how in the New Russia the ways of Orthodoxy and of Soviet life have suddenly come together."

From beneath the dropsical eyelids of a man with kidney or heart trouble, the old Misha suddenly glanced at me, merry, on the ball, playful, gallant.

"Of course they have. Aren't you afraid the church you are so keen to sign up with has turned into that local committee of the Young Communist League you once fled from? That everything has just been repainted in new colors, and when you finally get into the monastery you'll be bitterly disappointed and . . ."

I bit my tongue. No glib words came to mind.

"You were going to say I would kill someone again, blaming my problems on them?"

"No, of course not," I stammered, although that was indeed what I had been about to say. Misha and I seemed to be back on the same wavelength.

"That is exactly what you were going to say. I can only reply that I am afraid myself, of course, but I have nowhere else to go. If I stay here, I shall certainly end up in prison again. I felt better in prison, in a confined space. The monastery is like a labor camp, only with different guards. I need to live under guard. I can't control myself, seeing the kind of life we have around us."

"And what kind of life is that?"

"Cynical. I can't bear cynicism. That is why I started drinking."

"But why did you kill your woman friend? Was she cynical?"

"No, she was a very good person, and I can't remember why I killed her. I was drunk."

"So, at all events, you won't stay in the world."

"Under no circumstances. I couldn't stand it."

I didn't meet Misha again, but I do know that he didn't manage to get into a monastery. The paperwork dragged on. The Orthodox bureaucracy in Russia is much like the state bureaucracy, indifferent to anything that doesn't affect it directly. Misha went along to the Patriarchate, submitting forms, working as a watchman, actually living in a church. He gradually started to drink again. He turned up at Lena's a couple of times asking for money. The first time she gave him one hundred rubles; the second time she refused. She was quite right. She and her husband were not working to enable Misha to get drunk when he felt like it. Of course she was right.

Except that Misha threw himself under a Metro train. We heard about it much later, and only by chance. And we discovered that Misha, one of the most talented Russians I ever met, had been buried as homeless and unclaimed. More exactly, the authorities buried his ashes, because in such cases the remains are cremated. Nobody knows where his grave is.

Rinat

You can mount a frontal attack or you can make a detour. The compound of the Special Intelligence Regiment of the Ministry of Defense, its most elite unit, is not, of course, a place for civilians like me to be strolling around. Sometimes, however, it has to be done. I have been brought here by Rinat, one of the regimental officers. Rinat is a major. Nobody knows who his parents were. He was brought up in an orphanage. His face is Asian, with slanting eyes, and he speaks several Central Asian languages. His speciality was intelligence gathering. Rinat fought clandestinely in the Afghan war for years. He then infiltrated Tadjik armed bands in the mountains and on the Afghan-Tadjik border, catching drug smugglers red-handed. On behalf of the Russian government, he secretly helped some of the current presidents of former Soviet republics to come to power. Naturally, he spent a lot of time in Chechnya during both the first and the second wars. His chest is covered with medals.

Rinat and I are looking for a hole in the fence. He wants to show me the squalor in which, for all his medals, he lives in the officers' barracks; he wants to show me, too, the house in the military village that he had hoped to move into but then found himself out of luck. Although this regiment is highly trained and very famous, we find the hole we are looking for. An impressive hole it is, too, not just big enough for the two of us to squeeze through; you could drive a tank through it.

We walk on for five minutes, and there it is, the village where the spies live. It is morning. Around us we see the unsmiling faces of officers on their day off. The weather is far from cheering. Churned-up clay squelches underfoot. We are not walking but slithering, looking down at the ground in order to maintain our footing.

I look up and, wondrous vision, see before me, like a mirage among the other dismal five-story buildings, a fine new gray-green multistory block of flats.

"That's how it all started," Rinat says. "Of course, I wanted a flat. I've had enough of wandering the world. My son is growing up, and I am constantly away in wars."

The major falls silent in mid-sentence and suddenly embarks on a maneuver that puzzles me. He hides his face and doubles over as if we are being shot at and need to find a trench to shelter in. Rinat whispers quietly that we should pretend not to know each other; he also asks me not to look ahead and not to wave my arms or attract attention.

"But what's wrong?" I ask. "Is it an ambush?"

I'm joking, of course.

"We mustn't make him angry," Rinat says softly, continuing his distracting maneuver. Like well-trained spies, we quickly, deftly, and without fuss change direction.

"Whom mustn't we annoy?" I inquire when Rinat raises his head with a sigh of relief, indicating that the danger has passed.

"Petrov, the deputy commanding officer."

Our maneuvering is explained by the fact that Petrov had been driving toward us. His car had pulled up to the fine new block of apartments because that is where Petrov lives. Only after he had disappeared inside did Rinat relax and continue our stroll around the compound. We kept ending up back at the fine building, which Rinat gazed upon with longing and envy.

To tell the truth, I am perplexed. I know a little about Rinat's combat record, his fearlessness, and I am amazed. What is it, I wonder, that he fears most? Death?

"No, I have learned to live with death. I don't mean to boast."

"Being captured?"

"Yes, I am afraid of that, of course, because I know I would be tortured. I have seen it happen. But I am not all that afraid of being captured."

"What then?"

"Probably peace, civilian life. It's something I know nothing about. I am not prepared for it."

Rinat is thirty-seven. All he has done in his life is to take part in wars. His body is covered in wounds. He has peptic and duodenal ulcers, and his nerves are in tatters. He has constant, agonizing pain in his joints and cerebral spasms after several injuries to the head.

Recently, the major decided it was time to settle down, to come back from the wars to our ordinary world. He found he knew absolutely nothing about it. For example, who would give him a place to live? Surely he deserved a flat for all he had been through defending the interests of the state. Or some money?

As soon as Rinat started asking Petrov about such things, it became apparent that he could expect nothing. Rinat concluded that while he had been carrying out special government missions across mountains, countries, and continents, his state had needed him and had rewarded him with medals and orders. As soon as the major's health gave out and he decided to try to settle down, though, he found there was nothing waiting for him, and the military hierarchy was simply going to turn him out on the street. The army was even going to expel him from the squalid nook in the officers' barracks where he and his son were presently sleeping.

Rinat has a son, Edik, whom he is bringing up on his own. The boy's mother died several years ago, and for a long time Edik lived alone in the officers' barracks, waiting for his father to come back from numerous wars and important combat missions.

"I know how to kill an enemy so he doesn't make a sound," Rinat tells me. "I can climb a mountain swiftly and silently and take out those who are occupying it. I am an excellent rock climber and mountaineer. I can 'read' mountains from twigs and bushes and tell who is there and where they are hiding. I have a feel for mountains—they say it is a natural gift—but I am incapable of getting an apartment. I am incapable of getting anything at all in civilian life."

Before me is a helpless professional killer trained by the state. There are many like him now. The state sends people off to yet another war; they live in the midst of war for years, return and do not know what peaceful life is with its law and order. They take to drinking, join gangs, become hit men, and their new masters pay them big money to take out those they say need to be murdered in the interests of the state.

And the state? It doesn't give a damn. Under Putin it has effectively ceased to interest itself in officers who have returned from the wars. It seems as if the state is actively engaged in ensuring that there are as many highly trained professional killers in criminal gangs as possible.

"Is that what you are thinking of going into, Rinat?"

"No, I don't want to, but if Edik and I find ourselves on the street, I can't rule it out. I can only do what I am trained to do."

Rinat and I finally squelch through the mud and slush to a dismal shack. Called the "three-story building," it is the officers' barracks. We go up to the second floor, and behind a peeling door is a squalid, spartan room.

In his entire life the major has never had a home to call his own. First there was the orphanage in the Urals. Then there was the barracks of the military college he enrolled in from the orphanage. Later still, garrison hostels alternating with tents when he was on active service. He has been in the army sixteen years, a rolling stone under military oath. For the last eleven years, Rinat has moved constantly from one combat mission to the next. It is not a life that has led him to acquire possessions.

"But I was happy," the major says. "I never wanted to stop fighting. I thought it would last forever."

All that Rinat has acquired is now stored in one parachute bag. The major opens his standard-issue cupboard with an inventory number on its pathetic, battered side and shows me the bag.

"Sling it over your shoulder and go off on your next mission," he succinctly summarizes his values.

A boy is sitting on the divan and looking at us sorrowfully: this is Edik.

I interrupt the major. "You were married, though, so you must have had a household of some kind."

"No, we had nothing. We didn't have time."

While Rinat was fighting in Tadjikistan, helping President Rakhmonov to take power, he slipped away and got married in Kirghizia. The newlyweds had met during Rinat's previous combat mission, in the city of Osh, where the young woman lived and where Rinat had been sent because a bloody conflict had broken out there between ethnic groups.

They got married right there, their passion and love flaring up amid the butchery and the pain. Rinat then presented his young wife to his commanding officer. The commanding officer shrugged and asked him to leave his wife in Osh, because, for a spy, a sweetheart was

an Achilles' heel. Rinat left his wife behind and went back to Tadjikistan to join an armed group on the frontier.

One day his commanding officer told him that he had a son and that
his wife had named him Edik. Later still, in June 1995, Rinat's young
wife, a student at the local conservatory, was killed by people who had
discovered who she was married to. She had just turned twenty-one
that day and had been on her way to take her second-year exams.

At first, Edik lived with his grandmother in Kirghizia. The boy was
too little to live in officers' hostels, and in any case Rinat rarely spent
the night even in the grim, unswept rooms the state provided for him.
He was still engaged in secret operations and was at large in the mountains of our country. He was severely wounded twice more and spent
periods in various hospitals.

"Even so, I did not want a different life," Rinat says, "but Edik was
growing up."

The time finally came when he decided to collect his sons, and, after that, Edik stayed with his grandmother only when Rinat was away
on six-month military missions.

We are sitting in their cold, dismal little room. Edik is a quiet boy
with bright eyes that see everything. He is very grown up. He talks
only when his father goes out and only when he is asked a question: the
son of a spy, in a word. He understands that his father is going
through a difficult period now, and that this is why, in the next school
year, he wants to send Edik to the cadet officers' college. But the boy
does not like this idea.

"I want to live at home," he says calmly and in a very manly way,
without any suggestion of whining. Nevertheless he repeats it several
times: "I want to live at home, at home."

"And is this your home? Do you feel at home here?"

Edik is an honest boy. He knows that when you cannot tell the
truth, it is better to say nothing, and that is what he does.

Indeed, who could call this pen for combat officers, with the
drunken bawling of contract soldiers on the other side of the thin

walls, with its inventory of regulation furniture, "home"? Edik knows, however, that they are trying to drive his father even from here, so let this be home.

Relations between the regiment's commanders and the major began to sour when Rinat asked to be allocated a flat in that fine new building we had been walking around while hiding from the deputy commanding officer. The major supposed he was within his rights, since for many years he had been at the top of the waiting list for accommodations.

"When I asked Petrov, he was indignant: 'You haven't done enough for the regiment,'" Rinat relates. "Can you believe it, that is exactly how he put it? I was very surprised and told him, 'I have been fighting the whole time. I rescued pilots from a mountain when nobody else could find them. The state needs me.'"

The major had, indeed, been put forward for the country's highest award, Hero of Russia, for his actions when a military aircraft crashed in the mountains of Chechnya near the village of Itum-Kale in June 2001. Several search-and-rescue teams went into the mountains to find the crew but without success. The commanders remembered Rinat with his unique experience of combat, his feel for the mountains, and his ability to find men by reading twigs, sticks, and leaves.

He found the dead airmen in just twenty-four hours. One body had been booby-trapped by the Chechen fighters, and Rinat made it safe. So the families have graves to tend.

The active-service officers have a saying that commanders who lose their heads in combat and in the mountains are best in civilian occupations. Rinat told Petrov, "I know what kind of a hero you were in Chechnya, always skulking in staff headquarters." The deputy commanding officer responded, "Now you're really in the shit, Major. For that little remark, I'll make you a down-and-out. I'll discharge you without accommodations. You'll be out on the street with that son of yours."

Petrov set about implementing his threat with a vengeance. First he humiliated the major by ordering him to decorate the parade ground and also to manage the regimental club, organizing film shows for the soldiers.

Petrov next ordered Rinat to design posters for the parade ground (he is an excellent artist), which was the job of Petrov's wife. She simply ceased to turn up for work, and all the officers knew that Rinat was making the posters while she took her ease in that fine new block of flats.

Then Edik was taken ill and had to go to the hospital. The doctors told Rinat he should stay at his son's bedside. Rinat was constantly asking for time off, and Petrov, ignoring the medical certificate provided by the doctors and backdating the record, took to recording him absent without leave. Petrov convened an officers' court, manipulated the minutes, and used them to remove the major from the waiting list for an apartment. He was agitating to have Rinat summarily dismissed from the army without any privileges. In short, Rinat is in deep trouble.

"What have I done?" Rinat bows his head, aware that he is being outmaneuvered.

The wars our country takes part in continue afterward, wherever those who were involved in them find themselves—primarily within the units to which they return after completing their missions. The staff officers there are pitted in a fight to the death against the field officers. The latter find themselves discharged for disobedience, their past records ignored, with a barrage of insults hurled at them. Rinat is not the only one. The officers in the army now divide into two unequal categories. The first are those who have actually taken part in combat operations, who have risked their lives, who have crawled their way through the mountains, burrowed into the snow and earth for days at a time. Many have been wounded on numerous occasions. You feel desperately sorry for them. It is difficult for them to find a place in the civilian life that seems so normal to us. They can't find a common language with the second group, the staff officers, who have also been in Chechnya, so they rebel and get drunk and feel miserable. The staff officers, as a rule, outmaneuver them at every opportunity: they bear false witness against them, they run to their superiors, they tell tales, they plot. Before you know it, the awkward squad is being lined up for discharge. What have they done? They have been themselves, of course. By the mere fact of their presence in the units, the field officers daily remind the staff officers who is who in this world.

And the staff officers? They rise through the ranks faster than a speeding bullet. They take care of themselves very nicely, get all the flats and dachas.

In the end, Rinat gave up. He gave up the army that he loved so much and went off to who knows where with Edik, a homeless, penniless field officer. I fear for him, because I can guess where he has gone. I fear for all of us.

HOW TO MISAPPROPRIATE PROPERTY
WITH THE CONNIVANCE
OF THE GOVERNMENT

Moscow, February 2003. A bolt from the blue: President Putin appoints a new deputy minister of internal affairs and head of GUBOP, the Central Agency for Combating Organized Crime. He is Nikolai Ovchinnikov, a modest, low-profile deputy of the state duma who never speaks at its sessions, has no known involvement in its legislative work, and appears to be politically inert. He isn't even one of Putin's former cronies from Saint Petersburg, which in terms of current appointments policy is unusual. After the announcement, Ovchinnikov gives an interview saying he will do his best to be worthy of the president's trust and that he sees his mission as being to reduce corruption "to a minimum" and to ensure that the "healthy sector of society" is no longer at the mercy of the criminal minority. These are splendid sentiments, so why does the new deputy minister's pronouncement give rise to such merriment in the Urals?

Let us look at his new job. Where does it rank in Russia's bureaucracy?

The director of GUBOP occupies no ordinary position in Russia. This is a key portfolio in the power structure. In the first place, organized crime—the Mafia—is rooted in monstrous corruption, and permeates everyday life. We say in Russia that where money talks, it can't be silenced.

In the second place, the office carries so much clout because of its history. One of our country's top bureaucrats and power brokers, a man who has stayed afloat under Yeltsin and now under Putin, is Vladimir Rushailo.[8] Formerly minister of internal affairs, recently he headed Russia's National Security Council. He began his career as director of GUBOP. When he was appointed minister of internal affairs, he maintained an interest in his old field and did his utmost to beef the agency up. He inflated its staffing levels relative to other agencies and gave its officers sweeping powers, allowing them to carry out operations involving the use of force without prior approval, unlike other sections of the police. He also actively advanced his political appointees out of the agency and into the highest offices of state, with the result that nowadays "Rushailo men" are a factor to be reckoned with in the law-enforcement ministries. Their numbers are comparable only with the Petersburgers, as those who worked with Putin in Saint Petersburg and who followed him to various bureaucracies in Moscow are known, and the "Cheka men," products of Putin's old stomping ground, the KGB.

If we look at Nikolai Ovchinnikov the man, everything about his appointment to GUBOP seems respectable. He deserved the office. According to his official record, before entering the duma, he had been a provincial police officer for thirty years. At the time of his election as a parliamentary deputy, he was chief of police in Yekaterinburg, which is no sleepy provincial center nostalgic for past glories. It is the capital of the Urals, the hub of Sverdlovsk Province, which in turn is the Urals' major industrial region. When Yeltsin invited the regions of Russia to "take as much sovereignty as you want," there were serious plans to create a republic of the Urals, with Yekaterinburg as its capital. The city's chief of police was a celebrity known to all of Russia. The Urals are a region of great mineral wealth and possess natural and industrial resources sufficient for any country to survive on. Additionally, Yekaterinburg is traditionally the turf of one of the most powerful Mafias, formerly of the Soviet Union and now of Russia. Its official designation is the Uralmash crime syndicate. Whether he likes it or not, the top police officer of Yekaterinburg finds himself combating the Uralmash Mafia.

As might be expected, a good deal of important information is not to be found in Ovchinnikov's official service record—perhaps, indeed, anything that really matters. What kind of police chief was he? What priorities did he set? Which elements of the Mafia did he prosecute? What were his achievements? And what was the result: What kind of place was Yekaterinburg under Ovchinnikov, and what kind of place is it today?

It is not my wish to show how a police officer in the Urals rose to giddy heights in Moscow. I am much more interested in that phenomenon of Russian life known as corruption. What, in fact, is corruption? What constitutes the Russian Mafia—not as it was under Yeltsin but as it is in the Putin era? And why has Putin advanced the career of Ovchinnikov? If we analyze the way in which Ovchinnikov came to be appointed as Russia's principal champion for combating the Mafia, we can identify the guiding principles behind appointments under Putin and his administration.

The story goes back a long way.

FEDULEV

On September 13, 2000, a news story rocked Russia. At the time, the second Chechen war was being waged, and Putin had been appointed prime minister because, unlike the other candidates, he was willing to start the conflict. In Yekaterinburg one of Russia's largest engineering enterprises, the Uralkhimmash Corporation, its output used throughout the Russian chemical industry, was seized by the Mafia. Citizens armed with baseball bats, supported by the Yekaterinburg OMON Special Police Unit, burst into the factory's administrative offices, caused major disorder there, and attempted to install their own director in place of the incumbent, Sergey Glotov.

Urals television duly showed the local Communists shouting, "Hurrah! The people are taking power into their own hands! Down with the capitalists!" The local trade-union leaders repeated the slogans, declaring the seizure of Uralkhimmash a "workers' revolution" and promising that similar revolutionary renationalizations would spread throughout the country in the near future.

Although nothing was heard from President Yeltsin, nobody was surprised, because he was known to be ill. As the newly appointed prime minister, Putin was also silent. In fact, Moscow was silent. Vladimir Rushailo, then minister of internal affairs, had nothing to say in public about police officers under his authority who had stormed an enterprise on behalf of one of the sides in a dispute.

Moscow's failure to comment spoke volumes. In Russia, such events don't just happen. But nobody in the capital was talking.

By the evening of September 13, the workers' revolution had quieted down somewhat; the old Uralkhimmash management, unwilling to step down, had barricaded itself in the director's office. At this point, a veritable armored column, an armada of dapper black Jeeps, swept into the factory grounds. The special police respectfully made way for them.

From one of the Jeeps stepped a nondescript, rather short citizen wearing a good suit, expensive spectacles, and several gold chains. He was an archetypal New Russian, his face ravaged by a recent drinking spree. On his progress to the director's office, he enjoyed the protection of a powerful bodyguard provided by the Yekaterinburg police. The special police forcibly cleared the way for them; the workers moved back grudgingly.

"Pashka's spoiling for a fight again. He's here for a showdown," the Uralkhimmash employees muttered.

"Pavel Fedulev, the leading industrialist of our province and deputy of the Yekaterinburg Legislative Assembly, is attempting to restore justice in accordance with court rulings," broadcast Yekaterinburg television, switching from shots of the concerned expression on the face of the leading industrialist to the bloodied faces of the enterprise's defenders. Iron bars were now to be seen among the baseball bats.

The citizen in designer glasses proceeded inside and presented the beleaguered management of Uralkhimmash with a pile of documents, court rulings showing that he, the bearer, was co-owner of the enterprise and that it was his intention to install as director a person of his choosing. Accordingly, all unauthorized persons were to vacate the premises.

The citizen sat down, uninvited, in the director's chair, his brazen demeanor reflecting his proprietorial status. After a time, during which the displaced management acquainted itself with the documents he had brought, he received a torrent of abuse (which left him unfazed) and a different collection of documents and court rulings showing that the present director was in fact the real director.

To make sense of this situation, we must embark on a further excursion into Yekaterinburg's recent history. How did a society develop in which the seizure of such a large enterprise as Uralkhimmash was possible? And who is Pavel Anatolievich Fedulev? And why, when I asked all sorts of people in Yekaterinburg what on earth was going on, did I always receive the same reply: "It's all Fedulev's doing"?

How It Started

Ten years ago, when Yeltsin was in power and democracy, as we said then, was on the rampage, Pashka Fedulev was a small-time hoodlum, extortionist, and thug. In those days Yekaterinburg was still called by its Soviet name, Sverdlovsk. Major criminal brigades were operating there, carving out their spheres of influence, but Pashka was not associated with any of them. He was a sole trader. Although he had criminal offenses trailing behind him like a bridal train, the militia did not go after him because Fedulev was small fry. In those years such individuals were jailed not because of the crimes they committed but because it was "time to put them inside," if they failed to reach agreement with other hoodlums, spoke out of turn, or, in general, tried to throw their weight around. Behavior of this sort was not in Pashka Fedulev's repertory. At that time he was amenable to reason.

In the early 1990s, Pashka became a businessman, like the majority of his comrades. Pashka, however, was poor. He had no access to the funds of the criminals' central bank, despite the fact that Yekaterinburg, famous for its underworld, had one of the largest such banks in the country. As a small-time hoodlum, Pashka did not qualify for credit and thus had to accumulate his own capital. This he duly did.

Fedulev built up his capital quickly with a fiery home-produced vodka called "palenka." The mechanism was simple. In the remoter towns and villages of Sverdlovsk Province there had existed, since the Soviet period, a number of small liquor factories. In the early Yeltsin years they, like the other state-owned factories of the era, began to fall apart; there came a time when anybody could buy, for a nominal sum placed directly in the hands of the director, as much liquor as he could drive away.

Of course, doing so was flagrant theft from state factories, but at the time it was considered a normal feature of post-Soviet life. People were starving, and, to feed themselves, half the country robbed the other half, to nobody's surprise. People were surviving as best they could; their efforts were considered to be business, which was what we had been dreaming of.

The point of buying the liquor was that the spirit, which cost virtually nothing, could be diluted with water, poured into bottles and sold instantly as cheap vodka. Excise duty had not yet been thought of, and the police, even if they had wished to do anything, were powerless in the battle against Palenka. In any case, they did not wish to interfere, since they, too, preferred survival by any means available, which meant participating in illegal business. The underground vodka purveyors paid the police to protect them from their competitors.

This was when Pashka Fedulev, crook and bootlegger, first made the acquaintance of Nikolai Ovchinnikov, police officer. Like everybody else at the time, Ovchinnikov was eager for money. Police officers' wages were wretched, and frequently not paid at all. So Pashka and Ovchinnikov apparently came to an understanding. The officer would not notice what Pashka was doing, and Pashka, more successful by the day, would not forget Ovchinnikov. The policeman began to have more than enough for his daily bread and butter.

The moment finally arrived when Pashka's accumulated capital was sufficient for him to start playing a bigger and, more important, legal game. His trajectory has been typical in Russia: just as every soldier dreams of becoming a general, so every little crook dreams of graduating into legal big business.

It was, and still is, a peculiarity of the economy that there are three conditions for success in big business. First, you have to initially get a slice of the state pie—that is, a state asset as your private property. This is why the vast majority of big businessmen in Russia are former members of the Communist Party *nomenklatura* or the Young Communist League, or were party workers.

The second condition is that, once you have been successful in appropriating state assets, you stay close to the government—that is, you bribe, or feed, officials regularly. The kickbacks should guarantee that your private enterprise will prosper.

The third condition is to make friends with (i.e., bribe) the law-enforcement agencies.

Not being in a position to meet the first condition in the early days, Fedulev nonetheless concentrated on the second and third.

The Forces of Law and Order

A certain Vasily Rudenko, deputy director of the Yekaterinburg's Criminal Investigation Unit and a friend of Ovchinnikov, lived in the city. Everybody knew Rudenko, whose position required that anyone who wanted to succeed in business needed to keep on his good side. Rudenko weeded the personal files of new businessmen (and erstwhile gangsters), in effect relieving them of their criminal pasts.

Fedulev, too, was drawn to Rudenko. This period was not the most straightforward in Pashka's life. He had already made a reputation in Yekaterinburg as a liquor baron and was being invited to sponsor local almshouses and orphanages. He was flying to Moscow for weekends to enjoy the nocturnal entertainments now provided there, taking with him (a special privilege, testifying to his intimacy with the authorities) officials of the provincial administration. As a result, it was time to set about cleaning up his image. Pashka no longer needed to have the documentary record of his criminal past preserved in the archives of the Yekaterinburg police.

No sooner decided upon than done.

Fedulev was introduced to Rudenko by a man named Yury Altshul. All who knew Altshul remember him warmly, even with admiration. Not originally from the Urals, he had been sent there by the motherland. Altshul was a soldier, a military spy; he had arrived in the Urals as captain of a special operations company of the GRU (the Central Intelligence Directorate of General Headquarters, Russia). The unit had been pulled out of Hungary after the Berlin Wall came down, when the army group in the west was disbanded.

Altshul retired from the army and stayed on in Yekaterinburg. The country was not paying its servicemen, and Altshul couldn't wait to go into business. Like many other members of special units who left the army at that time, he set up a private security service, as well as a private detective agency and a charity for veterans of special units.

In Russia there are many such organizations, built on the ruins of
the army. Any large city has its veterans, whose main occupation is to
protect its traders. Fedulev thus became one of Altshul's clients, and it
was the former GRU officer who helped Pashka, through the agency
of Rudenko, to delete his picaresque past from the computer database
of the Yekaterinburg police. Pashka's wish had come true.

Altshul was soon not only Fedulev's bodyguard but his trusted lieutenant. It was he—astute, decisive, and educated, unlike Fedulev—
who introduced the latter to the Urals stock market. Pashka soon
found his footing there and became an adept player. Because he was
short of money, he allied himself with Andrey Yakushev, famous in the
mid-1990s as director of the Golden Calf, a successful Urals company.

Together with Yakushev, Fedulev was successful in buying up the
shares of a number of enterprises, including the Yekaterinburg Meat
Processing Factory, the largest such operation in the Urals. The scale
of the meat deal brought Pashka to within an inch of the status of a
Yekaterinburg oligarch, with corresponding access to the provincial
governor, Eduard Rossel.

At this point it became evident that Fedulev did not like to share success. He was able to form alliances to overcome difficulties but was unwilling to include others in the financial and social spoils. Now, for the
first time in his career, word got out that he had hired a hit man, and the
mood in Yekaterinburg became ominous. People were afraid of Fedulev,
recognizing that he had outgrown his earlier limitations. That is how it
is in Russia now: you kill someone, you gain respect.

Around this time, Fedulev borrowed a large sum of money from
Yakushev for another deal. Although the transaction yielded a profit
many times in excess of the stake, Pashka categorically refused to re-
pay the debt. Yakushev wasn't pressing him, but in any case he had no
opportunity to do so: on May 9, 1995, in the entrance to his own
house, in front of his wife and child, Andrey Yakushev was shot dead.

A criminal case? Well, yes. A case was opened, and it even has a
number: 772801. The prime suspect was said to be Fedulev.

Then what? Then nothing. A case with this number sits in the archives to this day. It is still open, in the sense that nobody investigated it or is currently looking into it. There were to be other similar cases involving Fedulev in the years to come, and every time the same thing happened—or, rather, didn't happen. Everybody in Yekaterinburg who had any involvement with Fedulev knew that he had made his most profitable investment yet: he had bought the city police force, and it would henceforth loyally shield him from any awkwardness.

This is the period when Rudenko and Ovchinnikov became Pashka's constant partners. They helped him to grow into a new Urals industrialist and to increase his fortune. It appears they may have used the technique that had been tried out on Yakushev.

One day Fedulev offered to cooperate with another Yekaterinburg oligarch, Andrey Sosnin. Fedulev and Sosnin pooled their financial resources and pushed through a speculative campaign on the Urals stock market that to this day remains unparalleled in its size. Sosnin became the owner of a controlling share in the region's prime enterprises—in effect, of its entire industrial potential, which had been created by several generations of Soviets, beginning during the Second World War, when the largest and most important factories of the European part of the Soviet Union were evacuated to the Urals. Among the enterprises of which Sosnin and Fedulev gained a significant measure of control as a result of their speculative coup were the Nizhny Tagil Metallurgical Complex and the Kachkanar Ore Enrichment Complex (both of international renown), Uralkhimmash, Uraltelekom, the Bogoslovskoe Ore Agency, and the three hydrolytic factories in the towns of Tavda, Ivdel, and Lobva.

The takeover was a major success for the businessmen, of course, but what about the state? Neither Sosnin nor Fedulev had development in mind for these enterprises. The provincial officials carried the two speculators shoulder high, not asking what they were planning to do with the factories, just anticipating their share of the proceeds. Corruption was attaining new heights. The two companions left nobody disappointed. They shared what they had stolen, because these were people they could not afford to disappoint.

And then came the moment to divide the spoils between themselves: Which goodies should each of them receive? The earlier pattern was repeated. Shortly thereafter, Andrey Sosnin died from a gunshot wound. Another criminal case was opened on November 22, 1996—No. 474802 this time—and the main suspect was again Fedulev and . . . and nothing.

It's not much good having connections if they don't work when you need them. By the time Sosnin was murdered, Fedulev's police friends were among the more prosperous of Yekaterinburg's citizens. Everyone could see that the richer they became, the more successful their patron, Fedulev, was in business. Case No. 474802 was closed. It was not even archived; it was simply forgotten.

LIQUOR WARS

Besides the Urals factories of which, by the end of the 1990s, Fedulev had seized control, he had achieved something even more significant. Yekaterinburg is primarily Uralmash, the most important institution in the Urals. Not Uralmash the vast machine-tool factory but the Uralmash crime syndicate, the largest Mafia grouping in Russia, a detachment many thousands strong with a strict hierarchy and representatives at every level of the state. It is one thing to bribe officials and bump off your partners but quite another matter to come to terms with the crime bosses of Uralmash. In 1997, Fedulev pulled that off, too. He joined forces with Uralmash to complete the buy up of the shares of the Tavda Hydrolytic Factory. The transaction made a lot of sense for Fedulev, who was leading a life of luxury and found himself short of cash for gambling on the stock market. Uralmash had money, it had the Trough bank. The only real surprise is that the bank's managers decided to do business with Fedulev, knowing the kind of maverick he was.

The reason why Fedulev and the Uralmash bosses were so interested in hydrolytic factories is that they produce spirit, from which Palenka vodka is made. There is tremendous demand for spirit in Russia, and it costs next to nothing to produce. Owning a spirit-producing facility is the perfect way to make fantastic profits in return for a minuscule investment, and the profits are in ready cash, don't involve credit, don't go through the banks, and are invisible to the Tax Inspectorate.

Accordingly, Fedulev and the Uralmash bosses bought 97 percent of the shares of the Tavda factory. They then proceeded to asset-strip it in a fairly standard way: both partners set up firms, assets were transferred away from the factory to those firms, the shares were divided, and the firms were then either wound up or took over the manufacturing activity. It became clear that the hydrolytic plant as such no longer existed.

Soon after the deal was completed, Fedulev broke the initial agreement on the proportions due and did not even allow Uralmash representation on the new board of directors, which he packed with his appointees.

Why? He wanted to be the first among the first and needed to shake off all partners, even the highly influential Uralmash. Incredibly enough, he got away with it. The Uralmash bosses did not shoot him, as might reasonably have been expected, but simply slunk off.

The reason for their leniency was simple. When the Tavda factory was taken over, Fedulev enjoyed more than just links with the police. He was, to all intents and purposes, in charge of the provincial police force. He had excellent personal relations with Governor Rossel. It was Pashka who decided on the most senior police appointments, choosing, for example, who would head the provincial UBOP agency, the top anticrime official whose job was to combat Fedulev himself and organized crime in general. That person turned out to be Rudenko. And Pashka had Nikolai Ovchinnikov appointed chief of police for Yekaterinburg.

The Uralmash bosses were made from the same mold, however, and they had ties of their own to pit against those of Fedulev. The day eventually came for them to lock horns, when a Uralmash squad arrived at the Tavda factory and took the property back by force of arms. Fedulev responded in full measure. A special rapid-reaction police unit was deployed, and the state's police paramilitaries were ready to use force as well.

But against whom? It turned out that it was against other police paramilitaries. Those going head to head in the fight at the Tavda factory were not so much the heavies of the Fedulev and Uralmash gangs but the forces of the people behind them. On Fedulev's side were Rudenko and Ovchinnikov with one unit of armed police. On the other side were Uralmash, supported by the head of the entire provincial police force, General Kraev, and the police under his command. In other words, those on either side of an armed stand-off over the illegal division of the province's property were the police forces at the disposal of those whose task it was to maintain the rule of law.

How did the Ministry of Internal Affairs in Moscow react? The agency presented the matter as a conflict within the police force in Yekaterinburg, as a personality clash between Kraev, on the one hand, and Rudenko and Ovchinnikov, on the other. Kraev and Rudenko were removed from their posts. Kraev was publicly accused of having close links with the Uralmash crime syndicate (although his career later led to deputy director of the Russian prison system), while Rudenko was declared to have been the victim of an irreconcilable power struggle against the most serious criminal group in the Urals. As the wronged party, he was transferred to Moscow, where the minister of internal affairs, Vladimir Rushailo, had him appointed director for UBOP in Moscow Province. Since then, that agency, under Rudenko's direction, has been causing alarm bells to ring in the capital.

Back in Yekaterinburg, meanwhile, there were vacancies to be filled in the wake of Rudenko's departure. The staffing of the Urals UBOP was arranged personally by Fedulev. Rudenko's replacement as director was Yury Skvortsov, not only Rudenko's right-hand man but someone to whom all of Fedulev's affairs had been confided over many years. As Skvortsov's first deputy, Fedulev appointed a certain Andrey Taranov. In the Urals, he was believed to be the protector (or "roof") within the police force of Oleg Fleganov, the region's leading supplier of wines and spirits. Fleganov was key to the marketing of bootleg vodka, since most of it was sold through his retail network. The other deputy whom Fedulev chose for Skvortsov was Vladimir Putyaikin. His task was to purge the ranks of the police throughout the province. He began by forcing out anybody who still had anything to say against the Mafia and anybody who refused to work under the tutelage of Fedulev.

The servile Putyaikin set to work with a will. We shall give just a single example of how he went about it. On one occasion Skvortsov demanded documentary evidence from Putyaikin regarding who in the police was working against Fedulev. Putyaikin had no such documents. That night he took home a young member of the UBOP team, got him drunk, and demanded that he should immediately denounce any of his colleagues who were opposed to Fedulev and his stooges in the police. The young officer refused to be an informer, whereupon Putyaikin appears to have bullied him into shooting himself with his service revolver.

"This is unbelievable!" I hear my reader cry.

Believe me, it fits the picture. This is exactly how, during the Yeltsin years, organized-crime syndicates were born and grew to maturity in Russia. Now, under Putin, they determine what happens in the state. It is precisely to them—powerful, influential, and superrich—that the president is referring when he says that any redistribution of property is impossible and that everything should stay as it is. Putin may be God and czar in Chechnya, punishing and pardoning, but he is afraid of touching these Mafiosi. Money is in play here beyond the dreams of most of us, and the price of a life, or a man's honor, is peanuts when the profits are counted in millions.

THE UNTOUCHABLES

With the coming of the Fedulev group, the Urals stopped living by the rules, to use the criminal jargon that has found such fertile soil in Russia that even the president employs it in his speeches.

I asked people in the streets of Yekaterinburg whom they respected: Governor Rossel? Fedulev? Chernetsky, the city's mayor? Their answer: "Uralmash." Taken aback, I asked them how they could respect crooks. The answer was simple: "They live by their thieves' law, but at least they have laws. The new crooks do not even observe those."

This is what we have come to: respect for one Mafia in preference to another, because the one is much worse than the other.

Let us go back to 1997. Fedulev had the Yekaterinburg police in his pocket and had taken over the illegal vodka market. He continued to play the stock market and defrauded a certain Moscow firm—not just any old firm, but one that belonged to the consortium of a well-known metropolitan oligarch who was sponsoring Yeltsin and his family. In those days to try to defraud him was tantamount to committing suicide. Twice the firm reported fraud to the Sverdlovsk UBOP, but any information that could embarrass Fedulev was blocked there, and the CID refused to open a criminal case. Only after the intervention of the prosecutor general's office was Criminal Case No. 142114 opened: in Moscow, not in Yekaterinburg. Fedulev went on the lam. An all-Russia arrest warrant was put out for him.

Remember Yury Altshul, the former spy who became Fedulev's minder? Remember that all who knew him spoke of him as a thoroughly decent person, a man of his word and entirely fearless?

Having set up his own detective agency and security firm, Altshul continued to provide the Russian security services with intelligence. Information passed by him to the prosecutor general's office and the FSB put several big wheels of the Urals underworld behind bars. Altshul did, however, have a particular obsession: the struggle against the Uralmash crime syndicate. Although the idea may seem bizarre, this was exactly what drew Altshul to Fedulev.

Faced with an all-Russia warrant for his arrest and knowing about Altshul's idée fixe, Fedulev summoned him for a talk. Fedulev was afraid that during his enforced absence, Uralmash would take control of the two other hydrolytic factories in Sverdlovsk Province in which he maintained an interest. Fedulev asked Altshul to defend, by any means at his disposal, Fedulev's interests against Uralmash. In return, he promised Altshul 50 percent of the profit from the Lobva Hydrolytic Factory, which he was in the process of completing his takeover.

Altshul went off to Lobva, a town with nothing apart from the hydrolytic factory. There he observed the deliberate running down of the factory's production capacity. Altshul could not help asking himself why Fedulev was buying up so many shares.

Before Fedulev had become involved, the Lobva factory had been operating fairly successfully. Once he began transferring its assets to his other companies, they started selling or processing spirits illegally. The money from these sales naturally came back to the Lobva factory through his companies' accounts, but not in full. Month by month, Fedulev sucked the factory dry.

When Altshul arrived at Lobva, the workers had not been paid for seven months. The factory was one step away from bankruptcy. Because the community had developed around the factory, without it the town would die.

At this point, Altshul decided to act on his initiative rather than on Fedulev's behalf. He gave the workers his word that he would restore order and that as a first step there were two individuals the workers would not see at the factory again, because Altshul would not let them through the door. They were Sergey Chupakhin and Sergey Leshu-kov, Fedulev's hatchet men.

Chupakhin and Leshukov had formerly been officers of the Seri-ous Fraud Office of the province's Directorate of Internal Affairs. They were also personal friends of Vasily Rudenko and colleagues of Nikolai Ovchinnikov, and had left the police in order to look after their financial interests in Fedulev's businesses.

Some time passed before Fedulev was finally arrested—in Moscow, naturally. Even from his isolation cell he did everything he could to in-fluence the course of events in Yekaterinburg. Members of the police who were under his control (Rudenko was, after all, in Moscow by now) arranged for Altshul to come, on Fedulev's summons, to see him in prison. At this meeting, Fedulev insisted that Altshul should hand the management of the factory back to Chupakhin and Leshukov. Not wishing to lose his share in the business, Rudenko was demanding this of Fedulev.

But Altshul refused and flew back to Yekaterinburg, with Ru-denko following in his wake. Altshul was summoned to the UBOP for a talk, and there Rudenko insisted that he give up the Lobva factory.

Again Altshul categorically refused. A couple of days later, on March 30, 1999, the former army spy was shot in his car. A criminal case was opened, this time No. 528006. Once again the prime suspect was Fedulev. This was the third criminal case in which he was impli-cated in contract killings, but can you guess what happened? Nothing. Case No. 528006 was shelved, like the others.

Fedulev's calculation was criminally simple: with Altshul out of the way, the factory was his. Altshul, however, had left a friend and deputy in Lobva: Vasily Leon, another ex-spy and special operations veteran. Leon categorically refused all the demands from Fedulev's people that he should get out.

The Rudenko-Chupakhin-Leshukov trio presented Leon with a

compromise, or rather an offer not meant to be refused. Leon could stay on as director, but Chupakhin and Leshukov would return to handle the wholesale side of factory liquor sales, which was what really mattered. The three didn't just ask Leon to agree; they intimidated him. He was openly summoned by Skvortsov, Fedulev's head of the UBOP, who did his best to cow Leon into submission. In the meantime, Rudenko had been further promoted and transferred to the Ministry of Internal Affairs.

The third source pressuring Leon was a certain Leonid Fesko, a friend of Rudenko's and another high-ranking police official in Sverdlovsk Province. Fesko was shortly to depart for Moscow to manage the so-called Defense and Aid Fund for Members of the Sverdlovsk Province UBOP. Funds like it were a familiar institution for legally transferring illegal payments, bribes, and bonuses; they had been devised by gentlemen like Fedulev in the mid-1990s. Large numbers of them still exist.

Fesko later became Fedulev's deputy for security and discipline in the enterprises Fedulev's Mafia controlled. In emergencies, if competitors were turning up the heat, it was Fesko's job to mobilize the special operations police units to crush the resistance. It was Fesko, in fact, who masterminded the seizure of Uralkhimmash in September 2000.

In 1999, however, Vasily Leon showed his defiance. But then, in December of that year, Yevgeny Antonov, an agent from Skvortsov's entourage, claiming self-defense, shot Leon's chief assistant, the very person who supervised the wholesale marketing of liquor at the Lobva factory. According to the official written statements about the events leading up to the shooting of his colleague that Leon made to the FSB in the aftermath of the killing:

In mid-January [2000] I had a conversation with Sergey Vasiliev, departmental head of UBOP. He complained stridently that by my presence at the Lobva factory I had deprived UBOP of financing. He further said, "You have stolen the Trough of the FSB, UBOP, and other security agencies of the province." Vasiliev categorically demanded that I should work with them. I asked what that work would consist of, and Vasiliev replied, "You are to bring money here!"

Every line of Leon's statements testifies to a criminal case that should at least have been opened. Once again, however, things got bogged down. Appeals by Leon to the prosecutor general's office, the Ministry of Internal Affairs, and President Putin himself produced not the slightest reaction.

Nevertheless, great concern was shown for the fate of Fedulev. In January 2000, on the personal instructions of Vasily Kolmogorov, deputy prosecutor general of Russia, Fedulev was freed from prison. Just like that.

On his return to Yekaterinburg, the authorities welcomed him like a conqueror. Governor Rossel showered favors upon him. On Rossel's initiative, Fedulev was declared Urals Entrepreneur of the Year. Following his spell in jail, the shooting of Altshul, the intimidation of Leon, and the murder of his colleague, Fedulev had attained the exalted status of Yekaterinburg's leading industrialist. From this time on, the mass media of the Urals invariably used this formula when writing about him. A little later, Fedulev was elected a member of the Provincial Legislative Assembly, thereby receiving parliamentary immunity.

If we step back a bit and look at the bigger picture, what do we see? Fedulev is a Urals oligarch, a member of the provincial legislature, a major property owner. What really matters, though, is that he is the founder of what the Russian criminal code calls an organized crime syndicate. By the autumn of 2000, when Uralkhimmash was seized, which is where we came in, Fedulev's syndicate had all the attributes of a fully fledged Mafia entity. The only snag was that, with Russian corporate law, at best, unclear, the godfather was in prison, and while he was there, his factories and industrial complexes started slipping out of his control. The syndicate panicked: "What about our money?" At that point, Fedulev was released.

The New Deal

Fedulev's release from prison was a turning point in the modern history of the Urals. As soon as his release became public, even before he returned to Yekaterinburg and before his countless hugs from Rossel, those in the know realized that matters were not straightforward. There was going to be a redistribution of property, and Fedulev was expected to make it happen. He had been released for good reason— certainly so that he could get back what he had controlled before but also so that those working for him (and perhaps whoever he was working for) should again receive their remittances.

Fedulev did not disappoint his supporters. His first priority on being freed was to restore his control of the Lobva Hydrolytic Factory.

Here is how he did it. As Vasily Leon put it in a statement to the FSB: "Fedulev informed me that previously matters had been resolved through the law courts: privatization, acquisition of shares. Now, however, things were settled by force."

Leon's statement is dated February 2000. At that time, he presented the FSB with a written request for help to resist the Mafia. He asked to be protected from blackmail by an organized crime syndicate. First, he was being blackmailed by members of the provincial UBOP, who were pressuring him to leave the Lobva factory in favor of Fedulev. Second, he was being blackmailed by Fedulev himself, who, on his release from prison, demanded not only that Leon leave but that he should pay Fedulev $300,000 in compensation.

Leon's request went unanswered. The state renounced the rule of law and left the factory to be torn apart by the Mafia.

On February 14, 2000, Fedulev decided to set up a committee of creditors of the Lobva factory. He did so by personal invitation despite having no legal authority. His aim was to push out the factory's current management and replace it with one under his control.

Of the five principal creditors, Fedulev managed to bend only two to his wishes. A forged proxy then appeared from a third creditor, thereby providing a quorum. This committee adopted the resolution Fedulev required: that the meeting of creditors should be held not in Lobva but in Yekaterinburg, at Fedulev's office. Nobody made any bones about why it had to be held there. If some of the real creditors suddenly turned up, they would need to be stopped, and cordoning off the office would make doing so a simple matter.

As the day of the meeting approached, Rudenko flew in from Moscow. The main issue he and Fedulev needed to resolve before the meeting was what to do about Leon.

Twenty-four hours before the meeting, on February 17, Fedulev sent a couple of his employees to the UBOP. These two gentlemen were well known there, because for many years they had been coming in for questioning as suspected hit men in the sluggish investigation into the murder of one of Fedulev's partners. On this occasion these heavies wrote a denunciation to the UBOP claiming that Leon had extorted $10,000 from them. In a single hour, with a rapidity unheard of in the Russian legal system, a criminal charge was brought against Leon, naturally without any preliminary investigation, recorded interview, or checking of facts. Simultaneously, a police car was cruising the streets of Lobva giving out flyers to the effect that Leon was evading arrest and could no longer be regarded as the factory's managing director.

The day of the creditors' meeting in Fedulev's office arrived. Everything began, quite properly, with registration. The entrance, corridors, and offices were under the control of men in police uniform armed with assault rifles, the guys from the UBOP. Seemingly nothing could derail Fedulev's strategy.

But then something unforeseen did happen. Galina Ivanova, the representative of the factory's trade-union committee, who had a right to be present at the meeting on behalf of the factory's workforce, suddenly pulled a power of attorney out of her handbag. It was an immensely valuable proxy from the main creditor; Leon, while on the run, had found time to prepare it. The proxy represented 34 percent of the votes, so how Ivanova voted would determine the outcome.

Fedulev gave the order and Ivanova was removed to the UBOP offices, by plainclothes UBOP officers mingling with the crowd in the hall. She was held for precisely three hours and twenty minutes, until Fedulev called to say that the registration had been completed.

Alexander Naudzhus was Vasily Leon's deputy. Here, taken from his official statement to the FSB, is how he describes events during the night after the meeting:

> I arrived at the factory at about 22.30. At about 1.30 I went to sleep. At 4.30 I was awakened. The door to the factory management offices had been broken down, also the grilles on the windows. There were a lot of armed people around, and about 30 cars and a bus. We were allowed through to the management offices, where the factory's security officers were standing with their hands up. They were being guarded by people with assault rifles and wearing police uniforms. Oleshkevich, a UBOP lieutenant, was sitting at the table. I went into the office of the commercial director. Fedulev was sitting there. I asked, "On what grounds has this occupation taken place?" I was shown the minutes of the creditors' meeting and the contract with the new director. The contract was unauthentic.

Thus was the joint operation of Fedulev and the provincial UBOP to illegally seize the Lobva Hydrolytic Factory crowned with success. There were manifest violations of the law and *ultra vires* actions by civil servants.

As we look back from the heights of 2004, the fourth year of the dictatorship of law proclaimed by Putin, who has been called to account? Nobody. Not so far, at least. Today the Lobva factory ekes out a miserable existence. Fedulev has sucked it dry and moved on, as was to be expected. In 2000, having reconquered Lobva and acquired a pile of cash during the following months (since there was no one to stop him), Fedulev started moving in on the minerals market. The first item on his menu was Kachkanar.

KACHKANAR

The internationally known Kachkanar Ore Enrichment Complex is one of Russia's national assets. It is one of the few enterprises in the world that mine ferro-vanadium ore. Its output provides an essential component for blast-furnace smelting. In our country, at least, not a single rail for the railways network would have been produced without the factory.

In the mid-1990s, like many other important Russian enterprises, the Kachkanar OEC was subjected to a succession of privatization measures that left it financially crippled. The situation became particularly dire in 1997–98. At this point, Fedulev became chairman of the board of directors and proceeded, as he always did, to emasculate the enterprise. By the end of 1998, Fedulev had brought Kachkanar to the point of bankruptcy, and only the arrest of the Urals Entrepreneur of the Year made a revival possible as other shareholders became able to play an active part. They hired a team of knowledgeable managers under the direction of Dzhalol Khaidarov, and large-scale investors appeared on the scene.

In 1999 the enterprise was transformed. Production rose to capacity, the net asset value increased, the workers began to be paid their wages again. Kachkanar's situation was similar to that of Lobva's. The town had grown up around the plant, and ten thousand people, almost the entire working population, were employed there.

The results of the recovery were obvious: the plant's shares again became sought after on the stock market.

In his entourage almost every Russian provincial governor has the kind of individual that Yeltsin had in Putin: an astute and loyal assistant, proclaimed as his patron's heir apparent because someone is needed to cover the principal's back when he retires from the political arena, to ensure his continuing financial well-being and personal security.

For Eduard Rossel, governor of Yekaterinburg, this person was Andrey Kozitsyn, the Copper King of the Urals, who managed the smelting factories of Sverdlovsk Province. As the next election for governor approached, Yekaterinburg saw Copper Kozitsyn expand into the iron industry, under Rossel's patronage, of course. Rossel was not going to be governor forever, so with reelection time approaching, he took steps to concentrate the juiciest bits of Urals industry in Kozitsyn's hands.

As you may recall, one of Fedulev's first visits in Yekaterinburg after his release from prison was to Governor Rossel. What they talked about we do not know exactly, but immediately after the audience, Fedulev transferred, to a trust managed by Kozitsyn, his shares in two enterprises, the Kachkanar OEC and the Nizhny Tagil Metallurgical Complex. To all appearances this was a straightforward deal between Fedulev and the governor. Fedulev bought himself the right to do as he pleased in the province, and Kozitsyn moved in on Kachkanar.

It has to be said that at that moment Fedulev's ownership was down to only 19 percent of the shares of the Kachkanar complex, and even those were a bit suspect, as we shall see. Because the shares transferred to Kozitsyn did not confer control, it wouldn't be easy to parachute in a director of their choosing. In any case, the managers, headed by Khaidarov, opposed the new Fedulev-Kozitsyn invasion and had the owners of 70 percent of the shares behind them.

What was to be done? Usurpers use force to get their way. At the end of January 2000, the Kachkanar complex was seized by armed men. There was shooting, there were forged documents, and the law-enforcement agencies were actively involved in the mayhem. In fact, the melee was a repetition of the scenario used at the Lobva Hydrolytic Factory. There was also active noninvolvement on the part of Governor Rossel, just as in Lobva. At dawn on January 29, the complex was vouchsafed a new director, Andrey Kozitsyn, and Pavel

Fedulev strolled proprietorially through the empty offices of the management. *Plus ça change* . . .

It was clear, however, that the power of these cuckoo birds would last only until the first shareholders' meeting, which could simply throw them out. The insurgents concluded that they should make two moves: not allow a shareholders' meeting and bankrupt the enterprise as soon as possible, to deprive the shareholders of their powers. Under Russian legislation, shareholders of an insolvent enterprise become nonvoting owners.

Fedulev and Kozitsyn prevented the meeting by a method successfully practiced in Chechnya. They simply blocked off all entry to and exit from the town. The shareholders on their way to the complex, accompanied by the dispossessed managers, were stopped at police checkpoints. How was that possible? Easy! Sukhomlin, the mayor of Kachkanar, issued Emergency Directive No. 14, banning the entry into Kachkanar of "citizens from other cities." All the shareholders and managers of the complex came from cities other than Kachkanar.

It was ridiculous, of course, a farce, but a farce taking place in real life. The shareholders' meeting was not held, and the partners in crime set about implementing the second half of their plan: the artificial bankrupting of the Kachkanar OEC.

How was this to be done, since the complex was functioning successfully?

Kozitsyn took a credit of $15 million from the Moscow Business World Bank, secured on the assets of the complex. He had no trouble getting it, because who would not like to get their hands on the Kachkanar plant? Equipped with this credit, he issued promissory notes from the enterprise. The money was invested not in the complex but in another of his businesses, Svyatogor—also located in Sverdlovsk Province—supposedly to create a joint enterprise. The next step was for Kozitsyn to seemingly transfer the Kachkanar promissory notes to Svyatogor.

Why "supposedly" and why "seemingly"? Well, none of these transactions actually took place. All the transfers were virtual, and the promissory notes from the complex ended up in the hands of a tiny firm. This firm, a front, was registered at the address of a modest Yekaterinburg apartment apparently belonging to a woman who subsequently, despite everyone's best efforts, could not be traced; this virtual proprietor was instantly transformed into the main creditor of the most influential ferro-vanadium producer in the world. How? The ephemeral firm bought the complex's promissory notes for 40 percent of their nominal value and promptly presented them to the enterprise for payment at 100 percent. It then declared the enterprise bankrupt because it could not buy back its promissory notes at 100 percent of the nominal value. In this way, the phantom woman was found to have 90 percent of the votes at the creditors' meeting. This fraud was played out brazenly under the nose of the provincial government: the creation of a straw creditor and an artificial debt, and the theft of millions of dollars from the real owners of the enterprise, who found themselves without any rights to the assets or refund of their investments.

While this was going on, an around-the-clock guard was mounted in Kachkanar by the provincial UBOP to avoid any annoying intrusions like a new Galina Ivanova, chairwoman of the trade-union committee. The guard was the same group as in Lobva when the factory there was seized.

A thief nobody stops becomes bolder. Which brings us back to Uralkhimmash. Just as Lobva was followed by Kachkanar, so Kachkanar was followed by Uralkhimmash. In September 2000, that enterprise, too, was seized by force of arms, following the same scenario. During 2001, there was a quiet stifling of the shareholders by artificially bankrupting the enterprise, again with the indulgence and connivance of the authorities. The "managed democracy" proclaimed by Putin was on the march.

Or perhaps it was just cowboy capitalism under the management of Mafia syndicates that had the law-enforcement agencies, a corrupt bureaucracy, and a tainted judiciary in their pockets.

The Urals Judiciary:
The Most Corrupt in the World?

Let us recall that, on the night following the seizure of Uralkhimmash, Fedulev and the supporters of the deposed director were waving a collection of mutually exclusive legal rulings at each other.

The documents were not forgeries. As soon as you start looking into the documents relating to Uralkhimmash, the Kachkanar OEC, and the Lobva factory, you see that the armed invasions were sanctioned by the courts of Sverdlovsk Province. We find certain judges on the side of one party, while other judges are on the side of the other. It is as if no laws existed, as if there were no constitution. Even as the Mafia syndicates of the Urals were slugging it out to claim their territories, a civil war was going on within the judiciary. The courts were being used, and continue to be used, as rubber stamps for decisions in favor of one party or another.

Here is an excerpt from a letter to Vyacheslav Lebedev, chairman of the Supreme Court of Russia, from I. Kadnikov, Award of Merit of the Russian Federation, former chair of the October District Court of Yekaterinburg, and V. Nikitin, former chair of the Lenin District Court of Yekaterinburg:

> It is Ovcharuk [Ivan Ovcharuk, chair of the Sverdlovsk Provincial Court from Soviet times until the present] who over a period of years participates directly in the formation and training of the bench in the Urals, personally chooses and controls the selection of judges for each appointment. Without his personal approval not a single candidate can be appointed to the bench, and none of us can have his appointment extended. Any judges who fail to find favor with him personally are squeezed out and persecuted. They are compelled to leave their jobs, and individuals are often selected for membership of the bench who have neither qualifications nor experience of the work but who are in some respect vulnerable and hence manipulable. At the present time a great

number of highly qualified judges who have worked for many
years and have immense experience, who possess such important
qualities as high moral principles, independence and firmness in
arriving at verdicts, incorruptibility and courage, have been forced
out of judicial work. The sole reason is that if you are not corrupt,
it is impossible to work normally under the direction of Ovcharuk.

What, in the opinion of Ovcharuk, are the characteristics of a
good judge?

Anatoly Krizsky, until recently the chair of the Verkh-Isetsk District Court of Yekaterinburg, was not just good; he was "the best in the
profession." For many years it was Krizsky who loyally looked after
the interests of Ivan Ovcharuk. What did that entail?

The Verkh-Isetsk court is the quirkiest in Yekaterinburg. Yekaterinburg prison is located on its territory, which means that, in accordance with the law, this court examines all cases relating to the
shortening of sentences of inmates in the prison. Everybody in Yekaterinburg knows that the main factor influencing the early release of a
prisoner is not the nature of the crime, not what the inmate actually
did and hence whether or not he remains a danger to society, but—
quite simply—money. A crook from a powerful crime syndicate will
usually spend less time in prison than other criminals. His colleagues
will simply buy him out.

For certain district courts, this situation leads to prosperity. Russia's
district courts are, in general, as poor as church mice. They are chronically short of resources, even of paper; plaintiffs have to bring their
own. The judges' salaries are barely enough to make ends meet. At the
Verkh-Isetsk court, the picture is quite different, however. The building
is surrounded by Jeeps, Mercedes, and Fords costing several thousand
dollars. The owners who emerge from these vehicles in the mornings
are modest district judges whose salaries are a few thousand rubles. One
of the flashiest cars invariably belongs to Anatoly Krizsky.

Krizsky had a close relationship with Pavel Fedulev. For many
years it was Krizsky who presided over cases in which Fedulev figured

in one capacity or another. Krizsky never allowed these cases to get bogged down in red tape. For the cases in which Fedulev was involved, the judge would always apply the fast-track system, letting nothing hold him back: neither the need to call witnesses nor the question of whether his decisions were in accordance with the law. If Fedulev asked Krizsky to rule that certain shares belonged to him, for example, Krizsky would not bother with the necessary proof. He would simply state: "These shares belong to Fedulev." With such rulings under his belt, Fedulev appeared at Uralkhimmash after the armed invasion.

Another curious detail is that Krizsky's rulings-to-order were sometimes obligingly made in the comfort of the customer's place of business. Krizsky would record his decisions on Fedulev's writs not in the courtroom, as the law specifically requires, but in Fedulev's office. Sometimes it was not even the judge who made the ruling but Fedulev's lawyer, in his own handwriting, with Krizsky merely adding his signature.

When in the autumn of 1998, Fedulev began to have problems with the prosecutor general's office over his defrauding of a Moscow company, it was Krizsky who, accompanied by Fedulev's lawyer, flew to Moscow to see the then prosecutor general, Yury Skuratov, to argue that the criminal proceedings against Fedulev should be dropped. Skuratov, who had been on friendly terms with Krizsky since they were young, received him personally, and although no one knows how it happened, the case was closed. On his return to Yekaterinburg, Fedulev's wife met Krizsky. She made no secret of the fact that she thanked him for his trouble, and Krizsky, in turn, made no secret of how pleased he was: a few days later he bought himself a new Ford Explorer.

To the Western reader, Krizsky's purchase may seem like no big deal. The chairman of a North American or European court is hardly going to be a beggar, so it is not surprising if he drives an expensive car. But for the chairman of a district court in Russia to afford such a car means one of two things: either he has just come into a large (by our standards) inheritance, or he is taking bribes. There is simply no third explanation. In Russia a Ford Explorer is something only a successful businessman can afford, and under Russian law, the chairman of a court is not permitted to engage in business. A Ford Explorer costs the equivalent of a judge's salary for twenty years.

Nor was this the end of Krizsky's miraculous good fortune. Barely a month had passed after the appearance of the Ford Explorer when Fedulev was again in trouble with the prosecutor general's office. The judge again flew off to talk to Skuratov, not in Moscow this time but at the Black Sea resort of Sochi, where the prosecutor general was on holiday. The storm clouds hanging over Fedulev were again dispersed. Krizsky exchanged his Ford Explorer, which had already sent shock waves through Yekaterinburg society, for a Mercedes 600, the ultimate status symbol of a New Russian.

Krizsky's birthday parties were the talk of Yekaterinburg, festivals of conspicuous consumption to rival the name-day celebrations of overstuffed prerevolutionary merchants. On those occasions the court was suspended, and, by order of the chairman, the doors were locked. Krizsky hired a restaurant in the center of town, money flew right and left, and vodka flowed in torrents. Every bureaucrat in Yekaterinburg kicked over the traces under the astonished gaze of the mostly impoverished public. What did those drinking and dancing care that a judge had no business conducting himself in such a manner, not only according to unwritten rules of common decency but according to the writ of law? The law on "the status of judges in the Russian Federation" requires that they maintain a modest demeanor outside work (and certainly during business hours). They are to avoid any personal associations that might adversely affect their reputation, and show the greatest circumspection at all times, in order to maintain the highest level of respect for the authority of the judiciary.

So what are we to make of the fact that it was Krizsky, with his associations with Fedulev and others like him, who was the favorite of

Ivan Ovcharuk, chairman of the provincial court? What was going on? At every assembly Ovcharuk would emphasize that Krizsky was one of the best judges in the Urals.

The simple truth is that most of us living in Russia were born in the land of the Soviets and, to a greater or lesser extent, lived by the Soviet code of conduct. For Ovcharuk, the Soviet ways of thinking and behaving were second nature. In other words, he was a typical die-hard legal boss. He had been trained not, under any circumstances, to argue with his superiors; he had learned to do as he was told, carry out his superiors' orders, even try to anticipate their moods, which way their eyebrows would move. This is no journalistic exaggeration but a description of Soviet servility. Ovcharuk is what we have inherited from our past, a man whose career progressed because he never challenged the opinion of his superiors, no matter how lawless or stupid it was.

When the new times came, and democracy and capitalism with it, there was a moment, eyewitnesses tell us, when Ovcharuk panicked. Whom could he serve now?

His perplexity was soon dispelled. A special Soviet flair for sniffing out whom it was most profitable to subordinate himself to, who the new powers were, soon came to his rescue. Ovcharuk chose two new czars. The first was the nascent business world, where capital was accumulating at a vigorous pace. The second was the civil-service bureaucracy, which, however much people complained about it, remained as monolithic and as solid as a granite cliff. For Ovcharuk it was represented by Governor Rossel. Since these twin czars had united in Yekaterinburg in tender friendship and a new Mafia had emerged alongside the old Uralmash, Ovcharuk had no further qualms: he began serving Rossel and Fedulev.

Only at the end of 2001 did Yekaterinburg get rid of Krizsky as chairman of the Verkh-Isetsk District Court. It was a messy business, and the outcome was hardly satisfactory.

The provincial directorate of the FSB was well aware that Krizsky had been servicing Fedulev's criminal activities in the Urals for many years, but its agents had never caught him red-handed. In the end, covert (and illegal) around-the-clock surveillance was set up, and the chairman of the Verkh-Isetsk court was caught engaging in . . . pedophilia. The FSB presented its evidence to Krizsky himself, to his patron Ovcharuk, and to Rossel. The outcome? There was no public scandal. Krizsky was not stripped of his judicial status, but he was redeployed, to become the mayor of Yekaterinburg's legal adviser, and that was that.[9]

BUT WHAT ABOUT those judges who did not want to take part in turning an independent judiciary into one totally subservient to the criminal underworld?

In Yekaterinburg in recent years, a majority of judges have been found to be intractable. Those who chose not to serve the emergent crime syndicates have been dismissed from the bench by the dozens, and have had insult and abuse heaped on them.

Olga Vasilieva worked for eleven years as a judge, a fair stint. Outwardly she was a calm, unfussy person, the kind of judge who refused on principle to rubber-stamp the directives and rulings that Fedulev needed for the games he played. She simply refused. Vasilieva worked in the same Verkh-Isetsk District Court, with Krizsky as her immediate superior, and was subjected to immense pressure, including occasional threats to her life and her family. She remained unbowed, never once gave in, and turned down not only Fedulev but Krizsky when he demanded summary directives from her for the early release of one or another of the judge's criminal protégés.

The last straw was when Vasilieva accepted a writ against the chairman of the provincial court, Ivan Ovcharuk. Krizsky insisted she should have rejected it in order not to create a precedent. The plaintiffs were citizens of Yekaterinburg whom Ovcharuk had subjected to unreasonable judicial delay, willfully failing to examine their application to the court within a reasonable time because it was directed against the interests of high officials in Governor Rossel's administration.

For Yekaterinburg, a city under the heel of the Mafia, where everybody knew that stepping out of line in such matters usually ended not in a quarrel but in a shooting, accepting a writ of that kind was revolutionary. Other district courts, in order not to bring major trouble down upon their heads, would refuse even to register such writs, although by law they had no right not to do so.

The system took savage revenge on Olga Vasilieva for acting within the law. She was not only fired; she was endlessly vilified. Complaints were appended to her personal file when it was submitted, in order to have her expelled from the bench. They came from Krizsky's criminal protégés whom she had refused to release from jail. The complaints were written by inmates on official court forms that they could have received only by Krizsky's having brought them to the prison himself.

Vasilieva had to start a pilgrimage around official institutions to prove that the accusations against her were false. It took a year for the Supreme Court of Russia to restore her rank, but even then her difficulties were not over. The Supreme Court sat in Moscow, but she practiced in Yekaterinburg, where she was entirely on her own. As soon as she got back home, she handed the Supreme Court resolution to Krizsky, but he refused to allow her to return to work and wrote an official representation against her to the Provincial Judges' College of Qualifications, an institution of the Russian bench. He advised its members that, despite having been restored to office, Vasilieva "had failed to mend her ways," a formulation traditionally used in reference to prisoners.

Judges in Russia are required to have their status reconfirmed periodically—in effect, to be reappointed—and hence must obtain a recommendation from the College of Qualifications in their republic or province. Approval from the college leads to more or less automatic reappointment by directive of the president. Now, however, Ovcharuk added his weight to Krizsky's denunciation, and the College of Qualifications resolved "no longer to recommend" Vasilieva for appointment as a judge.

As might be expected, nobody in this Mickey Mouse College of Qualifications made any attempt to corroborate the facts. These were the very allegations, based on the statements of convicts, that the Supreme Court had just rejected as unsubstantiated.

Olga Vasilieva, a courageous, principled woman, applied once again to the Supreme Court, insisting on her right to justice. Years of her life are being wasted on this exhausting, debilitating campaign, however, and in the meantime she is being prevented from working for the good of the state.

Can we expect the majority to tread the path Olga Vasilieva has chosen? Many Yekaterinburg judges commented, begging me under no circumstances to publish their names: "It is easier for us just to rubber-stamp the rulings Ovcharuk demands than to find ourselves in Vasilieva's shoes." They had many harrowing tales about what had happened to colleagues of theirs. The story of Alexander Dovgii, another Yekaterinburg judge, is one such saga.

Dovgii's offense was the same as Vasilieva's. On one occasion he ignored Krizsky's demand to release a crony from prison. A few days later, the judge was savagely beaten with iron bars in the street. The police refused even to look for the attackers, although, as a rule, they investigate attacks on judges thoroughly. Dovgii was hospitalized for a long time, came out crippled, and, although now back at work, hears only divorce cases. He asks not to be given any other kind of case.

With things as they stand, professionalism is regarded as the ability
not to have one's own judgment. People who cannot dispense with
Bolshevik methods are appointed in the name of the State to admin-
ister justice. They wag a finger in admonition and see nothing amiss
in demanding the passing of a particular verdict. They call judges to
account before the present-day equivalent of the Communist Party
activists, the College of Qualifications. They see nothing wrong
with condemning or pardoning in our name and by our hand. . . .

These words were written by a promising young judge, who also
asked me to forget his name, after he had been pressured by
Ovcharuk and Krizsky in much the same manner as Vasilieva. He
buckled under the pressure and simply walked away. He wrote these
lines in a letter addressed to Krizsky, applying for retirement, adding,
"I request that the matter be considered in my absence," and left
Yekaterinburg for good.

This young judge had had no intention of resigning, but one day the
inevitable happened. A case involving the latest criminal machinations
of some Mafia groups came his way, and Krizsky demanded that he close
the case immediately. The young judge asked for time to reflect. He received threats from persons unknown, anonymous telephone calls to his
home, notes left where he would find them. "Coincidentally," he was
beaten up in the entry to his house, not too severely, just as a warning,
and his assailants were never tracked down.

The young judge wrote requesting permission to resign, and the
Mafia case was promptly passed to another judge. On the eve of the
hearing, the new judge received a telegram from the provincial court,
signed by Ovcharuk himself, instructing him to stop the proceedings.
The following day that case was closed.

Sergey Kazantsev, a judge of the Kirov District Court in Yekaterinburg, ruled that a certain Uporov, accused of robbery and grievous
bodily harm, should be imprisoned as a danger to society until his case
could be fully considered. Judge Kazantsev then moved to consider
another case. He was in a conference room and writing up the

verdict—a time when, under Russian law, nobody is allowed to disturb a judge. To do so virtually guarantees that the verdict will be set aside by a higher court. Nevertheless, Ovcharuk called Kazantsev to demand that he alter the restraining order and let Uporov out of prison. Kazantsev refused and was told by Ovcharuk that he would be sacked. He was sacked.

There are any number of such episodes in Yekaterinburg. As a result, the judges who are still working there are highly manipulable, willing to rubber-stamp any judgment, just as long as they can avoid unpleasantness from their superiors. Resistance has been crushed. It is the rule of duplicity under the guise of "the dictatorship of law."

The situation explains why, when Uralkhimmash was seized, the two sides had, in their hands, contradictory rulings on the matter. For years any sign of judicial independence was brutally suppressed, and judges were conditioned to servility. Senior judges have long experience working in the shackled Soviet courts. Where, under these circumstances, are courageous and fair judgments to come from? Anybody prepared to stand up and refuse has long since been dismissed. Those capable of saluting promptly when required to serve the cause of lawlessness are hard at work and progressing up the career ladder.

BEHIND EACH OF Fedulev's coups stood his special intimacy with the bench of the Urals. He was friends with judges, and they were friends with him. The most frequently heard names in this connection are those of Judges Ryazantsev and Balashov. Ryazantsev is a humble judge of the Kachkanar Municipal Court, which is subordinate to Ovcharuk. Ryazantsev it was who rubber-stamped the rulings Fedulev needed in the Kachkanar OEC case, validating the deals of the rogue firm that purchased promissory notes on the cheap and cashed them at face value, thereby sealing the fate of an enterprise of international importance. The second judge, Balashov, also very humble, works in the Kirov District Court of the City of Yekaterinburg. He ruled in favor of Fedulev in respect of Uralkhimmash and at several other significant moments in Fedulev's business career. Here is how he did it.

It was Judge Balashov who effectively fired the first shot in the Uralkhimmash affair. On Friday evening he accepted a writ in support of Fedulev's interests at the factory, and on Monday morning, with a rapidity unheard of in the history of Russian jurisprudence, he issued the ruling Fedulev needed. Balashov managed to do this without calling any witnesses, gathering supplementary information, or making inquiries of third parties.

In fairness, it has to be said that Balashov operates within the framework of the law. He is just very good at exploiting loopholes. The fast-track procedure he resorted to is entirely legitimate. The injunction he issued "in satisfaction of the plaintiff's demands" is appropriate in cases where the defendants have taken executive decisions and measures leading to the embezzlement of property. The primary task of such an injunction is to freeze the situation. The court is within its rights in intervening to forbid any managerial actions until the substance of the dispute is resolved.

Accordingly, Balashov's lightning resolution on Uralkhimmash had nothing to do with resolving the ownership dispute. He was merely preventing anyone from managing the plant or making use of its assets. On the surface, all was innocence, sweetness and light. The result, however, was asphyxia.

Under Russian law, if a verdict has already been given in a dispute, it is impermissible for another court to hear the dispute again. In granting the injunction required, however, Balashov purported not to know the crucial detail that an arbitration court had already pronounced on the dispute over Uralkhimmash. He had an entirely plausible explanation for his lack of information: there was no unified communication system in the province (which was true), and people in the district courts were the last to hear about cases elsewhere.

A few hours after his injunction was issued, the ink barely dry on his signature, Fedulev descended upon Uralkhimmash with his armed brigades, waving it before him.

An Important Detail of
Russian Court Procedure

If a court shows clear bias, openly favoring one side in a dispute, it can do so precisely because the courts in Russia are supposed to be independent. All that matters is whether a judge has the support of his superiors. If the top judges who oversee the procedural actions see eye to eye with those below them, the lower court can please itself. After the ructions at Uralkhimmash, Valerii Baidukov, chairman of the Kirov District Court and Balashov's immediate superior, called him in for an explanation. Balashov informed him that his judgment was what the provincial court had wanted; the ruling had been arranged with Ovcharuk. There were no further questions.

What about the perplexed public, however? The brazen seizure of Uralkhimmash did cause the Yekaterinburg public to ask plenty of questions.

Baidukov explained the circumstances straightforwardly. He assured the people that the courts understood that every minute counted when assets could be siphoned off to who knows where. That was why, in the interests of citizens and owners alike, a ruling had been given with such rapidity.

Incidentally, the Baidukov who was doing all this explaining is the chairman of the provincial council of the bench, the corporate conscience of the judiciary. The case of Olga Vasilieva had passed through his office several times, and each time he had endorsed it, as required by Ovcharuk. The council of the bench is another institution of the community of judges, like the College of Qualifications. Only people agreeable to Ovcharuk belong to either group, and whatever representations he makes to the members produce the desired conclusions.

Although Valerii Baidukov is chairman of the Kirov District Court, one has no sense that he is capable of standing up to, or for, anyone. If he ever does have an opinion of his own, it remains hypothetical. He can pontificate about the district court as "the basic link of the Russian judicial system" but falls silent when asked to discuss facts.

Ninety-five percent of all criminal and civil cases in Russia are heard in the district courts, and to that extent they are indeed the basic link in the country's judicial system. In reality, however, this is a fiction. The district court is highly dependent and manipulable, because the senior judges of the provincial and republican courts have no wish to implement reform and lose the control they enjoy over their inferiors in the district courts. The latter enjoy independence only according to the constitution, and the fact that this document has legal preeminence makes no difference. The district courts have simply not been given procedural independence.

The law gives provincial courts procedural control of district and municipal courts—that is, the responsibility for monitoring their judicial practice. The verdicts of district and municipal courts are reviewed and evaluated by the provincial courts, which decide whether they are correct or flawed. Procedural dependence develops into organizational and career dependence. A lower judge who does not play by the rules of the game is as vulnerable as a baby. A superior judge has the right to criticize and annul his verdicts as he sees fit, without any accountability. The provincial court can overturn the verdict of a district court without explaining what is wrong with it or how it should be improved.

The provincial court does not take responsibility for the final verdict, but it does keep statistics to show how many cases, and from which district judges, have been found to be "erroneous." Such data are the basis for calculating bonuses for judges, awarding or depriving them of various privileges, such as holidays in the summer or winter months, advancement in the waiting list for an apartment (which is in the hands of the provincial court and matters because judges' salaries are insufficient for them to buy flats), confirmation of their tenure of office, and so on.

This is the mechanism through which the district court judges—who, according to the constitution, are "fundamental" to the system—have found themselves more dependent on their superiors than under the Soviet regime. The constitution seems to preclude such hierarchical relations, since it declares that all judges are equal and independent, individually appointed by directive of the president. The reality is rather different. They may be equal when they are appointed, but they are not equal when they get the sack. The chair of a provincial court who wishes to get even with a district judge holds all the aces; but if the chair of a provincial court is objectionable to district judges, that is just their hard luck. They cannot facilitate his removal.

Thus the laws and rules regulating the bench, as they have developed since the end of the Soviet era, have allowed Ivan Ovcharuk to become what he is: the official who protects the Urals from judges who might deliver an unpredictable verdict. The legal system has no safeguards to curtail the activities of those at the top of the hierarchy who might go off the rails. The constraints are purely moral. The only way the system could function satisfactorily would be if the person occupying Ovcharuk's office had different moral and ethical attributes. What sort of a system would that be?

TO COME BACK to District Judge Balashov. Could he have acted differently in the Fedulev case, and, if so, what should he have done? He had only to postpone consideration of the injunction, which he had every right to do.

In the course of preparing their seizure of Uralkhimmash, Fedulev and his accomplices checked out many district courts in Yekaterinburg to see whether they would play ball.

They all agreed to act like Balashov with the exception of one, the

Chkalov court. Ivan Ovcharuk invited the chairman of that court, Sergey Kiyaikin, to work in Magadan, in the extreme northeast of the country. Traditionally, "to be sent to Magadan" has meant to be exiled there, but Kiyaikin, an obstinate judge who had grown up in Yekaterinburg, a man with roots and pride in the city and the Urals region who had graduated in chemical engineering from the prestigious Uralkhimmash, was only too glad to get as far away as possible from his native region. He did not want to be killed or to have his family attacked.

Balashov is a loyal guardian of Fedulev's interests. He has gotten the production of verdicts to safeguard his friend down to a fine art. Here, for example, is one of Balashov's rulings, delivered on February 28, 2000.

Fedulev had decided to sell Uralelektromash, not a factory but a company that handled transactions in shares he owned. They happened to include his shares in the Kachkanar OEC and in Uralkhimmash.

Fedulev decided to sell in exchange for a certain sum of money, as he had every right to do. Sometime later, the new owners of Uralelektromash discovered that, although they had paid the money, they had not received the corporation's documents. Fedulev had *sort of* sold Uralelektromash, but he had kept all the shares. The purchasers realized they had been swindled and naturally demanded an explanation. Fedulev told them he had changed his mind. They countered, "Give us our money back. Then you can keep everything yourself." Fedulev replied, "I'm not going to give you any money back. You haven't got any documents. You are nobody. Go away." His Uralkhimmash shareholding was in the same situation. Emerging from prison in Moscow and eager to hold on to what he had already sold for several million dollars, Fedulev said, "I know nothing about it. It wasn't registered in the prescribed manner. The deal is invalid." He went to Judge Balashov, who found in Fedulev's favor.

To understand what Fedulev did, you need to appreciate that Russian legislation still has many loopholes. In this instance the flaw was that any company, when it issues shares, is required to register the fact.

In the early days, nobody in Russia knew how to go about this. There had been no stock market in the Soviet Union and hence no shares. After the collapse of the Soviets, the relevant governmental institutions took a long time to find their bearings. They could neither explain nor decide how shares should be registered. As a result, shares in many companies were unregistered. They were, and still are, traded in. The stock market continued on its way.

What should be done? Naturally, it was assumed that you just needed to be honest with your partners. That is not the basis on which Fedulev operates, however. Having spotted an opportunity, he first contracted to sell the shares of Uralelektromash and only then applied to have them registered with the appropriate state agency, the Federal Commission for Securities. When the shares were eventually registered, after a long delay because the transactions were bogged down in a morass of discoordination, Fedulev informed his purchasers that the contract to sell Uralelektromash had been concluded before the shares had been registered. He looked them straight in the eye and said, "The money is mine, too. It was your mistake, and you have to pay for it." The court once again rubber-stamped in Fedulev's favor.

Is Fedulev so clever that, unlike most other people, he knows all the details and can exploit the system? Of course not. He is rich enough to hire the savviest lawyers who spot the loopholes. He has managed to create an oligarchic pyramid to ensure that, whatever he undertakes, all those involved are links in the chain. None can do without the others.

So Judge Balashov ruled in Fedulev's favor in the Uralelektromash case. The judicial process followed the pattern we observed with Uralkhimmash: a highly complex case—running to many volumes of evidence that could be made sense of only by calling in experts in the subtleties of the Russian stock market—was examined by Balashov in next to no time.

After that, things took off. The exiling of a judge to Magadan was the least of it. The writ regarding the disputed Uralelektromash shares was the prologue to the bloody events at Uralkhimmash.

Another budding Balashov, the obliging Judge Ryazantsev, works in the Kachkanar Municipal Court. In late January 2000, as we have seen, the Kachkanar complex was brazenly seized by Fedulev's armed heavies. How did the courts react? On February 1, Judge Ryazantsev found no infringement of the law in the conducting of a meeting of the board of directors under the muzzles of assault rifles. The hearing was conducted à la Balashov, at high speed, without any prehearing submission or involvement of those whose rights had been trampled. And, of course, the writ was presented the following day.

On February 15, just a fortnight later, the Judicial College for Civil Cases of the Sverdlovsk Provincial Court (i.e., Ovcharuk's diocese) confirmed Ryazantsev's ruling, again without a hearing. The process represented incredible speed for the Russian appeals machinery, which normally takes six months.

The mocking of Themis, goddess of justice, did not end there. On the same day, when it was clear that the provincial court was not going to overturn his earlier verdict, Judge Ryazantsev, to avoid the possibility of any further mishaps, prohibited the holding of any more meetings of shareholders of the Kachkanar OEC.

A municipal court has not the slightest right to do anything of the sort. More than that, nowhere in the Code of Civil Procedure is there provision for prohibiting acts of persons not party to a dispute.

But who among the guardians of the law in Sverdlovsk Province cares about that? Was Ryazantsev removed for acting illegally? No way. The courts rolled out their verdicts without even bothering to check whether Fedulev was the legal owner of the complex. In fact, the 19 percent of Kachkanar shares that Fedulev flourished so effectively did not actually exist. They had long ago been impounded in the course of an examination of Fedulev's affairs in Moscow by the investigative committee of the Ministry of Internal Affairs. In fact, the reason he had been imprisoned on fraud charges was that he had twice sold the same 19 percent to different companies.

After February 2000, people began to take notice of what was going on. The Supreme Court in Moscow tried to challenge the rampaging of the Sverdlovsk Provincial Court on more than one occasion, but nothing changed. Fedulev retained control of the Kachkanar OEC, those he had duped hid abroad, and the Kachkanar Municipal and Sverdlovsk Provincial courts enjoyed the benefit of a mass of cases ancillary to the effective recognition of the Kachkanar complex as bankrupt.

The judiciary of Sverdlovsk Province thus facilitated a succession of deals that, together, and as intended, brought about the complex's insolvency. Such connivance, incidentally, is a criminal act, but who is going to bother looking into it? As we have seen, when Putin came to power, he made it clear that his loyalty lay with the likes of Fedulev and Rossel. On July 14, 2000, shortly after his first election, Putin flew to Yekaterinburg. He participated in the solemn laying of the foundation stone of Mill 5000 at the Nizhny Tagil Metallurgical Complex, the largest enterprise of its kind in the world. The players at that complex are the same people as in Kachkanar. Fedulev has pride of place, and Mill 5000 is a major investment project of Eduard Rossel's. The image of the president laying its foundation stone was excellent PR for Fedulev's continuing expansion of his criminal empire. Indeed, new money followed Putin. In response to this beneficence, Fedulev and Rossel are active supporters of Putin and underwrite the functioning of the Urals section of his United Russia Party. They supported Putin in his reelection campaign in 2004.

On the surface, everything in Russia is going swimmingly and the nation is democratic. The principle of an independent judiciary has been proclaimed, and any obstruction of justice is a criminal offense. The federal law on the status of judges is progressive and supposedly safeguards their independence. The reality, however, is that these constitutional and democratic principles are violated with the utmost cynicism. Lawlessness is demonstrably more powerful than the law. The kind of justice you get depends on what class you belong to, and the upper echelons of society, the VIP level, are reserved for the Mafia and the oligarchs.

What about those who are not at the VIP level? Well, you don't miss what you never had.

Since we are now building capitalism, there is private property. As long as there is property, there will be someone who wants to get a hold of it and someone else who does not want to part with it. What matters is the methods used in resolving the issue, the rules by which people behave. In our corrupt nation, for the time being, we live by the rules of Pashka Fedulev.

One final scene before we bring down the curtain. It is March 2003 in Yekaterinburg. Life in the province is sluggish, but for several days in a row, from March 25 to 28, a protest demonstration has been taking place. The protesters are the civil-rights activists of Sverdlovsk Province: the International Center for Human Rights, the Social Committee for the Defense of Prisoners' Rights, and an umbrella organization called Our Union Is the Land of People's Power. They are collecting signatures demanding the immediate retirement of Ivan Ovcharuk. They chant that Ovcharuk, with his long-standing collaboration with the crime bosses of the Urals, is the mainstay of judicial arbitrariness in the Urals and of opposition to judicial reform. They tell anyone who will listen that Ovcharuk is continuing to choke off any signs of democracy and will fight to the death against the introduction of trial by jury: he declares that it "is contrary to the interests of the inhabitants of Sverdlovsk Province." As the protestors see it, his only real concern is to prevent any changes that might cramp the corrupt legal system he has created for the benefit of the criminal underworld of the Urals.

March 2003 again, but Moscow this time. The president has reappointed Ivan Ovcharuk as chairman of the Sverdlovsk Provincial Court.

MORE STORIES
FROM THE PROVINCES

THE OLD MAN FROM IRKUTSK

The winter of Putin's third year in office, 2002–03, was very cold. We are a northern country, of course: Siberia, bears, furs, that sort of thing. So you might expect that we would be ready for the cold weather.

Unfortunately, everything takes us by surprise, like snow falling from a roof onto your head. Because we are no more prepared for frost than for anything else, the following events came to pass.

In Irkutsk, in the depths of Siberia, an old man was found frozen to the floor of his apartment. He was past eighty, an ordinary retiree, one of the people the emergency services refuse to help because they are just too old. Their response to a telephone call is straightforward and unreflecting: "Well, what do you expect? Of course he's feeling ill. It's his age." This elderly citizen lived alone, a veteran of the Second World War, who freed the world from Nazism, with medals and a state pension. He was one of those to whom President Putin sends greetings on May 9, Victory Day, wishing him happiness and good health. Our old men, our veterans unspoiled by too much attention from the state, weep over these form letters with their facsimile signature. Anyway, in January 2003, he died of hypothermia. He stuck to the floor where he fell. His name was Ivanov, the most common Russian surname. There are hundreds of thousands of Ivanovs in Russia.

Ivanov froze to the floor because his flat was unheated. It should have been heated, of course, like all the apartments in the block where he lived; like all the blocks of flats in Irkutsk, in the third year of Putin's stewardship.

Why did this happen? The explanation is simple. Throughout Russia, the heating pipes wore out because they had been in service since Soviet times, and those times have been gone for more than a decade, and thank God for that. For a long time the pipes leaked and leaked, and Communal Services, whose responsibility they are, did nothing about the situation. Communal Services is a centralized, state-run monopoly. Every month we pay a substantial sum for the agency's nonexistent technical support, but it virtually ignore us, goes on not doing its job, and periodically demands a rate increase. The government gives way, but those employed by Communal Services are so used to doing nothing that nothing is what they continue to do.

The day finally came when the monopolized pipes, which had been leaking for so long and had not been repaired for just as long, burst. In the middle of winter, in severe frosts, it was discovered that there was no way to replace them. Communal Services had no money to pay for substitute pipes. Nobody knew what the money we had been paying the agency had been spent on. The communal facilities that had been in service since the Soviet period had finally deteriorated. The fact that there was nothing to replace them with was not to be expected, because we produce thousands of kilometers of all sorts of pipes every year. "The country has no funds available for this purpose," the agents of Putin's government announced with a shrug, as if the subject had nothing to do with them. "What do you mean, there is no money?" the opposition politicians parried feebly, making their customary show of standing up for the rights of the people. The president publicly ticked off the prime minister. And that was the end of the tale of the leaking pipes. The politicians agreed to differ. There was no scandal. The government did not resign. Even the appropriate minister did not step down. So what if people had to pace around their flats to keep warm, sleeping and eating in their winter coats and felt boots? The pipes would be repaired come summer.

The old man who died was hacked off the icy floor with crowbars by the other people living in his communal apartment and quietly buried in the frozen Siberian earth. No period of mourning was declared.

The president pretended that the tragedy had not happened in his country or to a member of his electorate. He remained aloof during the funeral, and the country swallowed his silence. To consolidate his position, Putin changed the subject. He gave a grim speech to the effect that terrorists were responsible for all of Russia's woes and that the state's priority was the destruction of international terrorism in Chechnya. Apart from that, national life would stumble on in its usual way. The people could not be allowed to reflect on the imperfection of the world as it developed before their eyes.

Soon it was spring. Putin began preparing for his reelection in 2004. There could be no regret at defeats suffered, only joy at victories. Accordingly, several new holidays were announced—in fact, an unheard-of quantity of them, including the observance of Lent.

The nearer summer came, the less people talked about the collapse of Russia's heating infrastructure the previous winter. Citizens were called upon to rejoice at the preparations for celebrating the tercentenary of Saint Petersburg, and to take pride in the sumptuousness of refurbished czarist palaces, fit to dazzle the world's elite with their splendor. And that is exactly what happened.

Putin invited the world's leaders to Saint Petersburg, and the city was subjected to an intensive repainting of facades. The old man in

Irkutsk, and even the old men in Saint Petersburg, were forgotten by everyone, including Putin.

"Mind you, if he had died in Moscow . . . ," the metropolitan pundits would say, suggesting that there would have been a scandal and a half, and that the authorities would have replaced the pipes before next winter.

Gerhard Schröder, George W. Bush, Jacques Chirac, Tony Blair, and many other VIPs proceeded to our northern capital and effectively crowned Putin as their equal. They were received with pomp and ceremony. They pretended to regard Putin with respect, and old Mr. Ivanov and the millions of Russian pensioners who can barely make ends meet weren't given a thought. Putin's reign reached its high point, and almost nobody noticed. He decided to base his power solely on the oligarchs, the billionaires who own Russia's oil and gas reserves. Putin is friends with some oligarchs and at war with others, and the process is called statecraft. There is no place for the people in this scheme of things. Moscow represents life-giving warmth and light, while the provinces are its pale reflections and those who inhabit them might as well be living on the moon.

KAMCHATKA: THE STRUGGLE TO SURVIVE

Kamchatka is at the farthest reach of Russia. The flight from Moscow takes more than ten hours. The planes on the Petropavlovsk-Kamchatsky route are basic and predispose you to muse on the immensity of our complicated motherland and on the fact that only a tiny proportion of our people live in Moscow, playing their political games, setting up their idols and knocking them down, and believing that they control this enormous country.

Kamchatka is a good place to recognize how remote the Russian provinces are from the capital. In fact, distance has nothing to do with it. The provinces live differently, they breathe a different air, and they are where the real Russia is to be found.

There are as many sailors living in Kamchatka as there are fishermen, indeed even more. Despite the massive cutbacks in the armed forces, the power base here remains the same: whoever the Kamchatka Flotilla of the Pacific Fleet votes for wins the elections.

As you might expect in a coastal town, there is a predominance of black and navy blue everywhere: reefer jackets, sailors' vests, peakless caps. The only thing missing is the fleet's legendary chic. The jackets you see are worn, the vests much laundered, the caps faded.

Alexey Dikiy is the commander of a nuclear ballistic missile submarine, the *Vilioutchinsk*. He is the elite of our fleet, and so is his vessel, part of the armament of the Kamchatka Flotilla.

Dikiy received an outstanding education in Leningrad—today's Saint Petersburg—and then made brilliant progress up the career ladder as a highly talented officer. By the time he was thirty-four, he was a uniquely qualified submariner. In terms of the international military labor market, every month of service raised his value by thousands of dollars. Today, however, Alexey Dikiy, captain first class, is eking out a wretched existence; there is no other way of putting it. His home is a dreadful officers' hostel with peeling stairwells, derelict and eerie. Everybody who could has left this place for the mainland, throwing military careers to the winds. The windows of many now-uninhabited flats are dark. This is cold, hungry, inhospitable terrain. People have fled mainly from the poverty. Captain Dikiy tells me that in good weather he and other senior naval officers go fishing in order to put a decent meal on the table.

On the table in his kitchen he has placed what our motherland pays in return for irreproachably loyal service. Dikiy has just brought a captain's monthly rations home from his submarine in one of the fleet's bedsheets. The rations consist of two packets of shelled peas, two kilograms of buckwheat and rice in paper bags, two cans of the cheapest peas, two cans of Pacific herring, and a bottle of vegetable oil.

"Is that all?"

"Yes. That's it." Dikiy is not complaining, just confirming a fact.

He is a strong, genuine man. More precisely, he is very Russian. He is used to privation. His loyalty is to the motherland rather than to whoever happens to be her leader at a given time. If he allowed himself to think any other way, he would have been out of here long ago. The captain acknowledges that anything can happen, including famine, which is precisely what his rations evoke.

These cans and paper bags contain the month's supplies for the three members of Captain Dikiy's family. He has a wife, Larisa, who qualified as a radiochemist. She has a degree from the prestigious Moscow Institute of Engineering and Physics, whose graduates are headhunted straight from their benches in the lecture room by the computer firms of Silicon Valley in California.

Larisa, living with her husband in a closed military township of the Pacific Fleet, is unemployed, however. This is a detail of no interest to naval headquarters or to the faraway Ministry of Defense. The recruitment policies of staff headquarters mean they stubbornly refuse to see the gold lying at their feet. Larisa cannot even get a teaching job in the school for submariners' children. All the posts are filled, and there is a waiting list. Unemployment among the nonmilitary personnel here runs to 90 percent.

The third member of Captain Dikiy's family is his daughter, Alisa, in second grade. Her situation is also unenviable. There is nothing in this military township to bring out the abilities of Alisa or the other children. No sports center, no dance floors, no computers. All the garrison's children can lay claim to is a dismal, dirty courtyard and a building with a video recorder and a selection of cartoons.

Truly, Kamchatka is at the outer reach of our land and at the extremity of state heartlessness. On the one hand, we find here cutting-edge technology for the taking of human life, and on the other, a troglodytic existence for those who supervise the fancy equipment. Everything relies entirely on personal enthusiasm and patriotism. There is no money, no glory, and no future.

The place where Dikiy lives is called Rybachie. It is an hour's drive

from Petropavlovsk-Kamchatsky, the capital of the Kamchatka Peninsula. Rybachie is perhaps the world's most famous closed military
township, with a population of twenty thousand. It is the symbol and
the vanguard of the Russian nuclear fleet. The township, packed with
the most modern weaponry, is where Russia's east-facing nuclear
shield is situated, and where those who keep it in working order live.

Because Captain Dikiy's submarine is one of the most important
constituents of this nuclear shield, it follows that Dikiy himself is a vi-
tal component. His submarine is a technologically perfect piece of
weaponry whose equal is to be found nowhere else on the planet. It can
destroy entire surface flotillas and the best submarines of the world's
military powers, including the United States. Under Dikiy's command
is a unique weapon armed with nuclear missiles and an impressive array
of torpedoes. While we have such a defense capability, Russia is not seriously vulnerable, at least not from the direction of the Pacific Ocean.

Captain Dikiy himself, however, is highly vulnerable, and primarily from the direction of the state he serves. But he rarely thinks along
those lines. Like many other officers, he is skilled at surviving without
money. His salary is low and paid irregularly; it is often as much as six
months late.

When there is no money, Dikiy declines to eat on board his submarine (though officers are entitled to meals there). He takes home his
entitlement in the form of a packed meal and shares it with his family.
He has no other way of feeding them. As a result, Dikiy is a pale
shadow of a man. He is unconscionably thin. His face has an un-
healthy pallor, and it is clear why: the captain of the main constituent
of Russia's nuclear shield is undernourished.

Of course, constantly being in a radiation zone also takes its toll. In
the past, the job had its compensations, because submariners were
highly eligible as bachelors, but circumstances have changed. Nowadays, young women look away when naval officers walk by.

"Actually, the poverty is not the real problem," Dikiy says. He is an
ascetic, a penniless romantic, an officer to the marrow of his bones,

almost a saint of our times, when values are assessed in the cynical language of the dollar. "You can live with poverty as long as you have a clear goal and understandable operational tasks. Our real misfortune is the perilous state of the country's nuclear fleet, the sense of hopelessness. They don't seem to understand in Moscow that these armaments have to be taken seriously. In ten years' time, if the present level of financing is maintained, there will either be nothing here in Rybachie, or NATO will be refueling at our piers."

To escape from the hopelessness of what is occurring in front of his eyes, Dikiy has decided to continue his studies at the General Headquarters Academy. He wants to write a dissertation about the state of Russia's national security at the end of the twentieth and beginning of the twenty-first centuries. He hopes, when he has concluded his research, to give an academically grounded answer to the question that troubles him: In whose interests was it to undermine Russia's national security?

Although his interim conclusions are not favorable to Moscow, the captain is not antagonistic or offended at what has been going on. He thinks it is appalling that Moscow behaves as it does, but there is nothing to be done about it. Except to tough it out, because we are stronger and more intelligent than our superiors.

In Dikiy's job, his life is not his own. He cannot live the way most people do. To be on five-minute standby for his submarine, he must always be on call. He can't just go into the countryside berrying, picking mushrooms, or walking with friends. He has to live at the post he has accepted and cannot pass his duties over to anyone else. He has to be with his officers to make sure they do not become demoralized. He must find time to look in at the barracks to keep a fatherly eye on what the naval enlistees are getting up to. He is a busy man.

Many military officers, although living like a beggar much as Captain Dikiy does, can at least earn a bit on the side after a day's work, to feed their families and to buy clothes and even their uniforms (a majority of officers have to do this). Captain Dikiy has neither the time nor the opportunity to take a second job. In the few hours that remain after work, he is *required* to relax, to catch up on sleep, to restore his equanimity. When he boards his submarine, he must be at ease. It is a requirement of the job. The consequences of nervous debility could be catastrophic.

"I have to be as calm and balanced at work," Dikiy explains, "as if I had just come back from vacation, as if everything was sorted and I didn't have to worry about how I am going to feed my wife and daughter tomorrow."

"You say you have to. It seems to me that this is viewing the situation the wrong way around. You are serving the state, and so surely it is up to the state to create the right conditions for you to come to work in a calm frame of mind."

Dikiy smiles a rather patronizing smile, and I am not sure who this strange, tough, special man is feeling more condescension toward: me for asking such questions, or the state for spurning those who serve it best. It turns out that it is toward me.

"The state is not able to do that at present," the captain says finally. "It isn't, and there's an end to the matter. What point is there in demanding something that isn't there? I am a realist and not quick to anger. All the sentimentalists and the bad-tempered people left here long ago. They resigned from the navy."

"I still do not understand, though, why you have not resigned. You are a nuclear specialist with an engineering qualification. I am sure you could find a decent job."

"I can't resign because I cannot abandon my ship. I am a commander, not one of the enlistees. There is no one to replace me. If I left, I would feel a traitor."

"A traitor to whom? The state, surely, has betrayed you?"

"In time, the state will come to its senses. For now, we just have to be patient and preserve our nuclear fleet. That is what I am doing. Even if the Ministry of Defense pursues a policy of betrayal, my duty is to Russia. I am defending the people of Russia, not the state bureaucracy."

There you have the portrait of a Russian submarine officer in our times. He is stuck out there at the farthest reaches of our land and, true to his military oath, he daily covers the embrasure with his own body because there is nothing else to cover it with.

To fulfill his obligations in the midst of the profound financial malaise that has befallen the armed forces, the commander must have complete dedication. He leaves home at precisely 7:20 in the morning and returns at 10:40 at night every day. He is on board his submarine for ten hours or more. The navy is collapsing before our eyes, and with technology that is not being properly maintained, incidents, including a major disaster, are possible at any moment. The only thing that hasn't changed at all is the raising of the flag. This ritual is observed every day at 8 A.M., come hurricane, blizzard, accident, or change of government.

Incidentally, Dikiy walks from his home to where the *Vilioutchinsk* is moored. It takes him precisely forty minutes. He walks not because the exercise is good for him but because, of course, he doesn't have the money for a car and because no other transportation is provided by the navy. The Second Flotilla, to which the *Vilioutchinsk* belongs, is in the throes of a fuel crisis, as indeed is the rest of Kamchatka. No cars or buses run to the jetties. The navy does not have enough gasoline in a country selling oil to all and sundry! But that is the least of it. What if the fleet runs out of bread? The garrison is constantly in debt to the local bread factory, which goes on supplying the ships on credit.

Can you believe it? The service personnel who maintain the nuclear shield of an international power are being fed on charity. I wonder how the president feels when he attends the G8 summit meetings.

Well, okay. All the officers in Rybachie walk to work in the mornings. On the road the officers' corps is usually buzzing like an angry beehive. Its members are discussing the questions on all their minds: How long can they put up with this situation? What kind of an abyss are we rushing toward?

Their heated political debates are fueled by the view in front of the officers. As you walk toward Pier No. 5, for example, where the *Vilioutchinsk* is moored, you can contemplate Khlebalkin Island, where there is a derelict ship-repair yard. Two or three years ago, fifteen or so submarines would be in the Khlebalkin yard for servicing. Today the surface of the water is calm and mirrorlike, and not a single vessel is to be seen. The officers were informed that even the servicing of submarines was now subject to a rigorous economy.

"It's an appalling sight," Dikiy says. "We know exactly what it signifies. Our technology must be properly maintained. You can't just go on expecting miracles. Submarines are not like spry old men who never need to see a doctor. Accidents are inevitable."

The disintegration has demoralized some of the Rybachie officers. It has turned others to debauchery. They have seen it all in the garrison of late: bizarre behavior and suicides.

"The present situation makes the officers bitter," Dikiy tells me. "That is why I am so insistent that everybody should be there for the raising of the flag on the dot of eight. The men should see the eyes of their commander, and read in them that everything is in order, everything is being held steady, we are continuing to fulfill our duty no matter what. In spite of everything."

"Officers' bullshit! Fine words for soft heads!" Many reading these lines may dismiss Dikiy's sentiments in that way. To some extent, they will be right. These really are lofty sentiments, but the situation of the officers who have not yet resigned from the disintegrating Pacific Fleet is that they perform their demanding duties solely because those fine words are their anchor. They are men with ideals and principles. That's why they are in the navy. They volunteered for the submarines because of the prestige and in the expectation of dazzling careers with high salaries. They have known different times and expect them to continue.

Because real life does not have the consistency of a film or a novel, the sublime coexists happily in Rybachie with the ridiculous and the routine.

"It's impossible to live the way your husband does. Sometimes at least a man needs time to himself."

Larisa Dikiy is a chortling beauty born in Zhitomir, in Ukraine, a woman who has sacrificed her own life to live on the verge of starvation so that her husband can fulfill his duty. She laughs mischievously in reply: "Well, actually I rather like things the way they are. At least I always know where my husband is. He has nowhere to hide from me, so I'm saved all those pangs of jealousy."

Dikiy is standing beside us. He smiles an awkward smile, like a schoolboy who has just received a declaration of love from the prettiest girl in his class. I discover that the captain is a shy man. He blushes. I could almost weep. I see clearly that the enormous burden of responsibility the commander of a nuclear submarine bears is incompatible not just with his standard of living and way of life but also with his age and appearance.

At home, without his uniform, Alexey Dikiy, captain first class, looks just like the boy at the top of the class, thin and melancholy. By Moscow criteria, where young people still mature rather late, that is precisely the situation. Dikiy, remember, is only thirty-four.

"But you have already clocked up thirty-two years of service in the navy. It's time you retired!" says Larisa.

"Actually, I could," the captain says, again embarrassed.

"What do you mean? You joined the fleet when you were two? Like the son of a noble family who was registered in a regiment when he was born and by the time he came of age already had a good service record and epaulettes?" I press him for an answer.

The captain smiles. I can see he is looking forward to what he is going to tell me. His father was indeed a naval officer, but is now, of course, retired. Dikiy grew up in Sevastopol, at the Black Sea naval base. "As regards my thirty-two-year service record at thirty-four years of age—" he begins, but is promptly interrupted by his vivacious wife.

"It means that he has spent his entire service life in the most diffi-

cult sector of all, the submarine fleet, in the immediate vicinity of re-
actors and nuclear weapons. One year's service there is counted as
three."

"You don't feel that on those grounds alone, the state should long
ago have showered you with gold?" I persist. "Are you not insulted
that you have to share your dinner among three people as if you were
a student?"

"No. I am not insulted," he replies calmly and confidently. "It
would be senseless for us submariners to come out on strike. In our
closed city everybody lives the same way I do. We survive because we
help each other to survive. We are constantly borrowing and rebor-
rowing food and money from each other."

"If somebody's relatives send them a food parcel, that family will
immediately organize a feast," Larisa tells me. "We have a visiting cir-
cle. We get fattened up. That's how we live."

"Do your parents send you parcels from Ukraine?"

"Yes, of course. And then we feed all our equally hungry friends."
She laughs loudly.

As one of our writers put it, you could make nails out of these people.

It is a curious fact that the years are passing—a great deal of time
already separates us from the fall of the Communist Party—yet certain habits from the past remain untouched. Foremost among them is
a pathological lack of respect for people, especially those who, in spite
of everything, work devotedly and selflessly, who love the cause they
are serving. The government has never learned how to thank the people who are dedicated to serving our country. You are working hard?
Well, great, carry on until you drop dead or we break your heart. The
authorities become more brazen by the day, crushing the will of the
best of our citizens.

With the single-mindedness of a maniac, they stake their money
on the worst. There is no doubt that Communism was a dead loss for
Russia, but what we have today is even worse.

I continue my discussion of lofty matters with Captain Dikiy at the central control point of the *Vilioutchinsk*. Rybachie is closed to outsiders and the inquisitive, and even officers' wives are not allowed access to the classified piers. For me, however, Military Intelligence has unexpectedly made an exception.

The predatory, combative ethos of the *Vilioutchinsk* is evident already from the shore. On the bow, on a black background, is a daunting piece of artwork: a grinning killer whale's head. The naval artist, in his desire to make the monster as intimidating as possible, has given it many more teeth than are likely to be encountered in nature. The whale's depiction there is not random. From the day it was built, the submarine was called *Kasatka*, "Killer Whale," and it was renamed only recently—for what reason is a puzzle to the officers, but they have no problem with the new name.

My introductory tour provides me with a crucial insight, which is probably why I was allowed on the submarine in the first place. I wander past the mouth of a terrifying volcano—God forbid it should ever be stoked up the wrong way. An atomic reactor with nuclear missiles is an explosive mixture. The submarine is packed with nuclear weapons, the economy is in crisis, and the armed forces are in a state of disarray. What could be more scary than that?

As we continue the tour, Dikiy hammers his views home, and on ideological matters he is quite pedantic. There can be no compromises in the armed forces, no matter what changes are taking place in society. He rejects the notion of a right to disobey a "criminal order," an idea that has been circulating stubbornly through army units since 1991. His view is that allowing a subordinate not to carry out even a single instruction or order because he considers it foolish or inappropriate will cause the whole system to collapse in a domino effect. The army is a pyramidal structure, and you cannot take that risk.

I see that both Captain Dikiy and the others who join in our conversation, all of them officers whose uniforms are decorated with ribbons for heroic submarine campaigns lasting many months, distinguish between two concepts. There is the motherland, which they serve, and there is Moscow, with which they are in a state of conflict. There are, they say, two separate states: Russia and her capital city.

The officers are frank. Viewed from Kamchatka, nothing of what goes on in the bureaucracy of the armed forces makes any sense. Why does the Ministry of Defense obstinately refuse to pay for the maintenance of the nuclear submarine fleet, when the military knows full well that not only is it impossible but indeed forbidden for officers to undertake such work locally, using their own resources? Why does the ministry mercilessly write off ten- to fourteen-year-old vessels that still have many years of life? Why, in fact, is the military systematically turning its nuclear shield, created by the efforts of the entire nation, into a leaky old sieve—and at a time when a real threat exists, primarily in the form of Chinese nuclear submarines lurking adjacent to Russia's territory?

Also present on my exploration of the *Vilioutchinsk* is the most important person in the region, Valerii Dorogin, vice admiral of Kamchatka and commander of the Northeast Group of Troops and Forces. In the near future, Dorogin is to end his military career to become a deputy of the state duma. The officers speak frankly in his presence, in no way inhibited by his seniority. One feels none of the hierarchical pressure or barriers of rank that are usual in a military setting.

In large measure, this is because Dorogin is flesh of the flesh of Rybachie. There is nothing the officers and their commander are going to conceal from one another. Dorogin has served here, in this closed naval township, for almost twenty years. For a long time he was, like Dikiy, commander of a nuclear submarine. Now his elder son, Denis Dorogin, is serving in Rybachie. Just like everyone else, the commander walks to the pier in the morning. Like everyone else, he observes the disintegration of the military. Like everyone else he is here without any means of subsistence, waiting for friends to "fatten him up."

The Northeast Group, the agglomeration to which Kamchatka belongs, along with Chukotka and Magadan Provinces, has been set up again as a result of the severe cutbacks. A similar grouping existed before the 1917 revolution and under the Bolsheviks in the 1930s.

In any grouping, one category of troops inevitably dominates. In Kamchatka, home of part of the nuclear shield, it is predictably the submariners, and, accordingly, a vice admiral is in command; he has under him infantry and coastal troops, aviation and antiaircraft forces. At first there was a certain amount of contention and dissent, but then everything settled down, due, to a large extent, to Dorogin's influence. He is a legend on Kamchatka.

The vice admiral has spent thirty-three years in the navy; his total service record comes to another fifteen years because of his time in submarines. Dorogin's legend is based not on his military past but on the present, however. He lives in Petropavlovsk-Kamchatsky. Until recently his monthly salary as the officer responsible for an enormous territory and second in rank only to the governors of three major Russian provinces was 3,600 rubles, or just over $100.

In reality, because of his pension, which he paid up long ago, he receives just under 5,000 rubles a month. By way of comparison, a city bus driver in Petropavlovsk-Kamchatsky earns 6,000 rubles a month.

Dorogin lives in a military apartment on Morskaya Street, in exactly the same conditions as the other officers. There is no hot water, and it is cold, drafty, and uncomfortable.

"Why don't you just buy a basic boiler?"

"We don't have the money. If we get some, we'll buy one."

The thing Dorogin values most is his reputation. His life is ascetic. The apartment is not bare, but there is no way it befits an admiral. His most precious possessions, concentrated in his study, are nautical knickknacks from decommissioned ships that once served in the Russian Far East. His great love is naval history.

"What about your house in the country? You must have a dacha. Every admiral in Russia has one."

"I do, certainly," Dorogin replies. "And what a dacha. Oh, dear! We'll go and take a look at it tomorrow. Otherwise you won't believe it."

Tomorrow arrives, and I see a patch of land planted with potatoes and cucumbers on the outskirts of Petropavlovsk-Kamchatsky. These vegetables will feed the vice admiral's family over the winter. A decommissioned iron railway carriage stands on bricks in the midst of the vegetable garden: a place to work. Compared with Moscow expectations about the living standards of a military commander, it is a disgrace.

Kamchatka, as we have seen, is not Moscow. People here are more straightforward and generous. Some fishermen present me with a sack of red fish they have just caught, silversides. I give the fish to Galina, the vice admiral's wife, feeling a bit awkward because I am sure the wife of the commander in chief of Kamchatka must have tons of such fish brought to her door, but I simply have no way of cooking them myself.

To my great surprise, Galina thanks me effusively and bursts into tears. In her poverty she sees these fish as good fortune. She cooks dinner and is able to invite guests, even to pickle fish for the future. To crown it all, some of the fish, by luck, have gold inside them: red caviar.

Galina Dorogina tells me that although the wives of the senior officers have lived all their married lives on the peninsula, they have seen little of exotic Kamchatka. "Our lives have passed in training courses and campaigns, brief reunions and long partings," she says.

For all that, Galina has no regret, not even for what have, in effect, been wasted years. "The truth of the matter is that nothing has changed much for the officers' wives. If twenty years ago we were cold and hungry and I had to stand in line all day for a dozen eggs and they wrote my number in line on my hand, the only difference now is that we have absolutely no money. There are eggs in the shops, but the officers have no money to buy them with."

Vice Admiral Dorogin's thinking is an ideological mishmash, an amalgam of Communist and capitalist notions. This probably is to be expected from a man who spent almost all his life under the Soviet regime, was a member of the Young Communist League and the Communist Party, and now has to live with the realities of the free market. From my point of view, his ideas are outmoded; they are the stale ideology that lost its validity with the demise of the Soviet Union. At the same time, the vice admiral fully understands democratic aspirations and why they are needed.

Toward which of these ideological poles is his heart really drawn, and in which of these dimensions does he feel at home? It is not easy to tell, but I decide to try.

Dorogin is answerable for everything in Kamchatka, from the submarines to the state of the military museum. Here is just one episode from his life.

Among the units of the Northeast Group is the Twenty-second Chapaev Motorized Division. It bears that name because it is the same division as was formed in the Volga region in 1918 by Vasily Chapaev, a legendary hero of the civil war. It was here that his girlfriend, Bolshevik Anka, who figures in hundreds of questionable Soviet jokes, was a fighter.

After the Second World War, the Chapaev Division was redeployed to the Far East, and today it is famous in Kamchatka for the fact that its first company retains a soldier's bed for Vladimir Ilyich Lenin, leader of the world proletariat. In 1922, Lenin was made an honorary Red Army soldier in the division and the bed was accordingly allocated. Since 1922, wherever the division has been sent, it has been a tradition to transport Lenin's bed along with the other equipment. Even today the bed enjoys a prominent position in the barracks. It is neatly made up, and the walls around constitute a Lenin Corner, with drawings on the topic "Volodya was a good student!" All these items are registered in a logbook kept in a secret location in the division.

In the view of the head of the First Lenin Memorial, Captain Igor Shapoval, twenty-six, the spirit of Lenin keeps his soldiers up to scratch.

"Are you serious?"

"Yes. They see this neatly made bed and try to emulate it."

I find this idea laughable, but then I find that Vice Admiral Dorogin believes no less than Captain Shapoval in the lofty ideological role of Lenin's bed.

"New recruits find it a bit odd at first, but they come to respect it," Dorogin says. "When democracy triumphed in Moscow, there were attempts to get rid of Lenin's bed in Kamchatka, but we managed to save it. It's hardly in the same category as your monument to Dzerzhinsky at the Lubyanka."

Dorogin does not believe in change for its own sake. History is what it is, and you didn't need to be all that clever to demolish a monument to the founder of the Bolsheviks' secret police. He also considers that since the Lenin Corner was established in the Chapaev Division by a special resolution of the Council of People's Commissars, at the very least it would require a directive from the government of Russia, signed by the prime minister, for the bed to be dispatched to the scrap heap.

We talk about which example soldiers in Kamchatka should now be invited to follow. The present commander of the division, Lieutenant Colonel Valerii Oleynikov, says unambiguously, "The example of those who fought in Chechnya and Afghanistan."

The previous head of the First Lenin Memorial had indeed fought in Chechnya. Lieutenant Yury Buchnev received the award of Hero of Russia for fighting in Grozny. We continue this conversation, and I suggest that encouraging soldiers to emulate the military's experience in Chechnya can hardly be a good idea. Dorogin keeps out of the discussion, which, as a senior officer, he should. He is serving his country, and as a matter of principle his political views should be of no concern to anyone. But about the future he is willing to speculate. Ideology is one thing; the army cutbacks are quite another. The officers feel they are sitting on a powder keg.

"We are half expecting that at any moment the state will give a raw deal to those who have served it loyally," comments Alexander Shevchenko, the division's chief of staff. The other officers, including

Dorogin, agree. None of those likely to be retired have civilian qualifications commensurate with their rank and status in the service, and
of course they will have nowhere to live. If they have to leave the
armed forces, they will lose their homes, because, at present, all of
them are living in military flats. Igor Shapoval, an engineer who main-
tains military vehicles, is skilled in the cold working of metals, so when
he ceases to be an officer, he can look forward to a career repairing
tractors, or serving the civilian population in a key-cutting kiosk.
Shevchenko already has experience of civilian employment. For two
of the three years he studied in Moscow at the Artillery Academy, he
earned money on the side as a watchman in a florist's basement, covering the twenty-four hours jointly with three other student officers.

The view in Kamchatka is that the Ministry of Defense does not
agree that, in principle, an officer should dedicate himself to his military duties and not fritter away his time by working on the side.

"With things the way they are, it is only too easy to draw a man
into illegal activity," says the vice admiral. "I myself have been offered
$2,000 in an envelope. This was by someone who was directed to me
by a friend. He offered the bribe in a very respectable way: 'You need
money for medical treatment for your wife.' At that moment he was
absolutely right. The condition was that I should approve a contract
for the sale of scrap brass on terms unfavorable to the army, not at
$700 a ton but at $450. Actually, my signature was the last in a series of
signatures of senior military figures. I could simply have thrown the
man with the envelope out, but I called in the prosecutor. I thought it
might be an example to others."

Of course, Dorogin is in many ways a saintly man. Like many
other officers, he is serving his country not for money but from a
sense of duty. Only here, at the farthest reach of our land, are such
spiritually healthy people to be found.

How long the patience of Dikiy, Dorogin, and others like them will
hold out nobody knows, not even they themselves. Today's navy is dependent on the older and middle generations of naval officers. There

are almost no young ones. They don't come out here. The few who do are not willing to resign themselves to the idea that they should devote all their strength to the navy and receive nothing in return. What kind of officers will the navy have left in a few more years?

"Patriotism?" A young captain second class from Rybachie smiles wryly. He is an officer on the submarine *Omsk*. "Patriotism is something you have to pay for. It is time to put an end to this nonsense, this playing at being paupers. We need to get back on our feet, not limp through life like Dikiy. He is a commander, yet he always has cheap sneakers on his feet and drinks cheap brandy. The way the fleet is being treated is out of order, and the only way to respond is by making up your own rules."

"What do you mean by that?"

By "making up your own rules" the young officer means making a living by fair means or foul. He says that all the officers of his age are quietly trading whatever they can get their hands on under the counter.

"I get fish and caviar brought to my home now," he says proudly. "Two years ago I was bartering spirits I'd stolen from the ship, and people had no respect for me then."

"For the young officers a good standard of living is beginning to be the main reason for being in the navy," mourns Vice Admiral Dorogin. In his opinion, any thought of responding to state neglect by "making up your own rules" is just as fatal for anybody in the service as questioning a commanding officer's orders.

OLD LADIES AND NEW RUSSIANS

Two old ladies, Maria Savina, a former champion milkmaid, and Zinaida Fenoshina, a former champion cowherd, stand in the middle of the forest, angrily shaking upraised sticks in the direction of a bulldozer. The machine is roaring away at full throttle, and they are shouting as loudly as they can for all to hear: "Be off! Away with you! How much longer must we put up with this sort of thing?"

From behind ancient trees, surly security guards appear and surround them as if to say, "Leave now while you still can, or we shoot."

Nikolai Abramov—a retired veteran, the village elder, and the organizer of the demonstration—spreads his arms. "They want to drive us off our own land. We shall defend it to the death. What else is left?"

The theater of operations is on the outskirts of the village of Pervomaiskoe, in the Narofominsk District of Moscow Province. The epicenter is the grounds of an old estate formerly owned by the Berg family. It dates from 1904 and is today protected by the state as a natural and cultural heritage site.

When they have calmed down a little, the old people shake their heads sadly. "There, in our old age, we've joined the Greens. What else can we do? There's only us to defend our park from this scum. Nobody else is going to."

The scum are New Russians who have hired soulless developers to erect thirty-four houses right in the middle of the century-old Berg Park. Maria and Zinaida are members of a special ecological group created by the village assembly of Pervomaiskoe to organize direct action against the despoilers of the environment.

Paying little attention to the Green activists, the trucks continue to drive and the bulldozer to roar among the precious ancient trees. After an hour's work, they have cut a swath through the woodlands. It is to be the central avenue of the future cottage settlement. Pipes, reinforcement wire, and concrete slabs lie all over the place. The building work, in full swing, is being carried out as if to maximize damage to the natural environment. Already 130 cubic meters of timber have been taken as rare tree species were felled. Wherever you look, there are notches on cedars and firs, marking them for slaughter. The machinery brazenly wrecks the environment, churning up layers of clay from the depths and pitilessly burying, deep beneath it, the ecosystem of the forest floor that has formed over the years.

"Have you heard of the Weymouth pine?" Tatyana Dudenis asks. She is head of the ecological group and a research associate at one of the region's medical institutes. "We had five specimens growing in the grounds of our heritage park. They were the only ones in the whole of Moscow Province. The Bergs made a hobby of propagating rare tree species. Three of these Weymouth pines have now been sawn down for no better reason than that the developers wanted to run a street for their new estate just where the trees were growing. Other precious species are under threat: the Siberian silver fir and larch, the white poplar, a white cedar, *Thuja occidentalis*, the only specimen in Moscow Province. In just the last three days we have lost more than sixty trees. It wouldn't be so bad if they were destroying the less outstanding or sickly specimens, but they have quite a different approach. They decide where they want to construct a road and cut down anything that's in the way. They decide where they want to put up a cottage and clear the site, taking no account of the rarity of the trees they are destroying. The forest here is legally classified as Grade One, which means it is against the law to touch these trees. To obtain permission to fell them, you have to demonstrate 'exceptional circumstances' and support your application with a recommendation from the State Ecological Inspectorate. For every such hectare—about two and a half acres—you need the express permission of the federal government."

When the fate of Berg Park was being decided, no such applications were submitted. The Pervomaiskoe Greens lodged writs with the Narofominsk court to bring the nouveaux riches into line. They petitioned Judge Yelena Golubeva, who had been assigned the case, for an injunction to halt the building work until the hearing, since otherwise, after the trees had been felled, a verdict in their favor would be of little use.

However, as we have seen, this is the age of the oligarchs in Russia.

Every branch of government clearly understands the language of rustling banknotes. Judge Golubeva did not even consider granting an injunction to halt the construction and, when the work was already in progress, deliberately failed to conduct a hearing.

Nearly all those unique trees were felled.

Valerii Kulakovsky emerges from the posse of guards. He is the deputy director of the Promzhilstroy Company, which calls itself a co-operative of home builders. Kulakovsky advises me to stay out of this dispute. He says that some highly influential people in Moscow have an interest in the estate; they are going to live here. The information is soon confirmed. I discover that the "cooperative" has managed to acquire property rights over the Berg hectares, which, according to the law, are the property of the nation. The takeover is illegal.

Kulakovsky just shrugs and tries to explain his position. "We are very tired of these endless demonstrations by the villagers. What do you expect me to do now, when I have put so much money into this, bought the land, started building? Who do you think is going to give it all back to me?"

He also says that the developers have no plans to back down.

They did not back down. Berg Park ceased to exist. The felling of our most precious forests in the interests of the oligarchs and their companies goes on throughout the land.

Not long before the Green old ladies of Pervomaiskoe mounted the desperate defense of their ancient park, the Supreme Court of Russia considered the same matter of principle as it applied to Russia as a whole. The case was known as the Forest Issue.

"Bear in mind the interests of the property owners. They have acquired the land, built the houses, and now you want to turn everything back." The lawyer in the Supreme Court case repeated, almost word for word, what Kulakovsky had said.

The ecologist lawyers Olga Alexeeva and Vera Mishchenko, who were defending the interests of society against the caprices of the New Russians, had a different take on the matter: "Every citizen of this country has the right to life and enjoyment of the national heritage. If we are truly citizens of Russia, then it is our duty to ensure that future generations receive no less a national heritage than today's generations enjoy. In any case, how can we take seriously property rights that have been acquired illegally?"

The essence of the Forest Issue was that Russian ecologists, under the leadership of the Moscow Institute of Ecological Legal Issues, or Eco-Juris, which brought the case, demanded the repeal of twenty-two orders of the Cabinet of Ministers transferring Grade One forests to the category of nonafforested land. These orders permitted the felling of more than 34,000 hectares of prime forest in Russia.

Russia's forests are divided into three categories. Grade One relates to those deemed particularly important either for society or for the natural environment. These are forests containing highly valued species, habitats of rare birds and animals, reservations and parks, and urban and suburban green belts. The Forestry Code of the Russian Federation, accordingly, recognizes Grade One forests as part of the national heritage. Berg Park was in this category.

The formal applicant for the change in categories and subsequent right to fell trees was, oddly enough, the Forestry Commission of the Russian Federation, or Rosleskhoz. It is the body that has the right to submit documents relating to the legal status of forests for signature by the prime minister. The twenty-two orders disputed by the ecologists had been made without the statutory state ecological inspection, with the result that the national heritage became the prey of short-term interests. Where forests were cut down, they were replaced by gas stations, garages, industrial parks, local wholesale markets, domestic waste dumps, and, of course, housing developments.

The ecologists consider this last option to be the least objectionable, but only providing that the new homeowners behave responsibly toward the magnificent forests surrounding their houses and do not destroy the roots in the course of laying drainage systems.

While the Forest Issue was being considered and the judges were taking their time, almost 950 hectares of top-quality forests were condemned to destruction under new orders signed by the prime minister. The greatest damage was done in the Khanty-Mansiisk and Yamalo-Nenetsk Autonomous Regions, where trees were destroyed for the benefit of oil and gas companies. Moscow Province also suffered: what happened to Berg Park was the result of deliberate judicial procrastination.

While the paperwork was being taken care of and nobody had the courage to dot the legal *i*'s or cross the legal *t*'s, the struggle for the forest in Pervomaiskoe became violent. When, at the request of the prosecutor's office, the ecological group went to record the results of the developers' activities with a videocamera, police reinforcements were brought in. A fight broke out, the camera was broken, and the ecologists, all of them elderly, were beaten up.

"Of course, we do not want to wage a war, but we have been left with no option," Nikolai Abramov, the village elder, says by way of explanation. "The estate was the last place in the village where we could go to walk. There were usually old people and mothers with strollers there. There is a school for three hundred pupils and a kindergarten on the grounds. All the rest has been turned into cottages for the New Russians."

The veteran ecologists are aware that they are at war primarily with the super-rich, people whose wealth vastly eclipses anything they themselves have ever seen. They have heard the money talk, however. At a village assembly, Alexander Zakharov, chairman of the Pervomaiskoe Rural District Council, openly declared that the sums of money involved were too great for there to be any possibility of reversing the situation. Here is what Igor Kulikov, chairman of the Ecological Union of Moscow Province, wrote to the provincial prosecutor, Mikhail Avdyukov: "The chairman of the council publicly stated to members of the ecological group elected by the assembly that he had given their names and addresses to the Mafia, which would deal with them if they did not stop their protests."

Zakharov is undoubtedly one of the central characters in this unseemly tale. If he had stood firm, not one dacha would have encroached on the grounds of Berg Park. At the foot of the documents that ultimately permitted the felling of the Pervomaiskoe trees, in contravention of the law and against the resolution of the village assembly, is Zakharov's signature.

The scenario is a familiar one. First, application is made to the upper echelons in Moscow for the "transfer of Grade One forests to the category of nonafforested land." A short time later, an order is drafted for signature by the prime minister. The felling of the forest ensues when, implementing the prime minister's order, the local forestry officials and the head of the district council give the go-ahead.

There is not much wrong with our laws in Russia. It is just that not many people want to obey them.

NORD-OST: THE LATEST TALE
OF DESTRUCTION

Moscow, February 8, 2003. No. 1 Dubrovskaya Street, now known to the whole world as Dubrovka. In a packed theater whose image—just three months ago—was flashed to all the world's newspapers, magazines, and television stations, there is an exuberant atmosphere. Black tie, evening dress, the whole of the political beau monde has assembled here. Sighs and gasps, kisses and hugs, members of the government, members of the Duma, leaders of the parliamentary factions and parties, a sumptuous buffet . . .

They are celebrating a victory over international terrorism in our capital city. The pro-Putin politicians assure us that the revival of the musical *Nord-Ost* on the ruins of terrorism is nothing less than that. Today will see the first performance since October 23, 2002, when the unguarded theater, its actors, and its audience were seized during the evening performance and held hostage for fifty-seven hours by several dozen terrorists from Chechnya, who hoped to force President Putin to end the second Chechen war and withdraw his troops from their republic.

They didn't succeed. Nobody withdrew from anywhere. The war continues as before, with no time for doubts about the legitimacy of its methods. The only thing that changed was that in the early morning of October 26, a gas attack was mounted against all those in the building, some eight hundred people, both terrorists and hostages. The secret military gas was chosen by the president personally. The gas attack was followed by a storming of the building by special antiterrorist units in the course of which all the hostage takers was killed, along with almost two hundred hostages. Many people died for lack of medical attention, and the identity of the gas was not even revealed to the doctors charged with saving lives. Already on that evening, the president was announcing, without a qualm, that this was a triumph for Russia over "the forces of international terror."

The victims of this murderous rescue operation were barely remembered at the gala performance on February 8. It was a typical fashionable Moscow get-together at which many seemed to forget what it was they were raising their glasses to. They sang, they danced, they ate, a lot of people got drunk, and everyone talked a lot of nonsense, which seemed all the more cynical because the event was taking place at the scene of a massacre, even if the theater had been refurbished in record time. The family members of those who had died in the *Nord-Ost* tragedy refused categorically to come to the celebration, considering it a sacrilege. The president was also unable to attend but sent a message of congratulation.

Why did he send congratulations? Because nobody could break us. His message was couched in typically Soviet rhetoric and proceeded from typically Stalinist values: it was a shame about the people who died, of course, but the interests of society must come first. The producers warmly thanked the president for his understanding of their commercial problems and said that audiences would be in for a treat if they came back. The musical had received a "new creative impetus."

But now: the reverse side of the medal, the individuals at the cost of whose lives the president consolidated his membership in the international antiterrorist coalition. Let us look at those whose lives were crushed by the events at the *Nord-Ost*. Let us look at the victims about whom today's state machine is trying to forget as quickly as possible, and to induce the rest of us to do the same by every means at its disposal. Let us look at the ethnic purging that followed the act of terrorism, and at the new state ideology Putin has enunciated: "We shall not count the cost. Let nobody doubt that. Even if the cost is very high."

THE FIFTH ONE

Yaroslav Fadeev, a boy from Moscow, is now the first named in the official master list of those killed during the *Nord-Ost* assault. According to the official version of events, the four hostages who died from bullet wounds were shot by terrorists; the special unit of the FSB, Putin's own service, does not make mistakes and hence did not shoot any of the hostages.

There is, however, no escaping the fact that a bullet passed through Yaroslav's head, although his name is not on the list of the "four shot by the terrorists." Yaroslav was the fifth to die from a bullet wound. In the "Cause of Death" column on the official form that was issued to his mother, Irina, for the funeral, there is a dash.

On November 18, 2002, Yaroslav, who was in the tenth grade of a Moscow school, would have been sixteen. There was to have been a big family celebration, but standing over the coffin of the now eternally fifteen-year-old boy, his grandfather, a Moscow doctor, remarked, "There now, we didn't get to shave together even once."

Four of them had gone to the musical: two sisters, Irina Fadeeva and Victoria Kruglikova, and their children, Yaroslav and Nastya. Victoria was the mother of nineteen-year-old Nastya. Irina, Victoria, and Nastya survived, but Yaroslav died in circumstances that have never been officially investigated.

After the assault and the gas attack, Irina, Victoria, and Nastya were carried out of the theater unconscious and taken to the hospital. Yaroslav completely disappeared. He was not on any of the interim lists. There was a total absence of precise official information. The telephone hotline announced by the authorities on radio and television was not functioning. Relatives of the hostages were rushing all over Moscow, and among them were friends of this family. They combed the city, dividing its mortuaries and hospitals into sectors to be checked.

Finally, in the Kholzunov Lane Mortuary they found Body No. 5714, which fitted Yaroslav's description, but they could not confirm it was him. In his pocket they found a passport in the name of his mother, Irina Vladimirovna Fadeeva, but the page for "Children" contained this entry: "Male. Yaroslav Olegovich Fadeev, 18.11.1988." The real Yaroslav, however, had been born in 1986.

As Irina explained later, "I put my passport into my son's trouser pocket. He did not have any identification documents on him. Since he was very tall, looking to be about eighteen, I was so afraid that if the Chechens suddenly started releasing children and adolescents, Yaroslav might not be included because of his height. So, right there in the hall, I crouched under the seats and wrote Yaroslav's data into my own passport, changing the year of his birth to make him seem younger."

Sergey, Irina's friend, came to see her in the hospital on October 27 and told her that Body No. 5714 had been found. He told her about the passport in the trousers and about the resemblance to Yaroslav. In spite of the frost, Irina ran out of the hospital, straight through a gap in the fence, just in what she was wearing.

The hostages who had survived and been taken to hospitals were still being held hostage there. By order of the intelligence services, they were forbidden to return home. They were not allowed to telephone or be visited by their families. Sergey had gotten into the hospital by bribing everyone he encountered: the nurses, the guards, the orderlies, the police. The total corruption of our system prizes open even the most firmly battened-down hatches.

Irina ran from the hospital straight to the mortuary. There she was shown a photograph on a computer monitor and identified Yaroslav. She asked to see his body, felt carefully all over it and discovered two bullet wounds in the head, an entry and an exit hole. Both had been filled up with wax. Sergey, who was with her, was surprised at how calm she seemed. She didn't sob or become hysterical. She was logical and unemotional.

"I really was very glad that I had found him at last," Irina tells me. "Lying in the hospital, I had already thought everything through and considered my options. I had decided how I would behave if my son was dead. In the mortuary when I saw that this really was Yaroslav and that my life was therefore at an end, I simply did what I had decided on earlier. I calmly asked everyone to leave the hall to which his body had been brought from the refrigerator. I said I wanted to be alone with my son. I had decided I would say that. You see, before he died, I had made him a promise. When we were stuck there, he said to me at the end of the last day, during the night, a few hours before the gas, 'Mom, I probably won't make it. I can't take much more. Mom, if something happens, what will it be like?' I told him, 'Don't be afraid of anything. We have always been together here, and we will always be together there.' He said, 'Mom, how will I know you there?' I told him, 'Your hand is always in mine, so we'll find ourselves there together, holding hands. We won't lose each other. Just don't let go of my hand, hold on tight.' But see how it turned out. I felt I had deceived him. We were never far from each other while he was alive. Never. That is why I was so calm: we were together in life, and over there, in death, we would still be together. Anyway, when I was alone with him in the mortuary, I told him, 'There now, don't worry. I have found you and I'm coming to be with you.' . . . I had never deceived him. . . . That is why I was so calm. I went through the side door in order not to see the friends who were waiting for me and asked the assistants to let me out through the service entrance. When I got outside, I flagged down a passing car, went to the nearest bridge over the

Moscow River, and jumped off it. I did not drown, though. There were ice floes in the river, and I fell among them. I can't swim, but I didn't sink. I could see I wasn't sinking and thought, 'Well, I may at least get a cramp in my leg,' but that didn't happen either. As ill luck would have it, some people pulled me out. They asked, 'Where are you from? What are you doing swimming?' I told them, 'I've just come from the mortuary, but please don't report me.' I gave them a telephone number to call, and Sergey came to collect me. Of course, I'm doing my best to cope, but I am dead. I don't know how he is getting on there without me."

When she had regained consciousness in the hospital on October 26, Irina found she was naked under the blanket. The other women hostages around her all had their clothes, but she had only a small icon clutched in her hand. When she could talk, she asked the nurses to give her back at least some of her clothing, but they explained that everything she had been wearing when she was brought in from the theater had been destroyed on orders from officers of the intelligence services, because it was soaked in blood.

But why? And whose blood was it? Irina had passed out in the theater clasping her son in her arms. The person whose blood it was must have been shot in a way that caused it to gush over her. It could only have been Yaroslav's.

"That last night got off to a very tense start," Irina recalls. "The terrorists were nervous, but then 'Mozart,' as we called him, Movsar Baraev, the ringleader, announced that we could take it easy until 11 A.M. A ray of hope had appeared. The Chechens began throwing juice out to us. They did not allow us to get out of our seats. If you needed anything, you had to put up your hand and then they would throw you some juice or water. When the government assault began and we saw the terrorists running up on to the stage, I said to my sister, 'Cover Nastya with your jacket,' and I put my arms tightly around Yaroslav. I didn't realize they had released gas, I just saw the terrorists becoming agitated. Yaroslav was taller than I, so that really he was shielding me when I held him. Then I passed out. In the mortuary I saw that the entry wound was on the side away from me. I had been shielded by him. . . . He saved me, although my one wish in those fifty-seven hours as a hostage had been to keep him safe."

But whose bullet was it? Was a ballistics test conducted? Was a blood sample taken from the clothing to establish whose it was?

Nobody in the family knows the answers to these questions. All information relating to the case is strictly classified, kept secret even from a mother. In the mortuary register, the cause of death was given as "bullet wound," but the entry had been made in pencil. This document, too, was later classified: "They'll have rubbed it out, of course," the family says with certainty.

"At first I thought it had been done by one of the Chechen women," Irina relates. "While we were stuck in there, she was nearby all the time. She saw that whenever there was any danger, any noise or shouting, I would grab my son and hold him tight. It was my own fault that I attracted her attention. . . . It seemed to me she was watching us all the time. At one point she said, staring at Yaroslav, 'My son is back there'—in Chechnya, that is. Nothing bad happened to us after that, but I felt she was watching us all the time wherever she was. So perhaps she had shot Yaroslav. I still can't sleep. I see her eyes in front of me, the narrow strip of her face."

Irina's friends later explained to her that the size of the entry wound on Yaroslav's body indicated the bullet was not from a pistol, and the Chechen women had only pistols.

So the question remains: Whose bullet was it?

"It must have been our people," Irina says. "Of course, we were sitting in a very unfortunate position, right by the doors. Anyone who came in was right there at row 11. When the terrorists burst into the auditorium, we were the first people they saw, so of course when our soldiers came in, we would have been directly in front of them, too."

Irina can analyze what happened, and how, as much as she likes.

What she thinks or imagines is of no concern to the authorities. The state's line is that four people were shot, and no one else. Yaroslav, the fifth person, falls outside the official version of events. Indeed, Yaroslav is not even officially included among the victims in Criminal Case No. 229133, being investigated by a team from the Moscow city prosecutor's office.

"It really hurts me that . . . the authorities are pretending there never was any such person," Irina muses.

Worse, however, is that as soon as Irina shared her questions and conclusions with journalists, she was summoned to the prosecutor's office. The investigator was angry. "What are you kicking up all this fuss about? Do you not understand it is impossible that he had a bullet wound?" He went on to do his best to scare the wits out of the unhappy mother, who was already in a perilous state: "Either you immediately write a statement to the effect that you told those journalists nothing and that they thought everything up themselves, whereupon we shall bring criminal charges against them for slandering the intelligence services, or we dig up your son's grave without your consent and carry out a postmortem examination!"[10]

Irina did not give in to this wretched attempt at blackmail. Instead, she took her leave after a four-hour grilling in the prosecutor's office and went straight to the cemetery to guard her son's grave. It was late November, which in Moscow is the depths of winter. Again she was saved from death by friends who looked all over the city when she did not return home that night.

Yaroslav was considered a quiet, studious boy. He graduated from music school while others of his age were running wild in the streets swilling beer and exercising their swearing muscles. He suffered a great deal because of this. He wanted to be "tough," to be assertive, bold, and unflinching.

He kept a diary, as many of us do at his age. Irina read it after the *Nord-Ost* events. He wondered which aspects of his personality he could say he liked and which he disliked. He wrote: "I hate it that I am such a coward, scared of everything and indecisive." "And what would you like to bring out in yourself?" the diary asked. "I would like to be tough." He had school friends, but they were not boys who were considered tough or whom girls fancied. At home he had a sense of humor, could show what he was made of, and be bold and assertive. It was outside that the problems began.

Irina is saddened by the things she never said to Yaroslav and by the fact she never properly told him how much she admired him.

"People consider me, for example, a strong person," Victoria, Yaroslav's aunt, tells me. "But in there I was completely distraught. There we three women were sitting next to him, the youngest of us, and it was he who encouraged us, like a grown man. My daughter's nerves went completely. She was shaking and sobbing, 'Mama, I want to live. Mama, I don't want to die.' But he was calm and courageous. He reassured Nastya, he supported us, he tried to take everything on himself, as a man is supposed to. For instance, one of the Chechen women saw we had put the children between us, trying to protect them. . . . Irina and I thought that if there was an attack, we would cover them with our bodies. Then the woman came up to us with a grenade in her hand. She touched Nastya's leg. I said, 'Would you mind going away?' but she looked at Nastya and said, 'Don't be afraid. If I am standing right next to you, it won't hurt. You will die instantly, while those sitting further away will suffer more.' Then the Chechen woman went away, and Nastya said to me, 'Mom, ask her to stay with us, ask her. She said it wouldn't hurt us.' Nastya was broken. I knew perfectly well that if we had that Chechen woman standing next to us, we really would be out of luck, but if she wasn't, there was at least some hope. . . .

"Another time the terrorists were frightening us by saying that if nobody came to negotiate, they would start shooting us, and that the first to be shot would be anyone in the police or the army. Naturally, many people quickly threw away their military ID, but the terrorists picked them up and called out the names from the stage. Suddenly we heard, 'Victoria Vladimirovna, born 1960.' That was me. Only the surname was wrong. . . . The situation was very bad. Nobody answered. The terrorists started going through people row by row. They came to me. Irina said, 'We'll go together.' The terrorists demanded that members of the law-enforcement agencies go off somewhere with them, and we all thought they were going to be shot. I told Irina that one of us needed to survive or our parents would be left completely alone. . . . The terrorists found the Victoria they were looking for, but while everything was still unclear, Yaroslav came and sat beside me. He took my hand and said, 'Auntie Vicky, don't be frightened. If anything happens, I'll come with you. Forgive me for everything. Forgive me.' I said to him, 'That's all right, everything is going to be fine.' . . . I don't know where he found so much courage. We thought he was just a child. . . .

"It really was very scary. They let us listen to what was being said about us on the radio. That's how we knew the president was saying nothing, and that [the radical right-wing politician] Zhirinovsky in typical hard-line fashion had said there was no point in the Duma wasting time on this terrorist act. It wasn't worth discussing because it was all just a hoax. . . .

"After we had gotten through the first day, we felt we could sit it out there for a week just so long as we could stay alive and the authorities could come up with a solution other than an assault on the theater. We found it hard. It was difficult to maintain your composure. But Yaroslav took it."

Irina's life has changed completely. She isn't working now. She couldn't bear to go every day to the job she was doing before, when Yaroslav was alive. Her colleagues were a cheery bunch. They knew one another well and would celebrate every exam Yaroslav passed, every top grade he earned. She can't bear even to walk around Moscow, because she walked all the streets with her son and wherever she turns, the memories flood back.

"Look, these are tickets for the overnight train to Saint Petersburg, for October 25–26, just when he died. We were going there to a tennis tournament, just the two of us. I had been wanting to go somewhere with him by train for a long time, because I always had the feeling that we didn't talk enough and in the train there would be just the two of us, and we would be able to have a heart-to-heart. It wasn't to be."

"Why do you say you felt you didn't talk enough?"

"I don't know. . . . We did talk a lot, but all the same, that is how it seemed. I wanted to talk and talk to him. . . ."

Everybody around her is trying to help and support Irina. She is fortunate in having the love of those closest to her, but still it is hard. It was too much even for the priest she sought out in order to unburden her soul. When he had heard her story, he broke down. "Forgive me," he said, "it's just too painful."

"I went to ask the priest what I could do. It was I who had dragged Yaroslav to *Nord-Ost*. It was all my idea. He wasn't all that keen to go," Irina says. In photographs taken before the terrorist ordeal, she is a beautiful, self-confident young woman, glowing with happiness, perhaps a little plump. Now she is shrunken and haggard, with a look of despair in her lackluster eyes. She seems far from young in her perpetual black coat, black beret, black shoes and stockings, always shivering, keeping her coat on even inside.

"Yaroslav and I went to the theater a great deal. That evening we had tickets for a different production in a different theater," Irina continues. "We had already changed to go out. Victoria and Nastya had come to collect us, and there, standing in the hallway, we realized the tickets were for the day before. Yaroslav was glad. He wanted to stay at home, but I insisted: 'Let's go to *Nord-Ost*. It's on nearby.' . . . I dragged him along, and then I failed to protect him. . . . The last thing he said to me was, 'Mom, I so much want to remember you, if anything happens. . . .'"

"Did you talk a lot like that in there?"

"No. For some reason it happened that this was the last time we talked together. You know, while I still had Yaroslav, I would get up in the mornings feeling I was the happiest woman in the world. . . . Now I think you probably aren't allowed to be so happy. . . . I brought Yaroslav to such a terrible end. The present I gave him for his six-teenth birthday was a fence for his grave."

"It is not you who did that to him."

"It's the war. There is a war being waged," Victoria says again and again. "And now we have become its victims."

No. 2251: Unidentified

Before I can tell you this story, there is something I need to explain. It is about the way we are living in Russia in the aftermath of the *Nord-Ost* events, and about the state of the Russian judicial system under Putin.

The fact of the matter is that our courts were never as independent as you might have thought from our constitution. At the present time, however, the judicial system is cheerfully mutating into a condition of total subservience to the executive. It is reaching unprecedented levels of supine *pozvonochnost'*.

This word refers to the phenomenon of a judge delivering a verdict in accordance with what has been dictated in the course of a phone call (*zvonok*) by representatives of the executive branch of the government. *Pozvonochnost'* is an everyday phenomenon in Russia.[11]

"The victims of *Nord-Ost*" is how people now refer to the families who lost relatives during the assault, and also to hostages who were crippled as a result of the gas attack. These victims have begun to serve writs on the authorities demanding compensation for the "moral" (i.e., emotional and psychological) harm inflicted on them and naming as defendant the municipal government of Moscow. The victims have claimed that the officials of the municipal government, not wishing to argue with Putin and the FSB, failed to organize timely medical assistance for the victims. The plaintiffs consider that the city of Moscow's culpability is the greater, since Yury Luzhkov, Moscow's mayor and director of the city's executive authority, was one of the people who agreed that the president should use chemical weapons against Russian citizens.

The initial writs were served at the Tverskoy Intermunicipal Court of Moscow (a district court) in November 2002. By January 17, 2003, when the first three were being examined by Federal Judge Marina Gorbacheva to see whether there was a case to answer, the number had risen to sixty-one. The compensation demanded totaled the ruble equivalent of $60 million, with the plaintiffs stating that this was the price of a state lie. What they primarily wanted to know was the truth about why their relatives had died. It had proved to be impossible to obtain, because the FSB had classified anything connected with the October terrorist attack as secret. Since Putin's FSB was involved, the build-up to the court hearings took place amid a barrage of propaganda directed against the plaintiffs by the state media, who accused them of brazenly attempting to raid the country's coffers and of trying to profit from the death of relatives. The better-known lawyers of Moscow had chickened out of representing the *Nord-Ost*ers because they feared the wrath of the Kremlin. Igor Trunov, who agreed to act for them, was besmirched in the press.

The authorities did their best to bulldoze their way out of the *Nord-Ost* claims, using the considerable PR machinery at their disposal, as if they were not the guilty ones themselves but rather the aggrieved party.

On January 23, 2003, Judge Gorbacheva, true to form as a "telephone judge" and basing herself on a technicality, rejected the claims of the first three plaintiffs. The federal law known as the Struggle Against Terrorism could be read in several ways, and there were contradictions between different provisions. One of them could be interpreted as meaning that the state was under no obligation to compensate victims of terrorist acts for any loss they suffered. In fact, the judge did a good deal more than merely reject the claims. She accompanied her rejection with a barrage of abuse as shameless as that of the authorities themselves, who had no doubt asked her to do so. The hearings developed into a succession of unforgivable insults and humiliations directed at the plaintiffs.

Here are some examples from the January 23 session.

"Karpov, sit down. I said, sit down!"

"But there's something I need to say—"

Judge Gorbacheva interrupts Sergey Karpov, plaintiff, in midsentence. He is the father of Alexander Karpov, a popular Moscow singer, poet, and translator who was asphyxiated during the gas attack.

"Sit down, Karpov, or I shall have you removed. You missed your opportunity to make a written submission before the hearing."

"I didn't miss the opportunity. I was never notified."

"Well, I say you did. Sit down, or I shall have you removed."

"I wish to submit—"

"I am accepting nothing from you!"

The judge has a hysterical look. Her eyes are vacant, and she sounds like a street trader. While berating the plaintiffs, she is cleaning the dirt from under her fingernails. It is a disgusting sight. She continues her haranguing of Sergey Karpov: "Karpov, do not put your hand up again."

"I request that my rights be explained to me."

"You are going to have nothing explained to you."

The crammed courtroom has not been swept for a long time. All the journalists have been forbidden to use dictaphones. Why, exactly? What state secrets are likely to be divulged? You are reluctant to talk to the victims—whose souls are in torment—because they immediately start crying. Relatives and friends have come to support them in case they are taken ill. The representative of the Russian bench continues, however, to drown everything in her vulgarity.

"Khramtsova, V. I.; Khramtsova, I. F.; Khramtsov, T. I. Are you present? No?" The judge reels off the names with a total lack of courtesy.

"I am present," a tall, thin young man replies.

"Khramtsov! You may speak!" From the tone of her voice you

would think she was saying, "Here is a ruble, my good fellow, and now be off with you!"

Alexander Khramtsov has lost his father, who played the trumpet in the *Nord-Ost* orchestra. He begins to speak but finds it difficult to hold back the tears.

"My father traveled the world with orchestras and to make personal appearances. He represented our country and this city everywhere. His death is an irretrievable loss. Are you completely unaware of that? It is you who let the terrorists in, you, the city administrators of Moscow. They strolled around unhindered. Of course the assault was not your responsibility, but why were four hundred people taken to No. 13 Hospital when there were only fifty staff on duty there and they couldn't treat people promptly? People died before they received any attention. That is how my father died."

The woman in the judge's robes, presiding up there on the bench, appears to be miles away. To kill time, she lazily shifts her papers from one place to another. She is weary and occasionally looks out of the window, adjusts her collar, checks her appearance in the dark glass. One of her earrings seems to be irritating her. She scratches her ear.

The son continues. He turns naturally to address the three defendants at a side table. They are the "representatives of Moscow," officers of the law departments of Moscow's government. Now the judge is checking her manicure.

"Why did you not at least allow medical students into the building if there was a shortage of doctors? Or on to the buses taking the hostages to the hospital? They could have looked after our casualties on the way there. People were choking and dying because they were lying on their backs."

"Khramtsov!" Gorbacheva interrupts tetchily, noticing who the plaintiff is addressing. "Who are you looking at? You must address your remarks to me."

"Fine." Alexander turns his eyes back to the judge's bench. "They were choking on the buses. Choking!"

He is crying. Who could remain unmoved?

Sitting immediately behind the witness stand, Valentina Khramtsova, his widowed mother, is also weeping. She is dressed completely in black. Gorbacheva cannot fail to see her. Next to her is Olga Milovidova, her face hidden in a handkerchief, her shoulders like two sharp humps, but nevertheless holding back her tears in order not to disturb the court. All the plaintiffs know they must not anger the judge, since she could simply have the court cleared and they would have to stand outside for several trying hours. Olga is in the seventh month of pregnancy. Her fourteen-year-old daughter, Nina, died in the audience at *Nord-Ost.* Olga had bought the ticket for her. "Why do you keep trying to humiliate us?" shouts Tatyana Karpova, the late Alexander Karpov's mother, wife of Sergey. "How have we deserved that?" Danila Chernetsov, a Moscow student asphyxiated by the gas, was twenty-one years old and earning a little money in the evenings at *Nord-Ost* as an usher. His mother, Zoya Chernetsova, gets up and walks out of the courtroom. Outside the door she can be heard wailing. "I was looking forward to grandchildren," she cries. Her son's pregnant young widow had a miscarriage nine days after his funeral. "And now I have a court case where I'm insulted to my face."

There is such a lack of decent legal tradition in this land of ours. We all know Judge Gorbacheva's situation. Those who employ her consider that they, rather than we taxpayers, are paying her salary. They could remove her and the privileges of her office, which do make life easier for her than for an ordinary citizen on a low income. Let us suppose there is nothing she can do other than reject every one of the unfortunate victims' demands.

But why does she have to be so rude? What need is there for all this derision, all these insults? Does she just enjoy kicking those who are already down? Who is Judge Gorbacheva, anyway, standing so zealously in defense of the interests of Moscow's municipal exchequer?

Do you think anyone wrote in these terms in the state-controlled press or spoke in this way about the *Nord-Ost* hearings on state-

controlled television? Some hope! Day after day the media informed citizens that the government supported Judge Gorbacheva in her defense
of the interests of the state, which take priority over personal needs.

Such is our new Russian ideology, Putin's ideology. And there is no
getting away from the truth that it was first tried out in Chechnya. It
was precisely at the time of Putin's ascent to the Kremlin throne, amid
the din of the bombing at the beginning of the second Chechen war,
that Russian society made a tragic, immoral error because of its traditional unwillingness to think clearly. Our society ignored what was really going on in Chechnya, the fact that the bombing was not of
terrorists' camps but of cities and villages, and that hundreds of innocent people were being killed. It was then that most people living in
Chechnya felt, as they still feel, the diabolical hopelessness of their
situation—when, taking away their children, fathers, and brothers to
who knows where and for who knows why, the military and civilian
authorities said baldly (and still say), "Stop whining. Just accept that
this is what the higher interests of the war on terrorism require."

For three years Russian society kept quiet. The vast majority of
citizens tacitly condoned the behavior in Chechnya and ignored
those who predicted that it would come back to haunt them: a government that has acted like this in one part of the country would not
stop there.

The *Nord-Ost* victims and the families of those who died are being
abused in exactly the same way. "Stop whining," they are told. "This
had to be done. Society's interests come before personal interests."

Well, perhaps the government is behaving a little better, some
50,000 to 100,000 rubles better, toward them, since this time it has
managed, at least, to pay for the funerals.

What about the reaction of the Russian people? Not much sympathy has been forthcoming—sympathy as a politically significant im-
pulse that the government could not afford to ignore. Quite the
opposite, in fact. A depraved society wants comfort and peace and
quiet, and doesn't mind if the cost is other people's lives. Citizens run

away from the *Nord-Ost* tragedy and would rather believe the state's brainwashing machine than face the reality.

One hour after Alexander Khramtsov's damning speech, Judge Gorbacheva rattled off her verdict, finding in favor of the government of Moscow. The courtroom emptied, leaving behind only the victors: Yuri Bulgakov, a lawyer in the city's Revenue Department, and Andrey Rastorguev and Marat Gafurov, advisers in the legal department of the metropolitan authority.

"Well, are you celebrating?" I couldn't help asking.

"No," all three replied sadly. "We are human, after all. We can see what is going on. It is a disgrace that our state is treating these people in this way."

"Well, why don't you stop doing this disgraceful work?"

They were silent. We went out into the dark Moscow evening, some to warm homes filled with the laughter of their families, others to echoing flats left empty forever on October 23. The last to leave was a stooping, gray-haired man with expressive eyes. Throughout the hearing he had sat with quiet dignity in the corner.

"What is your name?" I called after him.

"Tukai Khaziev."

"Were you a hostage yourself?"

"No. My son died there."

"Can we meet?"

Tukai Khaziev reluctantly gave me his telephone number.

"I don't know what my wife will make of this. You must understand, it is not something she has any wish to talk about. But you may call in a week's time. I will talk to her."

The Khazievs, a Moscow family, have been through a specifically Russian hell. They have not only lost their twenty-seven-year-old son, Timur, a musician in the orchestra of *Nord-Ost*. They have been on the receiving end of the very ideology that is now so widespread and that, without exaggeration, was Timur's real killer.

"Would it have been so difficult for Putin to find at least some sort of a compromise with the Chechens, the terrorists?" Tukai Khaziev keeps repeating. "Who needed that 'indomitability' of his? Not us, that's for sure. . . ."

Tukai is the one person in this house on Volgograd Prospekt in Moscow who can talk about the subject without crying. His wife, Roza; Tanya, Timur's young widow; and the eighty-seven-year-old grandmother cannot control their grief. Timur's three-year-old daughter, fair-haired Sonechka, ricochets around the grown-ups. Her daddy was not there to celebrate her third birthday because it came after *Nord-Ost*.

They set the table, and Sonechka climbs up on a chair. She takes the biggest cup. "This is for Daddy. It's Daddy's cup. You mustn't use it!" she warns in tones that brook no contradiction. Grandmother Roza has explained to her that Daddy is in heaven now, just like Roza's own daddy, and that he can't come back anymore. But the small girl cannot see why he can't come back when she, his beloved Sonechka, so much wants him to.

"I believed in the state," Tukai Khaziev says. "Almost to the very end of the siege I believed in it. I thought the intelligence services would think of something, would come to an agreement, make some promises, fudge some issues and everything would work out. What I really did not expect was that they would do as Zhirinovsky suggested a day before the assault. I remember him saying that what we should do was gas everybody. Everybody would sleep for a couple of hours; then they would wake up and just walk away. Only they didn't wake up, and they didn't just walk away."

All of Timur Khaziev's life revolved around music and the House of Culture at No. 1 Dubrovskaya Street. From childhood he had attended the Lyre Music Studio there, and there he had signed up for the orchestra of *Nord-Ost*, which rented the premises of the House of Culture. And there he had died.

His parents, Tukai and Roza, used to have a room in a communal apartment near the House of Culture, and both their sons, Eldar, the eldest, and Timur, learned to play the accordion there. The teachers recommended that Timur continue. He was a talented boy, and when, after tenth grade, it was time for him to choose a career, he completed the examination course for percussion instruments in a single year with help only from his accordion teacher. He entered a wind-instrument college, which he finished in three years instead of four, and then the prestigious Gnesins Academy of Music, as he had long dreamed of doing.

His teacher called him Rafinad, "Sugar Lump," after the refined way he held the drumsticks. He was a subtle, intelligent, even suave percussionist.

Timur combined his studies at the Gnesins Academy with playing in wind and symphony orchestras of the Ministry of Defense. He toured Norway with a military orchestra, and a tour of Spain had beckoned after October 23.

"There, I had his uniform all ready, and his morning dress for concerts," Roza says firmly, in order not to be overcome by emotion as she opens the cupboard. "They just won't come and take it back, the Ministry of Defense."

Sonechka, whizzing past us, promptly grabs the cap with its shiny rosette, plonks it on her head and gallops around the room: "Daddy's hat! Daddy's hat!" Tanya breaks down and leaves the room.

When he graduated from the Gnesins Academy, Timur was invited to play in the *Nord-Ost* orchestra. This was a third job, but he took it on. He was married, and had a growing daughter. Tanya, who had graduated from the Academy of Eurhythmic Art and was an actress and producer, was working as a kindergarten teacher at a low salary.

It is unfashionable to believe in mysticism or presentiments, but a month before the siege at the theater, Timur had trouble sleeping. "I would wake up toward morning," Tanya tells me, "and he would be sitting up. I would ask him what he was doing, ask him to come back to bed, but he would say, 'Something is making me feel anxious.'"

His family supposed that Timur was just very tired. His day began

early, when he drove Sonechka and Tanya to the kindergarten. From
there he immediately went to his parents' apartment, where he kept his
instruments, to practice. Recently he had been working on improving
his left hand and was pleased when he got his technique sorted out. In
another couple of years, he told Tanya, he would be a really good percussionist. When he had finished practicing, he would jump into the car
and drive off to rehearsals with the military orchestra. From there he
would give his wife and daughter a lift home from the kindergarten and
go on to the *Nord-Ost* performance. He would get home close to midnight, and the cycle started again early the next morning. He seemed to
be in a great hurry to live his life. Why? He was only twenty-seven, after all. Nobody has an answer to that question, or knows why, on October 23, Timur was even at the performance of *Nord-Ost*.

"It was a Wednesday," Tanya tells me. "We had a rule that Wednesday was our free evening for being together as a family. A different
percussionist played on Wednesdays, but on this particular day he
asked Timur to swap because his girlfriend was insisting that he spend
the evening with her. That girl saved her boyfriend's life, but at the
cost of the life of my husband. He was never any good at saying no,
and because of that he died."

"You don't want the belongings of someone close to you just left lying around, do you?" Roza asks rhetorically. "So we went there [to the
theater]. Of course there was no sign of his mobile phone. Timur had
just started having a bit of money and had bought one. No sign of any
of his new clothes, either."

In the theater Roza had broken down when she saw his belongings.
The only items returned to Timur's parents were his old jacket, with
an army bootprint on the back, and his shirt. That was it.

We seem to have become very primitive in the last few years, even
rather ignoble. The change in moral values is increasingly noticeable
as the war in the Caucasus continues and broken taboos increasingly
become familiar facts of life. Killing? Happens every day. Robbery?
What of it? Looting? Perfectly legal in a war. It is not only the courts

that fail to condemn crimes, but society as well. What was regarded in the past with repugnance is now simply accepted.

In those terrible October days when the hostages were seized, the whole country seemed to have united in a surge of concern, wondering how to help, praying, hoping, and waiting. But there was nothing we could do. The intelligence services let no one near, assuring us that they had everything under control. How can we reconcile ourselves to the fact that among the few allowed special access were people who took the opportunity to do a bit of looting? Whatever was nice and new. Whatever fit. There is no other explanation for the disappearance of the hostages' clothing and possessions. The families of those who died can never be free of what they felt in those days. Even if the government suddenly decided to give them all a million dollars in compensation, those memories would still remain.

Judging by the shirt that was returned, Timur had been lying outside in the open. Roza couldn't wash our famous Moscow street muck out of it, a mixture of gasoline and oil.

When Timur went to work for the last time, he had in his pockets some ten different forms of ID with his photographs, testifying to the fact that he was a musician in the *Nord-Ost* orchestra and in the orchestra of the Ministry of Defense. There were his passport, his driver's license, and an address book with the telephone numbers of his friends and relatives.

Nevertheless, on October 28 his body was returned to his family with a tag attached to the wrist by a rubber band that read: "No. 2551 Khamiev Unknown."

"How could that happen?" Roza Abdulovna asks.

"Why 'Khamiev' instead of 'Khaziev'?" In Russian the word has an insulting ring to it: to call someone a *kham* is to call him a rat. "And even if they were going to give his name as 'Khamiev,' what was the meaning of 'Unknown'? And why did we have to go to such lengths to find him? They had only to open his address book, call any number in it, and ask the person who answered if they knew Timur Khaziev. They would immediately have been given our telephone number."

Timur's mother is talking about the day after the assault, the long day of October 26, which the Khaziev family will never forget.

"From the morning until four in the afternoon there was no mention of his name anywhere, not in any of the lists of hostages given out by the authorities," Tukai Khaziev relates. "When we had already done the rounds of all the mortuaries and hospitals, it suddenly appeared. There was a short list, just some twenty people, and Timur was on it. It said there that he was alive and in No. 7 Hospital. I phoned my wife and told her that everything was fine. We wept with joy. Our friends congratulated us. Tanya and I went around to the hospital as fast as we could."

At the gate, however, a posted sentry would not let anyone in. He said the prosecutor's office had forbidden it. Tanya began to cry, and the guard, taking pity, whispered to Tukai that it was bad news that "your one" was in there. It meant there was no hope. Tanya heard and started begging to be let inside. The guard opened the gate.

The hospital corridors appeared to be deserted until a police officer came at them with an assault rifle cradled against his fat belly.

"You know, he was just someone without a heart. No word of warning. No 'Brace yourself for bad news.' He just said, straight in my face, 'He's dead. Go away.' Of course I was in hysterics for twenty minutes, and that brought some doctors running. 'Who let you in here?' they demanded."

When Tanya recovered her composure a bit and asked to be allowed to see Timur's body before the autopsy, she was refused. She begged and begged, but the policeman just said, "Go and ask Putin for permission." Three officials from the prosecutor's office turned up. "Why are you in such a rush?" they asked. "You'll have time to nail down his coffin lid." Then they said, "Surname? Khaziev? A Chechen?"

That turned out to have been Timur Khaziev's undoing. Once the forces of law and order had taken his Tatar surname to be Chechen, everything had automatically followed in accordance with the prevailing ideology.

The family is now convinced that Timur died because, having been taken for a Chechen, he was deliberately denied medical treatment. When the men of the Khaziev family collected his body from the mortuary, written on his chest, in large letters, was "9:30," the time of his death in No. 7 Hospital. There were no marks on his body from a IV drip feed, an injection, or the use of a ventilator. Instructions had been issued from above to wipe out all the Chechens, and Timur, mistaken for one, was not entitled to resuscitation. For four hours and more after the assault, he just lay there dying. Timur was killed by ideology.

"We have no rights in our own country. We are just human trash. That is why all this happened to my Timurka" are Tanya's parting words to me.

While Tanya and Tukai were standing outside the hospital gate on October 26, about twenty people tried to enter the flat where the young Khazievs lived, some in uniform and some in plainclothes. Their neighbor quickly intervened and just managed to head them off. Tanya was told they had been acting on a tip-off from the hospital that a Chechen lived there.

What should the Khaziev family do now? Accept the humiliations and keep their heads down?

"When we spoke as plaintiffs about all this in the Tverskoy court," Tukai recalls, "Gorbacheva pretended not to understand what we were talking about. She was certain that everybody, without exception, had received medical attention."

Naturally, the Khazievs have a death certificate, but it contains no mention of the cause of death. The space has been left blank. No hint that there had ever been a terrorist act. In addition to the state ideology that killed him, Timur and his family have, working against them, a system that avoids providing documentary evidence.

"I imagine you asked the officials at the prosecutor's office why the cause of death had been left blank."

"Of course, on October 28. They assured us this was simply a formality so that we could get on with preparations for the funeral. After the results of the postmortem were known, they said, they would be sure to make the appropriate entry."

"Did they?"

"No, of course not."

This is an illuminating answer. Nobody expects fair dealings from the government. The authorities are, at best, a source of trouble, despite all their popularity ratings, which are officially so high. Recently the president's office set up a special department to engineer a "correct" perception of the country and the president abroad. The idea is to reduce the spread of negative information, to make Russia look better in the eyes of foreigners. It would be even better, of course, if the government set up another special department to improve the image of the country and the president in the eyes of its own citizens.

"Could Putin really not have backed down? Could he not just have said, 'I am bringing this war to an end'? Our loved ones would still be alive today," Tukai keeps repeating. "All I want to know is, who is responsible for our tragedy? No more than that."

TANYA RECENTLY BOUGHT Kiryusha and Frosya, a tortoise and a cat, so as to have some company to come home to. Sonechka is still too little to understand what happened to her daddy, but she doesn't like coming back after kindergarten to a home without him. Recently the family was phoned by the producers of the revived *Nord-Ost* musical and offered free tickets. The family declined but were told that anytime . . . We really seem to have lost all sense of propriety.

SIRAZHDI, YAKHA, AND THEIR FRIENDS

Only a madman could envy the Chechens who live in Russia now. In years gone by, their situation was unenviable, but since the *Nord-Ost* siege, the machinery of racially based state retribution has been in overdrive. Racial attacks and purges supervised by the police have become commonplace. In a single moment people's lives are ruined, they lose their home, their jobs, any sort of social support, and for just one reason: they are Chechens. Their lives in Moscow and many other cities are intolerable: drugs are slipped into their pockets, cartridges are pressed into their hands, and they are promptly sentenced to several years in prison. They have been quite openly made into pariahs and find themselves at a dead end, with no chance of escape. It is a way of life that leaves nobody unscathed, regardless of age.

"When they started speaking in Chechen and interrupted the second act, I realized that things were serious, and that they were going to get worse. I somehow saw that very clearly straight away." Yakha Neserhaeva is a forty-three-year-old Muscovite, an economist by profession. She is a Chechen born in Grozny, but she moved to the capital long ago. On October 23 she went to see *Nord-Ost*. Her friend Galya, whom she has known for many years, is from the northern Russian town of Ukhta. She bought tickets for the thirteenth row of the stalls, and, although Yakha was not that keen on musicals, Galya begged her to come along.

"Did you tell them you were a Chechen?"

"No. I was frightened. I did not know whether it was better to tell them or not. They might have shot me for being a Chechen at a musical."

Yakha did not see the gas, although many of the hostages noticed white clouds of something in the air. From where she was sitting, she just heard people shouting, "They've released gas!" and a few seconds later, she blacked out.

She came to in No. 13 Hospital, to which many victims were taken, including Irina Fadeeva, mother of Yaroslav, the boy who was shot. Feeling sick, Yakha didn't have much idea of what was going on. Soon an investigator appeared.

"He asked my name, surname, where I live, where I was born, and what I was doing at *Nord-Ost*. Then two women came, took my fingerprints and took my clothing away for forensic examination. The investigator came back in the evening and said, 'I have bad news for you.' The first thing I thought was that the friend I had gone to the musical with had died, but he said, 'You are being arrested as an accomplice of the terrorists.' It was a shock, but I got up and walked after the investigator in hospital slippers and a dressing gown. I was first taken for two days to No. 20 Hospital [a special-purpose, secure hospital], where nobody asked me anything or gave me any treatment. In fact, I received no treatment at any time. At the end of the second day, the investigator came again. I was photographed, and they recorded a sample of my voice. A few minutes later, they brought me a coat and a pair of men's half-boots, put me in handcuffs, and said, 'You need treatment in a different hospital.' They put me in a police car, took me to the prosecutor's office for ten minutes or so, and then to the Marino Prison [a women's isolation holding facility in Moscow]. So there I was, with boots three sizes too big for me on my bare feet, in a dirty man's overcoat, unwashed and unkempt for a week. They took me to a cell, and all the woman supervisor said was, 'Well now, you plague virus . . .' "

"Did they question you frequently while you were in solitary confinement?"

"I wasn't questioned at all. I just sat there and asked the wardress for a meeting with the investigator."

Yakha speaks quietly, slowly, without emotion. She seems barely to be present. Her face is that of a dead person, her eyes dilated, her gaze fixed, her muscles immobile. The photograph in her passport seems to show someone else; the face is that of a proud and beautiful woman.

Yakha does sometimes attempt a smile, but it is as if in the two weeks she spent in prison her muscles forgot how to respond. She thought she was done for and that nothing could save her. The situation was as bad as it could be. The police officers who transferred her from No. 20 Hospital, the only people who had had anything to tell her about her future, had informed her that she would "answer for all of them," since all the other terrorists had been exterminated and she was the only one left.

As normally happens in musicals, however, Yakha's story had a happy ending.

Her friends rallied around and swiftly engaged a lawyer who managed by a miracle to break through the seemingly impenetrable wall surrounding Yakha Neserhaeva. After ten days she was released from prison. Surprisingly, in these racist times, the investigators of the prosecutor's office who were working on the team investigating the *Nord-Ost* incident, finding nothing that remotely incriminated Yakha, simply did the decent thing. They did not set about trying to frame her, or tailor the charge to the individual, plant evidence, abuse or mock her. They made no attempt to take revenge on a Chechen woman purely because she was Chechen. Nowadays that is quite something.

They went even further. When they advised Yakha that she was free to go, they apologized and had her driven home. For that, she has senior investigator and lawyer first class V. Prikhozhikh to thank. She also has the officials of the Bogorodskoe Department of Internal Affairs to thank. They issued Yakha's elder sister Malika, who had rushed from Grozny to Moscow to help Yakha get back on her feet, a special permit to remain in the capital because a relative was in need of constant care. They issued the permit in the knowledge that without it, any Chechen in Moscow today cannot go out of the front door without being arrested immediately.

AELITA SHIDAEVA, THIRTY-ONE, is a Chechen, too. Since the beginning of the present war, she has been living with her parents and daughter, Hadizhat, in Moscow. Aelita was arrested where she worked, in a café by the Mariino underground station. She tells me her story in a calm and restrained manner, without tears or hysteria, smiling politely. You might suppose she had experienced nothing out of the ordinary, if you didn't know that when she was finally released from the Mariino Park police station after seven hours of relentless interrogation, she promptly collapsed.

"It was all pretty weird. First there was this one policeman having his dinner in our café. Nothing unusual, they often eat with us. The police station is one hundred meters from our front door. I've never hidden from them that I am a Chechen who fled Grozny to get away from the war. Anyway, this policeman finished his meal and went out, and suddenly the rest of them came rushing in. About fifteen of them, headed by our local policeman, Vasiliev. He knows me very well, too. They stood us all up against the wall, searched us, and took me in."

"And what questions did they ask you?"

" 'What were my relations with the terrorists?' I said to them, 'You all saw me yourselves. I've been right in front of you for twelve hours every day, from eleven in the morning until eleven at night.' "

"What did they reply?"

" 'Which of the terrorists did you go to a restaurant with?' I have never even been to a restaurant in Moscow. It isn't something I do. They said if I did not confess to links with the terrorists, they would plant drugs or weapons on me. They took turns interrogating me. Some suspicious-looking men in uniform were passing by and staring at me. The investigator said that if I did not confess to links with the terrorists, he would give me to these guys and they would 'eat me alive.' He said they were just waiting to get at me because they could make anyone talk."

At the police station Aelita was informed that she had been dismissed from her job. The prosecutor said that the café owner had been ordered to fire her if he didn't want his business to be closed down. The authorities released Aelita only because her mother, Makka, a Russian-language teacher, was a born defender of civil rights. According to the police officers at the Mariino Park station, she "trumpeted the case all over Moscow." Makka called the Echo of Moscow radio station, mobilized the lawyer Abdullah Hamzaev and many others, and, despite police insistence that Aelita was not at the station, eventually pressured the officers into releasing her.

Aelita is no longer in shock. She fully understands the situation and says she just wants to get out of Moscow.

"Back to Chechnya?"

"No, abroad."

Makka opposes the idea. She is not against her daughter taking her granddaughter elsewhere: Hadizhat needs to go to school, in spite of what Movsar Baraev and his supporters did at the Dubrovka theater and in spite of the special interest the Moscow police take in young Chechen girls. Makka herself is reluctant to leave. She cannot imagine living anywhere else than Russia, but neither can she imagine what it is that Russia wants from Aelita, from herself, and from Hadizhat. One is an adult who spent the greater part of her life in the Soviet Union. Another is a young woman who has never lived a full life, who has known only the urgency of fleeing from one place to another, from one war to the next. The third is a young girl who is attentively watching and listening to the world around her and saying nothing, for the time being.

Hadizhat's teacher has just phoned Aelita, painfully embarrassed, to say she must bring in a form confirming her status as a single mother. Who issues such forms? Her other documents are perfectly in order, but if she doesn't produce this form, then she, the teacher, "just does not know what to do." They want to expel Hadizhat. After October 26, 2002, there is no place in the fifth grade of No. 931 School, Moscow, for a Chechen girl brought here by her family to study.

"I can't even work out," Aelita says, "whether my being a single mother is counted in favor of Hadizhat or against her. Who can you trust?"[12]

ABUBAKAR BAKRIEV ONCE held a modest technical position in one of the big Moscow banks. Now, however, he is free of any such ties. It all happened very simply and undramatically. Abubakar was called in by the company's deputy chairman for security, who said, "Don't take this the wrong way, but we are going to have problems because of you. Write a voluntary letter of resignation."

At first, Abubakar could not believe his ears, but then the deputy chairman added that "they" wanted him to backdate the letter—for example, to October 16—so that the resignation would look quite proper and nobody could accuse the bank of sacking him as part of an anti-Chechen cull after the *Nord-Ost* incident.

So there we have it: the executioners put you to death (and for any Chechen to be sacked today is the end: there is no way he or she is going to find another job), but they do hope you'll understand their predicament. It is a peculiarity of our times that a murderer approaches the victim and says straight out, "I am going to kill you, not because I am a bad person but because I am being compelled to do so. But I would ask you to make it look as if you haven't been murdered."

On that day, a Dagestani employee was "voluntarily fired" from the same bank, his "personal decision," too, being backdated. He occupied a modest position but was also ethnically cleansed, to avoid any further unwelcome questions regarding people of Caucasian origin working at the bank.

"The bank has been cleansed," Abubakar says. "The security services can sleep at night. I am fifty-four. I don't know where to go. The police have to come to my home three times to see how I live with my three children. You are turning us into enemies. You need to understand that we have no alternative now but to demand independence, because we do need a land, somewhere we can live in peace. Give us any place on earth you choose, and we will go and live there."

ISITA CHIRGIZOVA AND Natasha Umatgarieva are Chechen women who live in a temporary center for refugees in the village of Serebryaniki, in Tver Province. We met in No. 14 Police Station in Moscow. Isita was wiping off the ink after being fingerprinted. Natasha was crying inconsolably. They had just been released, a miracle in today's climate. The police had taken pity on them.

On the morning of November 13, 2002, the women were subjected to typical treatment. They had come to Moscow on an early train to collect aid from one of the civil-rights organizations. They were arrested at the station, a couple of meters from the organization's entrance, because Natasha was limping. Because she has an open sore on her leg from diabetes, she was suspected of being a wounded fighter. Isita is in the seventh month of pregnancy; she has an evident bulge under her jacket, just where suicide bombers wear their grenade belts. This, at least, is how Major Lyubeznov, who was on duty at No. 14 Police Station, explained the reason for their arrest. *Lyubeznyi* means "amiable" in Russian, but the major proved far from amiable. Indeed, to safeguard Russia from the terrorist threat, he felt obliged to personally grope Isita's Chechen bulge, to ensure that it was caused by pregnancy.

The story of Isita and Natasha ended well. The police officers just gave the women some bluster to the effect of, "If you kill us, we'll kill you." Major Lyubeznov didn't have time to disgrace himself any further, and, in addition, I was able to be of some assistance. First, I managed to intercept the women in the police station before they were carted off to the isolation and interrogation unit. Second, I persuaded Vladimir Mashkin, the superintendent of No. 14 Police Station (and he was perfectly open to persuasion) that people sometimes come to collect humanitarian aid just because they are poor, having no opportunity to get a job and no home of their own.

ZARA WORKED AS a vegetable seller by the underground station. The owner of the little market came to her and said, "Don't come to work here tomorrow, because you are Chechen." Zara provides the only support for a family consisting of three children and her husband, who has tuberculosis. What need is there for the police to involve themselves in a situation like this one?

ASLAN KURBANOV SPENT the first Chechen war in a tented refugee camp in Ingushetia. In the summer he left to enter a college in Saratov, then moved to Moscow to live with his aunt, Zura Movsarova, a postgraduate student at the Moscow Aviation Technical Institute. He found a job and was officially registered as having the right to live in the capital.

On October 28, 2002, CID officers from No. 172 Police District (Brateevo) came to his home. The day before, Zura had been fingerprinted at the request of the local police, so when the CID authorities said they wanted Aslan to come with them only to have his fingerprints taken, nobody suspected anything. Aslan put on his coat and went off in the police car.

Three hours later, Zura became anxious. Her nephew still had not returned, so she went to the police station herself. There she was informed that Aslan had been arrested for possession of drugs. What sort of story was that? He had gotten up, put his coat on, put some drugs in his pocket, and gone to give himself up to the police? Aslan managed to shout to Zura that he had been taken to a room, some cannabis had been produced from under the table, and he had been told, "This must be yours. We are not going to give Chechens an inch. We're going to shake all of you up like this."

Aslan does not even smoke cigarettes. On October 30 he spent his twenty-second birthday in the Matrosskaya Tishina Prison.

ON THE MORNING of October 25, 2002, police officers burst into the Moscow apartment of the Chechen Gelagoev family. Alihan, the owner of the flat, was handcuffed and taken away. His wife, Marek, rushed for help to the Rostokino police station but was told that no officers had gone out from there. She called Radio Liberty, which reported Alihan Gelagoev's abduction, and by evening he was released. She had pressed the right buttons.

Alihan told me that in the car the police had put a sack over his head and beaten him for a long time as they were going to Petrovka, the street where the Moscow Central Police Department is located. They shouted, "You hate us and we hate you. You kill us and we will kill you."

When they arrived at Petrovka, however, they stopped beating him and tried for many hours to persuade him to sign a confession saying that he was the ideological mastermind behind the terrorist attack on *Nord-Ost.* This is the sort of thing that used to happen in the Stalin years. The confession had even been written in advance, as was the practice in the earlier period. All Alihan had to do was sign at the bottom.

He refused, but to obtain his freedom he had no option but to sign a statement to the effect that he had come voluntarily to the Central Police Department and had no complaints to make against its officers.

Racism? Yes. Appalling behavior? Of course. It is also a travesty of a war against terrorism. I do not believe a single statistic produced by the police authorities on the progress of the antiterrorist "Operation Whirlwind," telling the world how many "terrorists' accomplices" they have caught. The figures are bogus. The police are bogus officers churning out bogus reports based on bogus investigations.

In the meantime, where are the terrorists? What are they up to? Who knows? The police have no time to think about that. Putin is presiding over a return to the Soviet methods of bogus activity in place of real work.

THE POLICE INTERROGATORS were very reassuring, thirty-six-year-old Zelimhan Nasaev tells me. "Don't worry," they said, "you'll get three or four years and then you'll be out. They may give you a suspended sentence. Just sign here. Make it easy on yourself."

Zelimhan has been living in Moscow for many years. His family, following his elder sister Inna, moved here to escape the second Chechen war.

"Were you beaten at the police station?"

"Of course. They woke me up at three in the morning and said, 'Time for the pressure.' They beat me through a hard surface [evidently a technique to leave no external sign of injury] on the kidneys and liver, to make me sign a confession, but I wouldn't. I said, 'Pressure me, then. Even if you shoot me, I'm not going to let you pin anything on me.' They kept saying, 'What's a Chechen like you doing here? Your country is Chechnya. Go back there and get on with your war.' I told them, 'My country is Russia, and I am in my own capital city.' They got very angry about that. To make me lose control of myself, one of the policemen said, 'Well, I've just come from fucking your mother.' "

If only that agent in the Nizhegorodsky police station had known whose mother he was claiming to have raped, whom he was beating up and trying to coerce into admitting to a crime he never committed, in order to boost the policeman's rating in the post–*Nord-Ost* campaign to "crack down on Chechen criminals in Moscow"! But perhaps it's just as well he didn't know.

Roza Nasaeva is the granddaughter, and Zelimhan the great-grandson, of the legendary Russian beauty Maria-Mariam of the Romanov family, a relative of Emperor Nicholas II who fell passionately in love with Vakhu, a Chechen officer of the czarist army. She eloped with him to the Caucasus, converted to Islam, took the name Mariam, bore Vakhu five children, was deported with him to Kazakhstan and, after his death there, returned to Chechnya. She died there in the 1960s, regarded almost as a Chechen saint. This lovely story of Russo-Chechen friendship and love, known throughout the Caucasus, is of little help at the moment, however, because nothing could save Zelimhan from the Moscow police. Even if he had the blood of ten emperors flowing in his veins, they would treat Zelimhan exactly as they treat any other Chechen.

There are parts of Moscow you really do not want to go to, grim places behind factories, within industrial zones, or beneath high-voltage electricity lines, and they are where you will find the Chechens who are still trying to survive in the capital city. Frezer Road is one such location, a dour strip of asphalt leading from Ryazan Prospekt out past barely habitable five-story brick buildings to industrial slums very remote from the life of the metropolis.

Actually, they weren't ever intended for human habitation. Officially, they are still the workshops of a milling factory that ceased to exist long ago, a victim of perestroika. Its workers departed, and today the factory bosses make a living by renting out the derelict workshops and other premises. In one such dirty, looted, former factory building, the first Chechen refugees appeared, in 1997. They had fled the criminal anarchy that reigned between the first and the second Chechen wars and were mainly members of families opposed to the Chechens Maskhadov and Basaev. The directors of the milling factory allowed the refugees to refurbish the workshops, convert them into living accommodations, and then pay tribute to the bosses.

The Chechens live there to this day, the Nasaevs among them, one of twenty-six families. The local police know them all perfectly well. Nobody is on the run or in hiding because nobody has any wish to do so, or indeed anywhere to run to.

When the *Nord-Ost* hostage taking occurred, the police from the Nizhegorodsky station headed straight here, explaining that they had orders to arrest a quota of fifteen Chechens "in every precinct." All the men of the twenty-six families were arrested and taken away in buses for fingerprinting.

It was Zelimhan Nasaev-Romanov's bad luck that he wasn't at home at the time. He had gone to deliver a batch of the pens the family assembles at home and to collect the components for the next assignment.

The police soon came back to the industrial shack where the imperial family's descendant lives. They needed his fingerprints, they said, and Roza let him go without a fuss. The parents began to worry only several hours later, when their son had not returned. Finally his mother and father set off to the police station, where they were told, in typically inane fashion, "Your son had a grenade and a fuse in his pocket. We have arrested him."

"I shouted, 'You have no right to do this! You took him away yourselves. He left the house with you and there was nothing in his pockets. There were plenty of witnesses,'" Roza tells me. "The policeman just said, 'Here Chechens don't count as witnesses.' I was so offended. Are we no longer citizens, then?"

When Zelimhan's mother returned to the police station the next morning, they told her, "Your son is also dealing in marijuana. You can't help him."

"We got there and they took me to an office," Zelimhan tells me. "They said, 'You are dealing in heroin.' The more senior officer was holding a small packet in his hand and announced, 'This is yours now.' I was handcuffed. They put the packet into my pocket. I began to protest. Then they said, 'All right, then, we'll add a fuse from a "lemon."' I saw the senior policeman was already wiping a fuse with a rag to remove other people's fingerprints. He shoved it in my hand and made a note. I again shouted, 'You have no right to do this!' And they told me, 'We have our orders. We have every right, and if you aren't a good boy and don't agree to help us by admitting to the crime, your relatives will follow you. We are going back to your house now to search, and we're going to find another part of the same grenade. Sign the confession.' "

Zelimhan refused to sign anything. The officers beat him and said they would continue to beat him until he couldn't be seen by any lawyer. They released him only because journalists and Aslambek Aslahanov, a deputy of the Duma, interceded. Now Zelimhan sits at home in his shack in a deep depression. He is afraid of every knock at the door. Depression is the characteristic mood of all the Chechens living among us. Not a single optimist is to be found among the young or the old. At least, I haven't found any. Everybody dreams of emigrating so as to have a chance to merge into the cosmopolitan background somewhere and never have to reveal one's nationality.

"There is an orgy of systematic police harassment of Chechens in Russia," claims Svetlana Gannushkina, director of the Citizens' Aid Committee for Assistance to Refugees and Displaced Persons. This is the organization to which people turn in their distress: Chechens whose relatives have been arrested, fingerprinted, and had drugs or cartridges planted on them; Chechens who have been fired from their jobs or threatened with deportation. (For heaven's sake, where do you deport Russian citizens to from the capital of Russia?) They come to Svetlana Gannushkina because there is nowhere else for them to go.

"The signal for this new wave of frenzied state racism, officially called Antiterrorist Operation Whirlwind," Svetlana continues, "was given immediately after the storming of the Dubrovka theater complex. Chechens are being expelled everywhere. The main problem is when they are fired from their jobs or driven out of their flats. This is a settling of scores with an entire group in retaliation for the acts of particular individuals. The main method used to discredit them as a nation is the false creation of criminal cases by planting drugs or cartridges. The policemen think they look cool when they mockingly ask their victims, 'Which would you like: drugs or a cartridge?' The only ones who get rescued are those with mothers like Makka Shidaeva. But what about all the others?"

And what sort of a nation are we, the Russian people?

One Chechen family has three daughters. One has passed the entrance exam and gotten into music school while the other two haven't. The parents have asked their successful daughter's teacher to give private piano lessons to her sisters. The teacher has refused. The head of the music school—where, of course, everyone knows everybody else's business—will not allow the teacher to continue, saying she has received orders to that effect from the Department of Culture. If the teacher continues to teach the Chechens, the security services will start taking an interest in her.

Playing fast and loose with people's livelihoods—and sometimes even their lives—is something that we, the Russian people, must own up to. The majority of us go along with the state's xenophobia and feel no need to protest. Why not? Official propaganda is highly effective, and the majority share Putin's belief that an entire people must shoulder collective responsibility for the crimes committed by a few.

The upshot, nevertheless, is that nobody yet knows, despite a war that has been going on for years, despite acts of terrorism, catastrophes, and torrents of refugees, what the authorities actually want from the Chechens. Do they want them to live within the Russian Federation or not?

IN CONCLUSION, HERE'S a straightforward story of ordinary people living in Russia and suffering from state-induced hysteria.

"Do you often get told off at school?"

"Yes." Sirazhdi sighs.

"And is there a good reason?"

"Yes." He sighs again.

"What do you do that is naughty?"

"I'm running down the corridor and somebody bashes into me and I always give them something back so they don't think they can hurt me, and then the teachers ask me, 'Did you hit them?' and I always tell the truth and say, 'Yes,' but the others don't and I get told off."

"Perhaps you shouldn't tell the truth either? You might not get into trouble."

"I can't." He sighs heavily. "I'm not a girl. If I did it, I say, 'I did it.'"

"You know, he tries to trip our children up so the little ones will hit their heads and die. . . ."

Great heavens above! This is not Sirazhdi talking about himself now; grown-ups are talking about him. Not about a special operations agent trained to destroy terrorists but about a seven-year-old Chechen boy named Sirazhdi Digaev. The words represent the publicly expressed view of a certain woman member of the parents' committee of Class 2b of No. 155 School, Moscow, which Sirazhdi attends.

"Well, do you know, my child complains, 'Sirazhdi never has anything, and I have and I have to lend it to him.'" This from another mother on the committee.

Why is this child complaining? Surely if the person next to you hasn't got something and you do, you should bloody well lend it to him.

"He's a nuisance to everyone. You have to understand that. My son told me he didn't write down his homework in the class because Sirazhdi was making so much noise that he couldn't hear the teacher. Sirazhdi is uncontrollable. Like all Chechens. You have to understand that," opines another mother.

The conversation continues as we sit in an empty classroom. The second-grade children have gone home, and now the parents' committee is discussing how to purge the school of a small Chechen so that "our children don't learn bad things from a possible future terrorist."

You think I must be making this up. Unfortunately I'm not.

"Don't get us wrong. Even though he is a Chechen, we don't discriminate between nationalities. No. We just want to protect our children. . . ."

From what? In November the parents' committee of Class 2b convened a meeting to warn Sirazhdi's mother and father that, if they did not take him in hand by the New Year, and unless, "in spite of being a Chechen," he started acting in accordance with the parents' committee's understanding of good behavior, they would demand that the head of No. 155 School expel him.

"Well, just tell me, why are they all piling into Moscow?" The real reason emerges when, one or two weeks later, a member of the parents' committee tries to explain why they adopted the resolution.

Well, why should "they" not come to Moscow? Are the inhabitants of the capital so special that being brought into proximity with other citizens of Russia might have a negative effect on their sensibilities?

"Why is it you say they are having a hard time?" another parent almost shrieks. "Who asks if we are having a hard time? What makes you think our children are having it any easier than he is?"

Why? Well, Sirazhdi was born in Chechnya in 1995. When his mother, Zulai, was pregnant, there was shelling and bombing all around her. She fled because when the first Chechen war started, she had no option. Today Zulai has complicated feelings when she sees that, even though they moved to Moscow in 1996 and her youngest son has been a Muscovite for most of his life, he is still terrified by fire-works and thunderstorms. He hides and cries but doesn't know why.

"Oh, so it's because they don't feel at home here yet," floats up the ratty voice of another member of the parents' committee. "They think they can impose their ways on us? No, thank you very much!"

The irritation has arisen because Alvi, Sirazhdi's father, came to the meeting, listening to everything the parents had to say to him, and then took the floor himself and dared to explain his problems—that in front of his children he had been cursed at by a policeman who marched into their room in his jackboots, and that he, a father, had been unable to do anything about it. The children had seen it all.

Alvi also told them that the main reason his family was in Moscow and not in Chechnya, in spite of how uncomfortable things were for them here, was to enable their children to go to school without a war taking place around them. Zulai was a math teacher, but she had to work at a market stall in Moscow, not something she was good at. They spent their evenings rolling chicken cutlets to sell in the morning. Everything he and Zulai did was for the sake of their children.

"Well, how about that! They're worming their way right into the center of Moscow! And they expect to be given a $500 apartment!" This was the reaction of the parents' committee to Alvi's appeal.

"I do not want my son or my daughter to be taught in the same class as someone like that." Such was the verdict Alvi and Zulai were given at that meeting.

"Who says we're wrong?" the members of the parents' commit-tee demand.

Well, nobody, of course.

It is worth remembering an incident that began in a similar way in the twentieth century but had a different ending. When the Fascists entered Denmark, the Jews were ordered to sew yellow stars on their clothing so they could be easily recognized. The Danes promptly sewed on yellow stars, both to save the Jews and to save themselves from turning into Fascists. Their king joined with them.

In Moscow today, the situation is quite the opposite. When the authorities struck at the Chechens who are our neighbors, we did not sew on yellow stars in solidarity with them. Instead, we are making sure that Sirazhdi never loses the sense of being a pariah.

At my request, he shows me his exercise book for the Russian language. His marks range from poor 2's to average 3's. Sirazhdi's handwriting is untidy, as Yelena Dmitrievna reminds him on almost every page. She is his class mistress and writes out her words of admonition in a trained calligraphic hand. She has been a teacher for thirty-five years, all of them in a primary school.

Yelena Dmitrievna did not support the parents' committee in its campaign to get rid of the Chechen boy, but neither did she take a stand. She did not categorically refuse to be part of the group's efforts to oust the youngster, although she could have done so, thereby halting in its tracks the Digaev family's persecution by the notorious Russian public opinion assault being waged by the committee.

Sirazhdi is spinning like a top. He really has no wish to show me his Russian exercise book. He does his best to divert my attention to his math book, where the situation is much happier. Sirazhdi is an ordinary boy who can't sit still. The main thing is that he very much wants to look good. Why should he be any different, a modest little boy keeping his head down as the parents' committee would like him to, to make him less of a Chechen?

Even his math book soon bores him. Promising to draw a "sword and a man," he goes off in a great rush. He does everything in a great rush. Soon he returns, bearing a pad with the outline of a strongman with powerful muscles from *The Lord of the Rings*, and a light saber represented by a smudge of yellow crayon.

"You know, we only wanted what was best for him," the parents of Class 2b now say, realizing that the story of their campaign against a small Chechen boy in the wake of the *Nord-Ost* hysteria has been taken up by journalists. "Only what was best . . ."

Is Sirazhdi going to believe in what they think is best for him? He does fight at playtime. In art lessons he throws paint at the wall. He trips up his classmates, too, and the more often he misbehaves, the more it is made clear to him that he is the odd one out in Class 2b.

THIS IS LIFE in Russia after *Nord-Ost*. The months have passed, and many Russians have gradually begun to understand that this appalling tragedy has its uses. In fact, it has come in handy for lots of people, for a lot of reasons.

First in line has been the president, with his folksy cynicism. He has taken to reaping international dividends from this horror and its deadly outcome. Nor has he balked at allowing other people's blood to be spilled for his PR purposes inside Russia.

At the bottom of the heap are the petty squabbles in a small school and the rank-and-file police officers who were only too glad to beef up their antiterrorist scores before the New Year in order to qualify for bonuses. The frantic anti-Chechen chauvinism of the days immediately following *Nord-Ost* have mellowed to a pragmatic, steady racism.

"Do we take up arms, then?" some of the Chechen men ask. You can hear them grinding their teeth in impotence. "I can't take this anymore," groan others. Their impatience and anger are a sign of weakness, of course, which does not suit them at all, especially since their children are watching. What should they do?[13]

AKAKY AKAKIEVICH PUTIN II

I have wondered a great deal about why I am so intolerant of Putin. What is it that makes me dislike him so much as to feel moved to write a book about him? I am not one of his political opponents or rivals, just a woman living in Russia. Quite simply, I am a forty-five-year-old Muscovite who observed the Soviet Union at its most disgraceful in the 1970s and 1980s. I really don't want to find myself back there again.

I am making a point of finishing the writing of this book on May 6, 2004. There has been no miraculous challenging of the results of the March 14 presidential election. The opposition has acquiesced. Accordingly, tomorrow sees the start of Putin II, the president reelected by an unbelievable majority of more than 70 percent. Even if we knock off 20 percent as window dressing (i.e., ballot rigging), he still received enough votes to secure the presidency.

In a few hours Putin, a typical lieutenant colonel of the Soviet KGB, a soul brother of Akaky Akakievich, downtrodden hero of Gogol's story "The Greatcoat," will ascend to the throne of Russia once again. His outlook is the narrow, provincial one his rank would suggest; he has the unprepossessing personality of a lieutenant colonel who never made it to colonel, the manner of a Soviet secret policeman who habitually snoops on his colleagues. And he is vindictive: not a single political opponent has been invited to the inauguration ceremony, nor a single political party that is in any way out of step.

Leonid Brezhnev was a distasteful figure; Yury Andropov was bloody, although at least he had a democratic veneer. Konstantin Chernenko was dumb, and Russians disliked Mikhail Gorbachev. At times, Boris Yeltsin had us crossing ourselves at the thought of where his doings might be leading us.

Here is their apotheosis. Tomorrow their bodyguard from Unit 25—the man in the security cordon when VIP motorcades drove by— Akaky Akakievich Putin will strut down the red carpet of the Kremlin throne room as if he really were the boss there. Around him the polished czarist gold will gleam, the servants will smile submissively, his comrades in arms, a choice selection from the lower ranks of the KGB who could have risen to important posts only under Putin, will swell with self-importance.

One can imagine Lenin strutting around like a nabob when he arrived in the vanquished Kremlin in 1918 after the revolution. The official Communist histories—we have no others—assure us that, in fact, his strutting was modest, but his modesty, you can just bet, was insolent. Look at humble little me! You thought I was a nobody, but now I've made it. I've broken Russia just as I intended to. I've forced her to vow allegiance to me.

Tomorrow a KGB snoop, who even in that capacity did not make much of an impression, will strut through the Kremlin just as Lenin did. He will have had his revenge.

Let us, however, run the reel backward a little.

Putin's victory had been widely predicted both in Russia and throughout the world, especially after the humiliation of such democratic, liberal opposition parties as the country possessed in the parliamentary elections of December 7, 2003. Accordingly, the March 14 result surprised few. We had international observers in, but everything was low key. Voting day itself was a contemporary remake of the authoritarian, bureaucratic, Soviet-style pantomime of "the people expressing its will," which many still remember only too well, myself included. In those days the procedure was that you went to the polling station and dropped your slip in the ballot box without caring whose names were on it because the result was a foregone conclusion.

How did people react this time? Did the Soviet parallel rouse anybody from inertia on March 14, 2004? No. Voters went obediently to the polling stations, dropped their papers into the ballot boxes, and shrugged: "What can we do about it?" Everyone is convinced that the Soviet Union has returned, and that it no longer matters what we think.

On March 14, I stood outside the polling station on my own Dolgoruky Street in Moscow. With the advent of Yeltsin, its name had been changed from Kalyaev Street. Kalyaev, a terrorist in czarist times, was later regarded as a revolutionary. It became Dolgoruky Street in honor of the prince who had his estate there in Kalyaev's time, before the Bolsheviks came.

I talked to people going in to vote and coming quickly out again after participating in the charade. They were apathetic, indifferent to the process of electing Putin for a second term. "It's what 'they' want us to do? Well, then. Big deal." That was the majority sentiment. A minority joked, "Perhaps now they'll name it Kalyaev Street again."

The return of the Soviet system with the consolidation of Putin's power is obvious.

It has to be said that this outcome has been made possible not only by our negligence, apathy, and weariness after too much revolutionary change. It has happened to choruses of encouragement from the West, primarily from Silvio Berlusconi, the Italian leader, who appears to have fallen in love with Putin. He is Putin's main European champion, but Putin also enjoys the support of Tony Blair, Gerhard

Schröder, and Jacques Chirac, and receives no discouragement from
the junior Bush across the Atlantic.

So nothing stood in the way of our KGB man's return to the
Kremlin, neither the West nor any serious opposition within Russia.
Throughout the so-called election campaign, from December 7, 2003,
until March 14, 2004, Putin openly derided the electorate.

The main feature of his contempt was his refusal to debate anything with anyone. He declined to expand on a single point of his own
policies in the last four years. His contempt extended not only to representatives of the opposition parties but to the very concept of an opposition. He made no promises about future policy and disdained
campaigning of any kind. Instead, as under the Soviet regime, he was
shown on television every day, receiving top-ranking officials in his
Kremlin office and dispensing his highly competent advice on how to
conduct whichever ministry or department they came from.

There was, of course, a certain amount of tittering among members of the public: he was behaving just like Stalin. Putin, too, was simultaneously "the friend of all children" and "the nation's first pig
farmer," "the best miner," the "comrade of all athletes," and the "leading filmmaker."

None of it went further than tittering, however. Any real emotion
drained away into the sand. There was no serious protest over the rejection of debates.

Meeting no resistance, Putin naturally became bolder. It is a mistake to suppose he takes no notice of anything, never reacts and only, as
we're encouraged to believe, forges ahead in pursuit of power.

He pays a lot of attention and takes account of what he sees. He
keeps a close eye on us, this nation he controls.

In this way he is behaving exactly like a member of Lenin's Cheka,
or secret police. The approach is entirely that of a KGB officer. First
there is the trial balloon of information released through a narrow cir-
cle of individuals. In today's Russia, that is the political elite of the
capital. The aim is to probe likely reaction to policies. If there is none,

or if it has the dynamism of a jellyfish, all is well. Putin can push his policy forward, spread his ideas or act as he sees fit without having to look over his shoulder.

A brief digression is in order here, less about Putin than about us, the Russian public. Putin has backers and helpers, people with a vested interest in his second ascent of the throne, people now concentrated in the president's office. This is the institution that today rules the country, not the government that implements the president's decisions, not the parliament that rubber-stamps whichever laws he wants passed. His people follow society's responses very attentively. It is wrong to imagine they aren't bothered. It is we who are responsible for Putin's policies, we first and foremost, not Putin. The fact that our reactions to him and his cynical manipulation of Russia have been confined to gossiping in the kitchen has enabled him to do all the things he had done in the past four years. Society has shown limitless apathy, and this is what has given Putin the indulgence he requires. We have responded to his actions and speeches not just lethargically but fearfully. As the Chekists have become entrenched in power, we have let them see our fear, and thereby have only intensified their urge to treat us like cattle. The KGB respects only the strong. The weak it devours. We of all people ought to know that.

Let us now go back to late February 2004. At some moment the Kremlin techniques for sounding out opinion warned that the public was beginning to tire of Putin's insolent refusal either to debate or to campaign and of the absence of any recognizable preelection campaign.

To reinvigorate the languishing electorate, the Kremlin announced that Putin had decided to take firm measures. These proved to be a Cabinet reshuffle three weeks before election day.

At first, everyone was taken aback by what appeared to be an act of lunacy. In accordance with the constitution, the entire Cabinet does, in any case, resign after an election. The newly elected president announces his choice of prime minister, who, in turn, proposes ministers for the president to confirm. What sense could it possibly make to ap-

point all the Cabinet members now, only to have to reappoint them after the inauguration? What was the point of a senseless activity that
could only further paralyze the functioning of a government riddled
with corruption, which already spent a good proportion of its working
days taking care of personal, commercial interests?

However, although replacing the Cabinet a month before the constitution required was entirely daft, it did indeed serve to reinvigorate
the election process. The political elite was stirred, the guessing game
about whom Putin would appoint occupied the television channels,
the political pundits were provided with news to pontificate about,
and the press finally got something it could cover during the election
campaign.

But this reinvigoration of politics lasted one week at best. Putin's
spin doctors daily intoned on television that the president had made
the appointments because he wanted to be "absolutely honest with
you"; he did not want to "enter the election with a pig in a poke" (by
which evidently was meant following the constitutional procedure for
replacing the Cabinet). He wanted to present his future course before
March 14.

It has to be said, alas, that people believed him: probably just over
half the electorate. The half that fell for and hailed this dishonest, absurd line of argument has an important distinguishing feature. They
are people who love and trust Putin without reservation, irrationally,
uncritically; fanatically. They believe in Putin. End of story.

In the week preceding the appointment of a new prime minister,
the media images were all of the now-familiar love for Putin. Those
with faith in the genuineness of his proclaimed reasons for changing
the Cabinet ignored the obvious non sequiturs.

You really do have to believe unreservedly, as if you have fallen in
love for the first time, if you are not immediately to be struck by the
obvious question: Why didn't Putin choose a less dramatic way of presenting his future course than firing the entire government? He had
plenty of other ways to provide a glimpse of his second term. He

could, for example, have taken part in televised debates. But no. The week after the dismissal of the Cabinet saw unprecedented levels of cynicism. The people of Russia watching their televisions were told that actually it didn't matter what happened on March 14. Everything had been decided. Putin would be czar. The spin doctors were all but saying, "He wants to show you his course in advance because it's the only choice you've got."

The day when the name of the new prime minister was to be announced was arranged with all the ceremony traditionally preceding the emergence of the hero of an opera to sing his first aria. The president will tell us tomorrow morning. In two hours' time. In one hour's time. Ten minutes to go. Moreover, the one whose name would be revealed might, we were assured over the air waves, possibly be the president's successor in 2008.

In Russia it is important not to look ridiculous. People make up jokes, and you turn into a Brezhnev. When Putin announced his new government, even his die-hard supporters fell to laughing. No one could fail to see that the Kremlin had been staging a bad farce. It was no more than a petty settling of scores—subjected, of course, to endless spin and veiled behind all manner of claptrap and rhetorical flourishes that invoked the greatness of Russia.

But the mountains truly had brought forth a mouse. Virtually all the old ministers stayed where they had been. Only the prime minister, Mikhail Kasianov, was let go. He had been getting up Putin's nose for many months in a big way, and in many small ways, too. He was a legacy of the Yeltsin era. When raising the second president to the throne, the first president of Russia had asked Putin not to remove Kasianov.

Prime Minister Kasianov, alone among the main actors in Russian politics, categorically opposed the arrest of the liberal oligarch Mikhail Khodorkovsky and the gradual destruction of his Yukos oil company. Yukos was the most transparent company in our corrupt country, the first to function in accordance with internationally accepted financial practice. It operated "in the white," as people say in Russia, and, what is more, it donated over 5 percent of its gross annual profit to financing a large university, children's homes, and an extensive program of charitable work.

But Kasianov was speaking out in defense of a man whom Putin had, for some time, counted among his personal enemies, on the grounds that Khodorkovsky was making major financial contributions to the country's democratic opposition, primarily to the Yabloko Party and the Union of Right Forces.

In Putin's understanding of political life, Khodorkovsky's donations represented a grave personal insult. The president has publicly shown, on many occasions, that he is incapable of grasping the concept of discussion, especially in politics. There should be no backtalk from someone Putin considers his inferior, and an underling who allows himself to demonstrate any independence is an enemy. Putin does not choose to behave this way. He is not a born tyrant and despot; rather, he has been accustomed to think along the lines inculcated in him by the KGB, an organization he considers a model, as he has stated more than once. Thus, as soon as anyone disagrees with him, Putin demands that the "hysterics" be dropped. This is the reason behind his refusal to take part in preelection debates. Debate is not his element. He doesn't know how to conduct a dialogue. His genre is the military-style monologue. While you are a subordinate, you keep your mouth shut. When you become the chief, you talk in monologues, and it is the duty of your inferiors to pretend they agree that the choreography is a political version of the misrule of officers in the army that occasionally, as with Khodorkovsky, leads to all-out war.

But to return to the government reshuffle. Kasianov was out. The ministers returned to their original portfolios and Putin ceremoniously parachuted in Mikhail Fradkov as the new prime minister. In recent times, Fradkov had been quietly enjoying a place in our bureaucratic hierarchy as the Russian Federation's representative to the European institutions in Brussels. He is a nondescript, amiable, forgettable gentleman with narrow shoulders and a big bum. Most Russians learned that our country had a federal minister named Frad- kov only when his appointment as prime minister was announced, which, in accordance with Russian lore, tells us that Fradkov is a low- profile representative of that same service to which Putin has dedi- cated the greater part of his working life.

The nation laughed out loud when it heard of Fradkov's elevation, but Putin insisted, and even started explaining his "principled" choice to the effect that he wanted to be open with the electorate and to en- ter the election with people knowing whom he would be working with in his fight against Russia's main evils, corruption and poverty.

The Russian people, both the half that supports Putin and the half that doesn't, didn't stop laughing. The Kremlin farce continued. If the country as a whole did not know Fradkov, the business community re- membered him only too well. He is a typical member of the Soviet *nomenklatura* who, throughout his career, from the Communist period onward, has been shifted hither and thither to miscellaneous bureau- cratic posts, independent of his professional background and exper- tise. He is a typical boss for whom it is not too important what he is driving, just as long as he is in the driver's seat. While he was director of the Federal Tax Inspectorate Service, it had a reputation as the most corrupt ministry in the Russian civil service. Its bureaucrats took bribes for just about everything—for every form they issued and every consultation. The service was consequently shut down, and Fradkov, in line with the undying traditions of the Soviet *nomenklatura*, was "looked after." He was transferred once again, this time to Brussels.

Prime Minister Fradkov hastily flew back to Moscow from Brus- sels, only to provoke further merriment. At the airport, in his first in- terview in his new capacity, he confessed he didn't actually know how to be a prime minister. No, he had no plans; it had all come like a bolt from the blue. He was waiting to see what arrangements had been made and what his instructions would be.

Russia is a country where much goes on behind the scenes and most people have short memories. Despite his ignorance of the arrangements and the lack of instructions from Putin, which never have been made public, the Duma confirmed Fradkov's appointment by a convincing majority, making reference to its duty to "fulfill the will of our electors who trust President Putin in all matters." This Duma, its composition the result of the elections of December 7, 2003, contains practically no opposition to Putin and is firmly under the control of the Kremlin.

March 14 arrived. Everything went off as the Kremlin had intended. Life went on as before. The bureaucrats returned to their tireless thieving. Mass murder continued in Chechnya, having quieted down briefly during the elections, to give hope to those who for five years had been hoping for peace. The second Chechen war had begun in mid-1999, in the run-up to Putin's first presidential election. In accordance with Asian traditions, just before his second presidential election, two Chechen field commanders laid down their weapons at the feet of the great ruler. Their relatives had been seized and were held in captivity until the commanders stated that they now supported Putin and had given up all thought of independence. Oligarch Khodorkovsky took to writing penitential letters to Putin from prison. Yukos was rapidly becoming poorer. Berlusconi came to visit us, and his first question to his pal Vladimir was how he, too, could get 70 percent of the vote in an election. Putin gave no clear advice, and indeed his friend Silvio would not have understood if he had. Berlusconi is, after all, a European.

The two world leaders went off on a trip to provincial Lipetsk, where they opened a production line for washing machines and watched a military air show. Putin continued to give dressing-downs to high-level bureaucrats on television. That is usually how we see him, either receiving reports from officials in his Kremlin office or tearing one of these bureaucrats apart in monologues. The filming is methodically thought through in PR terms. There is no ad-libbing; nothing is left to chance.

Instead of the risen Christ, it was Putin who was revealed to the
people at Easter. A service was held at the Church of Christ the Re-
deemer, Moscow's cathedral re-erected in concrete on the site of an
open-air Soviet-era swimming pool. Almost a month had passed since
his second election. At the beginning of the Great Matins service there
stood, shoulder to shoulder with Putin as if at a military parade, Prime
Minister Fradkov and Dmitry Medvedev, the Kremlin's new éminence
grise, head of the president's office, a man of diminutive stature with a
large head. The three men clumsily and clownishly crossed themselves, Medvedev making his crosses by touching his hands to his fore-
head and then to his genitals. It was risible. Medvedev followed Putin
in shaking the patriarch's hand as if he were one of their comrades,
rather than kissing it as prescribed by church ritual. The patriarch
overlooked the error. The spin doctors in the Kremlin are effective
but, of course, pretty illiterate in these matters and had not told the
politicians what to do. Alongside Putin there stood the mayor of
Moscow, Yury Luzhkov, who had been behind the rebuilding of the
cathedral and who alone knew how to invoke the protection of the
Cross in a competent manner. The patriarch addressed Putin as "Your
Most High Excellency," which made even those not directly involved
wince. Given the numerous ex-KGB officers occupying top government positions, the Easter Vigil has now taken over from the May Day
parade as the major obligatory national ritual.

The beginning of the Great Matins service was even more comical
than the handshakes with the patriarch. Both state television channels
did a live broadcast of the procession around the cathedral that pre-
cedes the service. The patriarch participated in this, despite being ill.
The television commentator, who was a believer and theologically
knowledgeable, explained to viewers that in the Orthodox tradition,
the doors of the church should be shut before midnight because they
symbolize the entrance to the cave where Christ's body was placed. After midnight the Orthodox faithful taking part in the procession await
the opening of the church doors. The patriarch stands on the steps at

their head and is the first to enter the empty temple where the Resurrection of Christ has already occurred.

When the patriarch had recited the first prayer after midnight at the doors of the temple, they were thrown open to reveal Putin, our modest president, shoulder to shoulder with Fradkov, Medvedev, and Luzhkov.

You didn't know whether to laugh or cry. An evening of comic entertainment on Holy Night. What is there to like about this individual? He profanes everything he touches.

At about this time, on April 8, nine-month-old twin girls were declared *shaheeds*—martyrs for the faith—in Chechnya. They came from the tiny Chechen farmstead of Rigakh and were killed before they had learned to walk. It was the usual story. After the March 14 election, relentless military operations were resumed in Chechnya. The army, in the form of the Regional Operational Staff Headquarters for Coordinating the Counterterrorist Operation, announced that it was attempting to catch Basaev: "A large-scale military operation is under way to destroy the participants of armed formations." They failed to catch Basaev, but on April 8 at around two in the afternoon, as part of the military operation, the Rigakh farmstead was subjected to a missile bombardment. It killed everyone there: a mother and her five children. The scene that confronted Imar-Ali Damaev, the father of the family, would have turned the most hardheaded militant into a pacifist for life, or into a suicide bomber. His twenty-nine-year-old wife, Maidat, lay dead, holding close four-year-old Djanati, three-year-old Jaradat, two-year-old Umar-Haji, and the tiny nine-month-old Zara. Their mother's embrace saved none of them. To one side lay the little body of Zura, Zara's twin sister. Maidat had had no room and evidently no time to think of a way of covering her fifth child with her own body, and Zura herself had had no time to crawl the two meters. Imar-Ali gathered up the antipersonnel fragments and established the number of the killer missile: 350 F 8-90. It was not difficult; the number was easy to read. Family members and friends started burying the bodies, and the mullah, a Muslim scholar from the neighboring village, declared all those who had been slain to be martyrs. They were interred the same evening, their bodies unwashed, without burial clothes, in what they were wearing when death claimed them.

WHY DO I so dislike Putin? Because the years are passing. The second Chechen war, instigated in 1999, shows no sign of ending. In 1999 the babies who were to be declared *shaheeds* were yet unborn, but all the murders of children since that time, in bombardments and purges, remain unsolved, uninvestigated by the institutions of law and order. The infanticides have never had to stand where they belong, in the dock; Putin, that great friend of all children, has never demanded that they should. The army continues to rampage in Chechnya as it was allowed to at the beginning of the war, as if its operations were being conducted on a training ground empty of people.

This massacre of the innocents did not raise a storm in Russia. Not one television station broadcast images of the five little Chechens who had been slaughtered. The minister of defense did not resign. He is a personal friend of Putin and is even seen as a possible successor in 2008. Nor was the head of the air force fired. The commander in chief himself made no speech of condolence. Around us, indeed, it was business as usual in the rest of the world. Hostages were killed in Iraq. Nations and peoples demanded that their governments and international organizations withdraw troops, to save the lives of people carrying out their duties. But in Russia all was quiet.

Why do I so dislike Putin? This is precisely why. I dislike him for a matter-of-factness worse than felony, for his cynicism, for his racism, for his lies, for the gas he used in the *Nord-Ost* siege, for the massacre of the innocents that went on throughout his first term as president.

This is how I see it. Others have different views. The killing of children has not deterred people from trying to have Putin's term in office extended to ten years. This project is being conducted through the creation of pro-Putin youth movements on instructions from the Kremlin. The deputy head of Putin's office is a certain Vladislav Surkov, the acknowledged doyen of PR in Russia. He spins webs consisting of pure deceit, lies in place of reality, words instead of deeds. There is a great fashion at the present for bogus political movements created by directive from the Kremlin. We don't want the West suspecting that we have a one-party system, that we lack pluralism and are relapsing into authoritarianism. Suddenly there appear groups called Marching Together, Singing Together, For Stability, or some other latter-day version of the Soviet Union's Pioneer movement. A distinctive feature of these pro-Putin quasi-political movements is the amazing speed with which, without any of the usual bureaucratic prevarication, they are legally registered by the Ministry of Justice, which is usually chary of attempts to create anything remotely political. As its first public act, the new movement usually announces that it will attempt to ensure the extension of the term of office of our beloved president. Putin was given just such a present for his inauguration on May 7. At the end of April, the members of For Stability set in motion procedures for prolonging his term. The group's underlying concept is that Putin is the guarantor of stability. At the same time, the members of this pocket-size movement demanded an inquiry into the results of privatization, a move that revealed them to be against Khodorkovsky, hence friends of Putin. The Moscow City Electoral Commission hastened to accept the application of the young members of For Stability for a national referendum on the president's term.

Such was the state of play on inauguration day, May 7, 2004. Putin has, by chance, gotten hold of enormous power and has used it to catastrophic effect. I dislike him because he does not like people. He despises us. He sees us as a means to his ends, a means for the achievement and retention of personal power, no more than that. Accordingly, he believes he can do anything he likes with us, play with us as he sees fit, destroy us if he wishes. We are nobody, while he whom chance has enabled to clamber to the top is today czar and God.

In Russia we have had leaders with this outlook before. It led to tragedy, to bloodshed on a vast scale, to civil wars. Because I want no more of that, I dislike this typical Soviet Chekist as he struts down the red carpet in the Kremlin on his way to the throne of Russia.

POSTSCRIPT

July 10, 2004, is just another day in the calendar of Russia. It happens to be the cutoff date for making changes to this book.

Late yesterday evening, Paul Khlebnikov, editor in chief of the Russian edition of *Forbes* magazine, was murdered in Moscow. He was mowed down as he left the magazine's office. Khlebnikov was famous for writing about our oligarchs, the structure of Russian gangster capitalism, and the huge sums of easy money certain of our citizens have managed to get their hands on. Also last evening, Victor Cherepkov was blown up by a grenade in Vladivostok. He was a member of our parliament, the Duma, and a prominent champion of the weakest and poorest of this land. Cherepkov was running for mayor of his native city, the most important municipality in the Far East of Russia. He had successfully gotten through to the second round and looked to have a real chance of being elected. As he left his campaign headquarters he was blown up by an antipersonnel mine activated by a trip wire.

Yes, stability has come to Russia. It is a monstrous stability under which nobody seeks justice in courts that flaunt their subservience and partisanship. Nobody in his or her right mind seeks protection from the institutions entrusted with maintaining law and order, because they are totally corrupt. Lynch law is the order of the day, both in people's minds and in their actions. An eye for an eye, a tooth for a tooth. The president himself has set an example by wrecking our major oil company, Yukos, after having jailed its chief executive, Mikhail Khodorkovsky. Putin considered Khodorkovsky to have slighted him personally, so he retaliated. Not only did he retaliate against Khodorkovsky himself, he went on to seek the destruction of the goose that laid golden eggs for the coffers of the Russian state. Khodorkovsky and his partners have offered to surrender their shares in Yukos to the government, begging it not to annihilate the company. The government has said, "No. We want our pound of flesh." On July 9, Putin strong-armed his loyal supporter Muhammed Tsikanov into the post of vice president of Yukos-Moscow, the parent company. Nobody has any doubts that the former deputy minister for economic development has been parachuted in for one reason only: to coordinate the delivery of Yukos into the hands of those whom Putin favors. The market is in turmoil, investors are running for cover, and all the remotely successful business executives I know spent May and June looking for ways to move their capital to the West.

They were wise to do so. On July 8, 9, and 10, lines a mile long formed at ATMs. The authorities had only to hint that a crackdown might close some of the banks; the result was the withdrawal from Alpha Bank, one of the most stable, of funds to the tune of two hundred million dollars in seventy-two hours. Other banks also saw a run on deposits.

It took just a hint. Because everyone expects the state to play dirty, the withdrawal of those two hundred million dollars in three days tells us all we need to know about Russia's current stability.

If we go by the official surveys of public opinion, conducted by polling firms that have no wish to lose their contracts with the president's office, Putin's popularity rating couldn't be better. He has the support of an overwhelming majority of the Russian public. Everybody trusts him. Everybody approves of what he is doing.

AFTER BESLAN

On September 1, 2004, a horrible act of terrorism, one without precedent, was perpetrated in Russia, and from now on the name of the little North Ossetian town of Beslan will be associated with a waking nightmare beyond the imaginings of Hollywood.

On the morning of September 1, a multinational gang of thugs seized control of No. 1 School in Beslan, demanding an immediate end to the second Chechen war. The hostage takers struck during the annual *lineyka*, a celebration of the beginning of the school year that is observed throughout Russia. By tradition this is an occasion to which whole families come: grandmothers and grandfathers, aunts and uncles, and especially the relatives of the youngest children, who are going to school for the first time.

This is why almost 1,500 people were taken hostage: schoolchildren, their mothers and fathers, their brothers and sisters, their teachers and their teachers' children.

Everything that happened during the period of September 1–3, and in Russia subsequently, has been the predictable consequence of the Putin regime's systematic imposition of the power of a single individual, to the detriment of common sense and personal initiative.

On September 1 the intelligence services, and after them the authorities, announced that there actually were not that many people in the school: just 354 in all. The infuriated terrorists told the hostages, "When we have finished with you, there really will be only 354." The relatives who had gathered around the school said the authorities were lying: more than a thousand people were trapped inside.

Nobody heard what the relatives were saying, because nobody was listening. They tried to get their message through to the authorities by way of the reporters who had converged on Beslan, but the journalists went on echoing the official tally. At this point, some of the relatives started beating up some of the journalists.

The authorities spent September 1 and the first half of September 2 in an unforgivable state of shock and disarray. No attempts were made to negotiate, since such a move had not been sanctioned by the Kremlin. Anybody attempting to lay the groundwork for negotiations was subjected to intimidation, while those whom the bandits called upon to come forward and negotiate—President Zyazikov of Ingushetia; President Dzasokhov of North Ossetia; Putin's adviser on Chechnya, Aslambek Aslakhanov; and Dr. Leonid Roshal (who had mediated in previous sieges)—kept their heads down or fled the country, displaying cowardice at the very moment when courage was essential. Each of them subsequently had his excuses ready, but the obstinate fact remains that none of them entered the building.

Against this background of official cowardice, relatives of the hostages were terrified that there would be a repetition of the government's tactic for ending the *Nord-Ost* siege at a Moscow theater in 2002, when they mounted an assault that resulted in the loss of an enormous number of innocent lives.

On September 2, Ruslan Aushev, the former president of Ingushetia, entered the beleaguered school. Reviled by the Kremlin for constantly calling for peace talks and a political settlement of the Chechen crisis, Aushev had been forced to "voluntarily" resign in favor of the Kremlin's candidate, FSB general Zyazikov.

Arriving in Beslan, Aushev had found a deplorable situation, as he later recounted. He discovered that, one and a half days after the school had been seized, none of those in the headquarters of the operation to free the hostages was at liberty to decide who should take part in negotiations. They were waiting for instructions from the Kremlin and paralyzed by the fear of losing favor with Putin, whose displeasure would signal the end of their political careers. Evidently this consideration took priority over concern for the predicament of the hundreds of hostages. The deaths of hostages could always be blamed on the terrorists, whereas running afoul of Putin would be political suicide.

Let me state unambiguously that all the top Russian government representatives in Beslan at that time were more concerned to work out what Putin wanted than to work out a way of resolving the monstrous situation in the school. When Putin did speak, no one dared to contradict. Dzasokhov, for example, told Aushev that Putin had personally telephoned him and forbidden him to enter the school if he didn't want to face immediate criminal charges.

Dzasokhov stayed put. Dr. Roshal fared no better. Although a pediatrician, he failed on this occasion to save anyone other than himself, having been warned by an unnamed intelligence source that the terrorists were calling for him as a negotiator only in order to kill him. He, too, stayed put.

The officials in the operational nerve center succeeded in saving their careers but failed to save the children. Even before the showdown on September 3, it was obvious that Putin's vertical system of authority, founded on fear of and total subservience to one individual, himself, was not working. It was incapable of saving lives when that was what was needed.

Faced with this situation, Aushev printed off the Internet a declaration by Aslan Maskhadov, the leader of the Chechen resistance in whose name the thugs claimed to be acting. Because Maskhadov had stated categorically that he was against the taking of children as hostages, Aushev took this declaration and went in to talk to the terrorists. In the course of the Beslan catastrophe, he was to be the only person to conduct negotiations of any sort.

For his pains he was roundly abused by the Kremlin and accused of collaborating with the terrorists.

"They refused to talk to me in Vainakh," Aushev related afterward, "although they were Chechens and Ingushetians. They would speak only in Russian. They asked at least to have a minister sent to negotiate—for example, Fursenko, the minister for education—but nobody was willing to go in without the sanction of the Kremlin."

Aushev was in the school for about an hour and carried three babies out in his arms. A further twenty-six small children were allowed to leave with him. At two in the afternoon on September 3, an assault was launched, and fighting continued in the town until late into the night. Many of the terrorists were killed, but many others broke through the cordons and escaped. Officialdom began counting how many hostages had died, and is still counting today. A field was plowed up on the out-skirts of Beslan and turned into an enormous cemetery with hundreds of new graves. At the time of this writing, more than one hundred hostages have simply vanished: they are classified as having disap-peared without a trace. Some people believe they were abducted by the terrorists who escaped; others, that they were incinerated by the incendiary warheads of the rockets with which the special operations units were equipped.

In the immediate aftermath of Beslan there was a further tighten-ing of the political screws. Putin announced that the tragedy had been an act of international terrorism, denying the Chechen connection and blaming everything on al-Qaeda. Aushev's courageous intervention was denigrated and the mass media, on instructions from the Kremlin, set about portraying him as the terrorists' principal accomplice rather than as the only hero of the hour. That role was reserved for Dr. Roshal, since the masses need heroes to admire.

In political terms, Beslan did not prompt the Kremlin to analyze and correct its mistakes. On the contrary, the Kremlin went on a po-litical rampage.

Putin's favorite slogan after Beslan was "War is war." His top-down authoritarianism must be strengthened. He knew better than anyone else who was responsible for what, and only if he held the reins would Russia be safe from terrorist acts in the future. The Kremlin intro-duced a bill in the Duma abolishing direct election of provincial gov-ernors; in Putin's opinion, it only led to their acting irresponsibly.

Not a word was heard about the fact that throughout the Beslan hostage taking, it was Presidents Zyazikov and Dzasokhov, effectively Putin's nominees, who behaved like cowards and liars. They provided about as much leadership as one can expect milk from a billy goat.

The proposed reform of the system for selecting governors was accompanied by a campaign of ideological brainwashing that asserted that the authorities had performed irreproachably throughout the Beslan catastrophe. Nothing could have been done differently, nothing could have been more effective. As a smoke screen, a commission of inquiry of the Russian Federal Council (the upper chamber of the Russian parliament) was set up to monitor the investigation into the hostage taking. The chairman of the commission, Alexander Torshin, was received in the Kremlin by Putin and sent off with some presidential advice: The commission has not been stepping out of line.

The people of Beslan got the distinct feeling that they were being disregarded. Television coverage concentrated on the good news: the help the hostages were receiving, the mountains of sweets and toys sent to them. The question of what had happened to all those who had disappeared without a trace was not looked into.

The traditional forty-day period of mourning passed and official memorial services were held. No air time was given to the heartbroken families.

Then it was October 26, the second anniversary of the *Nord-Ost* hostage taking in Moscow, when a band of terrorists seized the audience and the actors of a musical in the middle of a performance. Two and a half days into the ensuing siege, the security services mounted an assault using an unknown chemical gas that resulted in the deaths of 130 hostages.

After *Nord-Ost*, the only action undertaken by the authorities was to whitewash their behavior, award themselves medals, and preen. Not only were no attempts made to find a settlement to the second Chechen war, but the noose was drawn tighter. A campaign was launched to destroy or neutralize anybody who might be capable of

bringing a peace settlement nearer, or of preventing the Chechen crisis from again spawning terrorism in the region. It was a predictable
response to the state terrorism of Russia's antiterrorist operation directed against the peoples of Chechnya and Ingushetia. Antiterrorist
terror was the defining characteristic of life in Russia in the period between *Nord-Ost* and the Beslan atrocity. We are ground to dust between the millstones of terror and antiterror. The number of terrorist
outrages has increased exponentially, and the path leading inexorably
from *Nord-Ost* to Beslan is plain to see.

On October 26, 2004, at eleven in the morning, there was a
gathering on the steps of the theater on Dubrovka of all those
whose loved ones had died or whose lives had been blighted by the
Nord-Ost events: the hostages themselves and the relatives and friends
of those who died. Earlier that morning they had visited the graves
of those dear to them, as is the tradition in Russia, and the service of
remembrance at the theater had accordingly been scheduled for
eleven. The *Nord-Ost* aid association of those affected by the tragedy
publicized the event through the usual channels. The arrangements
for the service were broadcast over local radio. Invitations were sent
to the office of the mayor of Moscow and to the president's office,
and assurances were received that representatives would attend.

But now the priest was waiting as the clock ticked past 11:20, 11:30,
11:50. It was time to start. People began murmuring among themselves: "Surely they can't just not show up?"

Then it was noon. The crowd was getting edgy. Many people had
children with them, orphans of those who had died. "We want to talk to
the authorities. We came to ask them questions face to face." Finally,
more angrily, "We need help urgently. We are being ignored. Our children are no longer receiving free hospital treatment."

Still no sign of officialdom. There was no point in waiting any
longer: nobody turns up that late. Were the authorities afraid of looking their victims in the eye? The investigation of the *Nord-Ost* incident
had led nowhere. The truth about the disaster and about the gas used

remained classified information. Or was something else going on here?

The square around the theater had been sealed off by police, ordinary young men who had been sent to ensure that any mob passions were kept under control. They could hear what people were saying, and they were not looking happy. Eventually, it was the police officers who explained to the *Nord-Ost* victims that the authorities had already been to the scene and had already left. They had come for their own cozy, official memorial service while the families were out at the cemeteries, so as not to confront the victims of their actions. At ten in the morning, representatives of the mayor of Moscow and the president's office had come to Dubrovka to pay their respects to the dead for the benefit of the TV cameras. Official wreaths had been laid; a guard of honor had performed like clockwork; appropriate speeches, planned and approved by higher authority, had been delivered. It had all been highly dignified: no tears, no excessive displays of grief, and the sanitized charade was shown repeatedly on all the television channels on the evening of October 26. Russia could rest assured that the authorities were suitably mindful of this tragic incident and that everybody agreed they were doing the right thing. The official nationalization of Russia's memory of the events was slotted neatly into just a few minutes.

Of course, nothing stopped the thousand-strong crowd of friends and relatives, former hostages, and numerous foreign journalists from honoring the dead. Candles were lit on the steps of the theater where those gassed had lain barely alive, and where many of them died before medical help arrived. One hundred and thirty portraits of the dead were illuminated by the flickering flames of lovingly placed candles. It was raining, just as it had been two years before, and the rain mingled with our tears, just as it had then.

The rain could not, however, wash away the bad feeling left by this ideological cynicism. It was a sorry reaction by the state to the immense grief of those who had suffered from its incompetence, at the very place where its victims had lost their lives. The authorities' apparent contempt for citizens stems from their fear of us. They cannot face our grief; they cannot admit their shortcomings or acknowledge their responsibility for the many victims of so many terrorist acts, which they have no effective strategy for dealing with.

This, alas, is precisely the future awaiting those who have suffered at Beslan. The official version of the tragedy is likely to bear little resemblance to the unofficial one. Grief will be permitted, within bounds, but the truth will not be told. Few onlookers would wish to hear what those who were present have to say. Higher authority will decide what is appropriate. Spontaneous emotion is undesirable, just as it was under the Soviets. The ideological stance adopted by the authorities since the tragedy of September 1 is that nothing must indicate that the officials were incompetent (which they certainly were). Tears are admissible, but only in moderation—everything is, after all, under control. While the disaster should not be forgotten, excessive displays of emotion, which might suggest despair, should be discouraged. They have no place in the land of the Soviets, because Putin is watching over us and knows better than we how matters ought to be arranged. We are all fighting a war on international terrorism; we are, moreover, "united as never before."

On October 29 the Duma voted by an overwhelming majority to enact Putin's bill under which he would nominate candidates for the post of governor and the regional parliaments could rubber-stamp the name put to them. If a region's MPs should be so impertinent as to reject Putin's nominations twice, the recalcitrant parliament would be "deemed to have passed a motion of no confidence" and would be dissolved by a directive of, yes, Putin again.

The process, of course, makes a mockery of the constitution and demonstrates utter contempt for the Russian people, but the Russian people took the news only too calmly. Certainly the opposition held a few meetings, but they were quiet, local affairs and nobody paid any attention to them. Putin got his way. This is post-Beslan Soviet Russia in action.

So what is the situation after Beslan? "The Party and the People Are One," the old Soviet slogan ran. In reality, the rift grows wider by the day, while the images on television convey the opposite impression. Soviet-style bureaucracy is growing stronger, and bringing with it an old-style political freeze. No evidence of global warming here. Russia, which swallowed the lies about how the *Nord-Ost* siege was ended, now makes no demands for justice or an objective investigation of the Beslan atrocity. For two years after *Nord-Ost*, most of the population slept peacefully in their beds, or went out dancing at discos, occasionally rousing themselves long enough to turn out and vote for Putin. It is arguably we ourselves who allowed Beslan to happen as it did. Our apathy after the *Nord-Ost* events, our lack of concern for the ordeal of its victims, was a defining moment. The authorities saw they had us, once again, under their thumb and relapsed into the complacency that brought about Beslan.

We cannot just sit back and watch a political winter close in on Russia for several more decades. We want to go on living in freedom. We want our children to be free and our grandchildren to be born free. This is why we long for a thaw in the immediate future, but we alone can change Russia's political climate. To wait for another thaw to drift our way from the Kremlin, as happened under Gorbachev, is foolish and unrealistic, and neither is the West going to help. It barely reacts to Putin's antiterrorist policies, and finds much about today's Russia entirely to its taste: the vodka, the caviar, the gas, the oil, the dancing bears. The exotic Russian market is performing as the West has come to expect, and Europe and the rest of the globe are satisfied with the way things are progressing on our sixth of the world's landmass.

All we hear from the outside world is "al-Qaeda, al-Qaeda," a wretched mantra for shuffling off responsibility for all the bloody tragedies yet to come, a primitive chant with which to lull a society desiring nothing more than to be lulled back to sleep.

NOTES

1. The story of the fifty-four soldiers received extensive publicity, with the result that an official inquiry was held under the auspices of the chief military prosecutor's office. The investigation found that while in their training of the soldiers the officers had exceeded their authority, the soldiers' misconduct on the training ground had provoked the officers into losing their tempers. The case did not come to court, and none of the officers received a criminal sentence. The soldiers were dispersed to different units to prevent them from causing further trouble. This judgment of Solomon was produced by a legal system specifically for those in the armed forces. Such cases are investigated by military prosecutors and passed on to military courts. The prosecutors and the military judges are themselves members of the armed forces who have sworn an oath of loyalty and are subordinate to their superiors, and so on right up to the minister of defense. Accordingly, at every level, prosecutors and judges cannot be independent in their judgments.

2. This incident was handled in much the same way as the case of the fifty-four soldiers. An inquiry was held by the garrison prosecutor's office, whose employees were effectively subordinate to the commanding officer of the military unit in which the incident occurred. Again the prosecutor's office acquitted the officers. The illegal "sale" and "renting out" of soldiers as inexpensive laborers, usually by their junior officers and in order to carry out particular agricultural or building tasks, is common practice in Russia. Payment usually goes to the officers

for their role in the deal. It is extremely rare for the soldiers to be paid other than in food, cigarettes, and overnight accommodations. Occasionally no payment is involved. If the officer and the employer are decent people, the soldiers may be moved out of their units for a time simply because they can be more adequately fed away from the army.

3. Aslan Maskhadov was the leader of the Chechen resistance forces in the current Chechen war. In 1997 he was elected president of the Chechen Republic of Ichkeria, his legitimacy recognized both by the Kremlin and by the Organization for Security and Cooperation in Europe, which sent observers to the elections. In 1999, however, Putin declared Maskhadov to be de facto deposed. Maskhadov responded by heading up the resistance to the occupation of Chechnya by federal troops. He remained on Russia's most-wanted list and was assassinated in March 2005.

Islam Hasuhanov is married to Maskhadov's niece. He was renowned in Russia as a submarine officer, having served on one of the navy's elite missile cruisers. On completing his service contract, he was honorably discharged and worked for the Ministry of Defense of Chechnya during the period when Maskhadov was internationally recognized as the legitimate president. The situation did not save Hasuhanov from being sentenced to twelve years in prison—in effect, for working for Maskhadov. As the Supreme Court of the Republic of North Ossetia–Alaniya acknowledged, testimony against Maskhadov was extorted from Hasuhanov during the preliminary investigation by means of barbaric treatment. The record of these court sessions, containing the admission that torture had been used, was subsequently passed to Amnesty International, which continues to work on the case.

4. The Russian code of criminal procedure provides that the accused have access to an attorney irrespective of ability to pay. During the second Chechen war, however, the law-enforcement agencies began misusing the system to foist on accused persons defense lawyers who, more often than not, were the agencies' former employees. Such people are known as insider lawyers. There are also lawyers who work with the FSB and so have a better understanding of its needs than of the individuals they are supposed to be defending. The function of such lawyers is to be present on occasions when the law requires the presence of an attorney. FSB officers also appoint insider lawyers to represent suspects the FSB has abducted. The relatives know only that their family member has disappeared. The FSB deliberately hides him, informing the family neither of his whereabouts nor of the charges against him. Often no formal accusation is ever made. The detention of the disappeared person is illegal, but the family is prevented from appointing a defense lawyer for him. Such victims can "disappear" for weeks or months; in Hasuhanov's case, the period was about six months. Meanwhile, testimony is beaten out of them, as happened in Hasuhanov's case. His family had no idea what had happened to him or where he was. All the law-enforcement and security agencies

of the republic denied they were detaining anybody by that name, while in fact he was being tortured by the FSB despite the appointment of a lawyer.

5. The Red Cross is often unable to carry out its functions because the Russian authorities frequently withhold permission for prison visits.

6. Abdullah Hamzaev died in Moscow in June 2004 after a serious illness. During the Budanov trial he was subjected to extreme pressure for speaking out against the accused and all he stood for. Hamzaev was threatened with retribution, and members of his family were intimidated both by Russian nationalists from extremist paramilitary groups and by officers who were colleagues of Budanov. He had several heart attacks in the course of the trial and was taken to the hospital. Once he suffered infarction and clinically died, but later returned to the trial. Hamzaev succeeded in ensuring that Budanov was sentenced to a long term of imprisonment, something few people believed possible in the spring of 2000.

7. It is important to understand what changed the direction the judicial proceedings were taking, toward justice in accordance with the law. Psychological and psychiatric reports were crucial in the Budanov case. When it became apparent that Budanov might be released from detention right there in the courtroom, the Memorial Civil Rights Center and the director of the Independent Psychiatric Association of Russia, Professor Yury Savenko, sent a request to colleagues in Germany to produce a report for the trial based on the documentary evidence. Simultaneously, lawyers stated in court that they had no confidence in the politically motivated Russian psychiatric experts and demanded that respected foreign psychiatrists be officially invited to contribute to the trial. Despite the fact that the judge refused this demand, the German psychiatrists soon presented their conclusions, which were passed to members of the Bundestag. As a result, the spotlight turned onto the biased reports of the Russian psychiatrists, which were contrasted with the German specialists' conclusions. Then Gerhard Schröder brought up the case in conversation with Putin, who, while not much concerned about public opinion in his own country, is highly sensitive to criticism from abroad. Shortly afterward, the trial in Rostov-on-Don dramatically changed direction, which only goes to show, once again, the dependence of the courts on Russia's leaders. The state prosecutor who had spoken in favor of Budanov was replaced by one who was unbiased. Lawyers were allowed to call witnesses. The judge agreed to attach to the case file the long report by Dr. Stuart Turner, a fellow of the Royal College of Psychiatrists, in London. For Dr. Turner, Yury Budanov was not the politically sensitive figure he was for us; he was just another patient. Thus it was Western intervention that changed the direction of the Budanov trial.

8. Rushailo was removed from this post in May 2004, and moved into a new position with little power.

9. In addition to the pedophilia problem, the prosecutor general's office also

held an inquiry into the allegation that Fedulev's wife had given a bribe of $20,000 to Judge Krizsky, and into the closing of the case for which he had interceded. The inquiry found the allegation of "thanking" to be valid, but no criminal investigation followed. In accordance with Russian tradition, Krizsky was allowed to "resign at his own request" in order not to cause a scandal. And resign he did, into "honorable retirement" from the bench. Soon afterward, Prosecutor General Skuratov left office, having provoked a public scandal in which corruption figured prominently.

10. This was moral blackmail calculated to crush a woman in a state of extreme stress. Under Russian legislation, as the investigator must have known, exhumation can be authorized only after a court hearing. Where exhumation is authorized, it may take place only in the presence of the mother, father, or other close relatives whom the court recognizes as having suffered as a result of the death of the individual concerned. As a result of his misconduct, the investigator who attempted to blackmail Irina was moved to other work. Later he was quietly sacked.

11. "Telephone law" is the Soviet term for an informal system of governance based on personal acquaintance. Officials telephone judges directly, and the latter produce the verdicts required. "Telephone law" operates in every other sphere of our life as well, as is evident from the saying "What can't be done, can be done over the telephone."

12. An inquiry into the arrest of Aelita Shidaeva was conducted by the Moscow prosecutor's office after she lodged a complaint. None of the police officers involved were disciplined.

13. A wave of racism (not only against Chechens but against people of non-Slavic appearance) washed over Russia after the *Nord-Ost* events. Many complaints were investigated by Russian civil-rights organizations, primarily the Moscow Helsinki Group, the Memorial Civil Rights Center, and the Citizen's Aid Committee for Assistance to Refugees. Numerous petitions and appeals were sent to the president by Amnesty International and Human Rights Watch. They were fruitless. Nobody was punished. The international interventions did not halt the wave of racism largely because the Russian leadership took no action. Racist harassment and murders continue and show no sign of abating.

INDEX

mistreatment of soldiers (*cont'd*)
　Putin's influence on, 1–3, 23–24
　remains of Pavel Levurda, 3–13
　suffocation of Dmitri Kiselev, 19–20
　suicide of Yury Diachenko, 20–21
monopolized pipes, 160
Moscow
　case against Pavel Fedulev, 128
　compensating *Nord-Ost* victims, 197–98
　food shortage in, 87–89
　Kamchatya remote from, 162
　Mafia seizing Uralkhimmash
　　Corporation, 117
　motherland vs., 172
　murder of Paul Khlebnikov, 245
　Nikolai Ovchinnikov, appointment of,
　　114
　No. 14 Police Station, 217–18
　No.155 School, 225–29
　Nord-Ost tragedy in. *See Nord-Ost*
　　tragedy
　Red Square demonstration of 1968, 66
　slums, 221
　Yury Shuratov prosecuting in, 141–43
Moscow Aviation Technical Institute,
　218
Moscow Business World Bank, 138
Moscow Central Police Department,
　219–20
Moscow City Court, 12
Moscow City Electoral Commission, 243
Moscow Helsinki Group, 260
Moscow Institute of Ecological Legal
　Issues, 183
Moscow Institute of Engineering and
　Physics, 164
Moscow Province
　Berg Park, 184
　Dmitri Kiselev serving in, 19–20
　Fifteenth Guards Motorized Infantry
　　Regiment in, 11
　Pavel Levurda serving in, 5–6
mothers of soldiers
　Bryansk Committee of Soldier's
　　Mothers, 9
　defection from Twentieth Division,
　　14–18
　Nina Levurda suit against state, 3–13
　Svetlana Putintseva's correspondence
　　with son, 21–23

Volvograd Province Mother's Right's or-
　ganization, 16–18
Movsarova, Zura, 218
"Mozart," 191
Mozdok military base, 34
municipal courts, control of, 152–53
Musaev, Djamalaili, 77

Narofominsk District of Moscow
　Province, 180, 181
Nasaev, Zelimham, 220–25
Nasaeva, Roza, 221
Naudzhus, Alexander, 135
navy, nuclear submarines of, 163–70
neo-Soviet capitalism
　alcoholism in, 98–100
　bribing officials, 92–96
　Misha in. *See* Misha, example under neo-
　　Soviet capitalism
　Orthodox Christian bureaucracy under,
　　103–4
　personal independence under, 86–92
　religious belief in, 100
　Soviet regime vs., 83–86
　Tanya in. *See* Tanya, neo-Soviet
　　capitalism influencing
　translators in, 98
Neserhaeva, Yakha, 211–14
neurasthenia, 84
Nevmerzhitsky, Major Vitaly, 77
New Russians, 179–85
Nicholas II, Emperor, 221
Nikolaev, Misha, 18–19
Nizhergorodsky police station, 221–22
Nizhny Tagil Metallurgical Complex, 123,
　137, 157
No. 1 Dubrovskays Street, 186, 204
No. 1 School in Beslan, 247–52
No. 14 Police Station, 217–18
No. 172 Police District, 218
No. 20 Hospital, 212–13
No. 7 Zarechnaya Street, 46
No. U-729343. *See* Levurda, Lieutenant
　Pavel
No.155 School, 225–29
Nokhchi-Keloy, 77
nomenklatura
　big businessmen, 120
　Mikhail Fradkov in, 238
　Putin influencing, 82–83